IT
DOESN'T
HAVE
TO BE
AWKWARD

DR. DREW PINSKY
PAULINA PINSKY

IT DOESN'T HAVE TO BE AWKWARD

Dealing with **RELATIONSHIPS**, **CONSENT**, and Other **HARD-TO-TALK-ABOUT** Stuff

Houghton Mifflin Harcourt
Boston   New York

hmhbooks.com

The text was set in Adobe Garamond Pro and Bourton Hand.
Hand-lettering and illustrations by Ellen Duda
Cover and interior design by Ellen Duda

The Library of Congress Cataloging-in-Publication Data is on file.

ISBN: 978-0-358-39603-1

Manufactured in the United States of America
DOC 10 9 8 7 6 5 4 3 2 1
4500830727

TO THOSE WHO WANT TO SPEAK UP
BUT DON'T KNOW HOW

CONTENTS

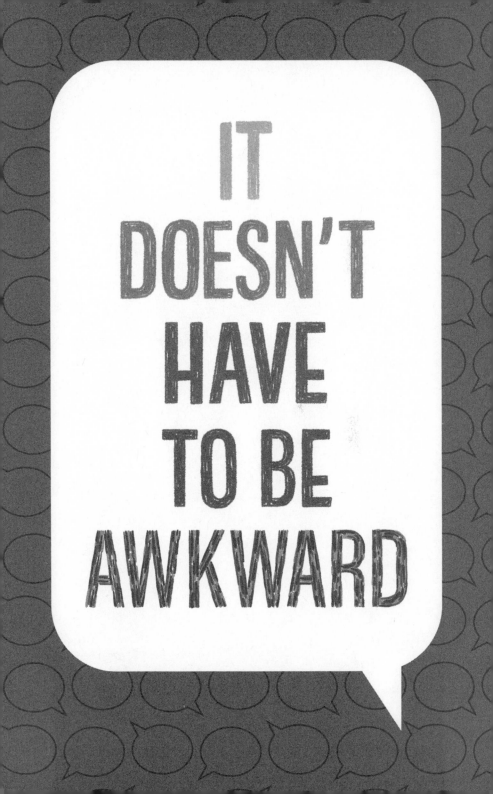

FATHER/DAUGHTER TEAM:
GET TO KNOW US

This is a book about relationships, so it's only fair that you know the people you're getting into this with: I'm Dr. Drew, and I've been talking about sex with teenagers for a long time—since I was twenty-four and in med school. I had a popular radio show where I answered questions from teens and twenty-somethings who wanted information about sex and relationships. Some of their questions were about basic and important health questions and, as a doctor, I had the answers they were looking for.

But many of their other questions were more complex. They wanted to know about sexuality, and attraction, and whether what they were doing—or wanted to do—was right or wrong, or normal or weird. To be fair, there *were* a whole bunch of confusing messages at the time. In the eighties, sex ed or health class in high schools usually focused on what was called "sexual literacy." The point was to just teach kids about the mechanics of their own bodies and (hetero)sexual relationships. My goal was to go beyond the basic biology and let people know they could ask me anything without feeling embarrassed.

And while I was talking to other kids about sex . . . I also had kids (triplets!) of my own. Naturally, I was confident I could give my kids the facts they needed to know about sex. By the time they were teens, I had learned that our most important conversations were about so much more. There is no doubt it was sometimes awkward (for everyone involved) to talk about the mechanics of sex, but it wasn't so hard to talk about how to have healthy, meaningful relationships (with all kinds of people, not just sexual partners). My kids are adults now, and I'm hoping that what I've learned can help you think more deeply about these topics, and offer some perspectives—backed by studies, science, and over thirty-five years of experience—that you may not have considered. But I'm not heading into this conversation with you alone. I'm bringing along one of my kids: my daughter, Paulina. She's a millennial, a writer, a comedian, and a feminist. She'll keep it real when I start to geek out on theory, and together we'll do our best to help you navigate the complex, confusing, and completely natural questions you have around sex, consent, and relationships of all kinds.

Oh, yeah. Dad's not kidding when he says it could be awkward. I remember when my parents first talked to me and my brothers about the birds and the bees. The five of us were all seated at one end of the mahogany dining table that is only used during holidays in my parents' home in Pasadena, California. I was in the fifth grade. The use of the formal dining table alerted me to the fact that the night was special, but I was ultimately unsuspecting. A pink plush version of a sexually transmitted infection (STI), syphilis, lay on the table and stared back at me with its phony sewn-on eyes. Dad had been given the toy as a promotion of some sort at KROQ, the radio station he worked at, and he thought it could be a nice little prop for our conversation.

Dad broke the news: "We are going to talk about se—" As soon as I heard what was about to happen, I covered my ears and shouted, "LA! LA! LA! School already told us about this!" I stood up and threw the stuffed STI onto the floor before running out of the room. My brothers were very confused and remained seated because they are better behaved than I am. Lucky for me, I went to a school that knew that sex ed was essential to my development. And wow, has that knowledge come in handy!

Okay, the "sex talk" must have been equally traumatic for me because I don't remember that conversation at all. What I do remember is one time driving in the car with Paulina and her brothers. They were probably in third or fourth grade. For some reason I was sitting in the back with the boys; Paulina was sitting in the front with her mother when she just burst out with "All right— can somebody please tell me what's the deal with this whole penis/ vagina thing?" My wife shot me a glance in the rearview mirror and I started right in, saying, "Okay. I'll explain the whole deal. Just tell me when you want me to stop." I started to describe intercourse, but within about twenty-two seconds, the boys were cracking up and Paulina was screaming, "STOP!" Maybe that's why I thought props would help the next time I was bringing up the topic.

So here we are: I've spent decades listening to people ask and talk about sex and relationships and coaching them to find solutions. I'm as old (or older!) than your parents, and even though I talked with my own teenagers about their relationships, I can understand if you think that I couldn't possibly get what you want to know about.

Maybe you feel like your world and concerns are invisible to adults. And when I listen to people your age, I hear that you have questions and challenges around your relationships today that I couldn't imagine when I first started giving advice. But the answers to navigating these issues are grounded in proven science—and evolving theory—about why people behave the way they do.

This is bound to be a complicated conversation. Know that I'm here to hold your hand. Remember, I'm not much older than you are and I'm having this conversation with my dad. I don't know your relationship to your parents, but know this: I am not easily embarrassed, I want my dad to be proud of the work I do, and I'm not afraid of difficult conversations. No matter where you come from, what your parents think, or what other people think about you: we are in this together.

. . . AND LEARN WHY WE WROTE THIS BOOK

When I was in college, Emma Sulkowicz was carrying her mattress around Columbia University's campus, where we both went to school. You might be too young to remember her performance art, but I saw it firsthand. The first time I saw her, she was alone, carrying her striped twin-XL mattress, dragging it across College Walk. I was confused. Why was she carrying it? Wasn't it heavy? Why wasn't anyone helping her?

But then someone told me: she was carrying her mattress until her rapist was found guilty.

The next time I saw her, five people were helping her carry it over their heads. I wanted to help, but there were already too many hands. She brought that mattress to every class. She carried it across the stage at graduation. The university did not give her a reason to leave it in her dorm. The student she had accused of rape remained on campus. Her charges against him were investigated by the university and dismissed. Their reasoning: How could sex that started out as consensual become nonconsensual?

And that's part of the reason this book exists.

When I attended graduate school at Columbia, I was required to do sexual harassment training. It was clinical and legal, and it was easy to skip through. It felt like a way for the institution to protect itself, rather than a way to protect its students.

This confusion about consent was compounded by my dating experience in my early twenties. I was Tindering a lot. On the app itself, I felt objectified and harassed by random people I did not know. If I did make it to a date, I sometimes found myself having sex just because it was easier to have sex than to say no. The sex was unfulfilling. I was left feeling empty and confused. I was exercising my sexuality, but I felt used, unappreciated, and unseen.

So I started talking about it with my friends. And the more I spoke about it, the more common I found the experience to be. It's never too late to start this conversation. Although I haven't talked about these parts of my life with my dad before, I know that being able to comfortably talk about relationships, sexuality, and consent is a skill worth having. Because talking about how you feel, and listening to how others feel, should be a lifelong conversation. All in all, it's safe to say I learned as much writing this book as I hope you will reading it. Relationships affect us all, and we are honored to be here as you just get started.

If you think that because I'm a doctor this book is going to be about all of the physical things you need to know about relationships and sex, you might be surprised. Without question, healthy sexuality comes from an understanding of how your body works. The good news is that our bodies are surprisingly easy to figure out. If you have questions about your health or physical self that haven't been answered in health class in school, or by your parents, there are plenty of places where you can find good information. (Start by checking out our recommendations in the back of this book.) What Paulina and I really want to talk with you about is how you can understand your own unique self to feel good about the decisions you make about how you act with other people.

My work with young people has opened my eyes to the fact that, for you, the landscape of relating is at best confusing, and at worst, scary. And when the #MeToo movement happened, I started thinking about what college students had told me years ago—that they had no idea what it really meant to communicate clearly, recognize power imbalances, and consciously respect boundaries around sexual encounters.

When Paulina and I first started talking about this book, we knew we'd tackle the subject of consent, since everyone seemed confused and, frankly, misinformed. But the more we talked, the more it became clear that so much more was at stake. The first step in clearing away confusion about all relationships, but especially sexual relationships, is being secure in what you know to be true about yourself.

Every relationship you have is different. And developing an awareness about different dynamics helps you interact with all kinds of people with confidence. We want you to start thinking of a relationship like a weird kind of math equation where 1 + 1 does not equal 2. Instead, 1 + 1 = 3. There's *you* and *someone else,* and then there's this third element: *the relationship.* People who study human connections call this third element a "cocreated experience." **These "cocreated" experiences stay with you. That's why, even when you're not literally with someone, you can have a physical and emotional response when you think about them. That third thing stays with you. That's why a great relationship can make you feel like you're walking around wrapped in a warm blanket, and a bad one can follow you around, lingering like that cold you just can't kick.**

Since a relationship is two different people coming together to make a third thing, it makes sense that each person has some responsibility in what this shared experience feels like. When it comes to your body and your health, you're in charge, even if you're not in control. If something isn't going right, you need to step in and take action. The same is true for your relationships. You're responsible for your actions with other people, even though you are not in control of their behavior. So how can you do your part to make your relationships good ones?

Healthy relationships that feel good happen when the people in them successfully balance a powerful trio of key ingredients: **trust, compassion, and boundaries**. We're going to talk about these three things a lot, so to make it easy to remember, just think of them as "**TCB**."

TCB works for me. No lie, I have *TCB* with a lightning bolt tat-

tooed on my rib cage. It's my first tattoo and a long story—I'll tell you about it later! But it's why I'm psyched to incorporate this kind of TCB in my life. Regular check-ins on whether trust, compassion, and boundaries are in balance mean you're doing your part to keep relationships strong and healthy. You'll be taking care of each other (and yourself).

The other big relationship topic that you might have heard about, particularly in regard to sex, is **consent.** Maybe you've learned in health class at school about consent. And maybe your takeaway is that "consent," especially when it comes to sex and relationships, means that everyone has the option to say "yes" or "no" and that everyone should listen. And that's true. But in this book, we are here to tell you that consent is much more than that. Consent is not simply a transaction (you say "yes" and something happens, or you say "no" and nothing does). **Consent is a way of constantly testing how TCB is holding up at any given moment in your interaction with someone else.**

So where does TCB come from, and how do you get good at it? How can you pay attention to how you use it to take care of yourself and your relationships? And how does it all come together in this idea of consent? We're going to break it down for you in the next few sections. There's a lot to think about here, but I know you can handle it. We are going to ask you to challenge some of what you may already believe about yourself . . . and about yourself in relationships.

HOW TO USE THIS BOOK

We are taking you very seriously here. We talked to tons of young people to find out what they really want to know about relationships and sex, and we know you have real questions and that the answers matter. Our advice works best when you start from the very beginning of the book, where we tell you things that you might not hear from other adults. We are asking you to begin taking responsibility for your place in the world by investing in understanding where we are coming from, so take the time to read all of part 1 from beginning to end.

After that, feel free to skip around and look for the questions, scenarios, or topics that matter most to you at any given time in your life. If you trust us—and trust our advice—before you know it, you'll be able to recognize and maintain trust, compassion, and boundaries in all the relationships that matter most to you!

One more thing: Throughout this book, you'll read about people in various situations that help us illustrate the topics we discuss. With two exceptions, the people and the scenarios are fictional. Any comparison to real life is coincidental.

PART 1

TRUST, COMPASSION, BOUNDARIES— CONSENT STYLE

Before we dive into the real stuff, I want to tell you why I got so excited when we realized that the first letters of the three key ingredients to good relationships were TCB. It has to do with a key relationship in my life that made me believe in the power of those three little letters. I cringe as I write this—but, for a decade or so, I was infatuated with . . . ELVIS PRESLEY. I loved listening to his music, I loved watching his movies, and I loved looking at him. But it wasn't just superficial, it was a spiritual connection.

From my obsession with Elvis, I knew that the rhythm section of his band, the part that held down the beat and drove the songs forward, was called TCB (which stood for taking care of business). I also knew that Elvis often wore jewelry that featured a lightning bolt and the letters *TCB*. And I begged my mom until she bought me a TCB necklace of my own.

From age five to eighteen, I was a competitive figure skater. Minutes before every performance, I'd whisper to myself, "Elvis, help me." I'd squeeze my butt cheeks and hold on to my lucky necklace, and then I'd go out and take care of business. (Okay, totally embarrassing, but we're being open with one another here, right? I still do this when I'm facing a big challenge. Like taking a test. Or writing a book. Or saying yes to going on a date.)

Just like Paulina, lots of us have rituals or good luck charms that give us confidence—things we say to ourselves to quiet down anxiety, or clothes that we think make us look a certain way. But these external things are just props. **Real power and confidence come from connecting to your authentic self.** So while a lucky necklace and a prayer to Elvis might temporarily boost your confidence, it isn't the same as the TCB we are talking about here. Knowing how to call on the real TCB—**trust, compassion**, and **boundaries**—will help you feel more secure when you're in challenging territory—whether it's walking up to that person you're attracted to and saying hi, deciding whether to have sex with someone, or having a hard conversation with a person you love.

chapter 1

TCB:
TELL ME MORE
?!

If you think about it, you'll realize that every interaction you have, from negotiating with your parents about that party that they think is a bad idea to talking about your crushes with your friends, from swiping right to meeting in real life, has some mix of TCB. When trust, compassion, and boundaries are all in the right balance, being with someone feels effortless. You are relaxed about being yourself. You look forward to spending time together. You care about them and trust that they care about you. You have deep feelings, but there's no drama. **But if just one of these three elements is out of whack, things can become problematic.**

TCB: WHAT IT MEANS

Trust is the ability to feel safe in a relationship. It is a belief you have in a person or situation that you will be safe. Trust is guided by instinct (after all, babies trust that their mother will care for them just seconds after they've met), but it is also affected by experience, and it has everything to do with how you approach relationships later in life. A baby who cries because they are hungry is expressing a feeling. And if their cries are ignored, they learn two things: they can't trust that the people closest to them understand them, and they can't depend on having their needs met.

Trust is something that must be earned, based on shared respect, clear communication, and lack of exploitation. Where there is mutual trust, compassion naturally follows, and **boundaries** are respected. Trusting someone means you know that your feelings are valued and appreciated by the other person.

For such a powerful thing, trust can be fragile. Think of it like a tower of blocks. You can spend a lot of time building a complicated structure, but with one false move, everything can come crashing down. It doesn't even have to be on purpose. Sometimes, an outside force sets things in motion. The most common example I can think of is someone who cheats in a relationship. Maybe they had been slowly pulling blocks out of the relationship with other untrustworthy actions (lies, evasions, omissions) until the structure was weak and one obvious act wrecked it all. Maybe they made a bad decision in a single moment. In any case, as soon as they cheated, they destroyed the trust between them and their partner. Breaking someone's trust can feel terrible, and losing the trust of someone you love feels even worse.

It can happen in friendships, too. The little things start to add up. It can start with your best friend still following your ex-boyfriend on Instagram, even though he lives in another state. Then you notice that they are posting pictures of group hangouts that you were not invited to. Little signals are being sent: you are not prioritized. If there isn't an open line of communication, this thing could lead to a blowout. Or even the end of the friendship.

Like a tower of blocks, trust can be rebuilt. Just like you can rebuild a tower one block at a time, you can begin to restore trust one consistent act at a time. Repairing trust that has been damaged takes patience. And, just like your tower of blocks, as you start to rebuild, you might question whether it is as sturdy as it was before. You might worry it's going to crumble every time you place a new block. It might wobble or sway. It might take longer to rebuild than it did to build the first time, but you keep building. Or you might even decide that it is going to take too much time to build it up again. You might just walk away. Once trust is damaged, there is slow, steady work that must be done to repair the relationship. And whether you keep going until you have something as strong and steady as before is mostly up to you.

Compassion is the ability to be open to the experiences of others without judgment or prejudice. For instance, if your friend tells you that their family cat died, you should extend your support in whatever way they need. You can be a listening ear, a shoulder to cry on, or whatever the situation demands. Compassion goes hand in hand with empathy, which is the powerful ability to step into another person's shoes. Empathy doesn't mean that you have had the same reaction to any particular experience as someone else, but when you have empathy, you can feel what someone else feels, and understand it fully, without being personally overwhelmed.

People who are empathetic pick up on other people's feelings easily. People who are less empathetic may have to start by imagining what the other person might be feeling. Either way, active effort to feel empathy leads to compassion, helping you to be aware of your own biases. Learn how to listen to different experiences. Compassion without empathy can feel patronizing, and empathy without compassion is essentially impossible. There are definitely times when I wish I had more empathy and compassion. Especially for my brothers when we were growing up. One time, Douglas had been playing *Crash Bandicoot* and he was on the final level, but I wanted to watch the TV. YOINK! I pulled the plug to the game console out of the wall. He immediately started crying—weeks of working on getting to that level, gone. When I did it, I was only thinking of myself. I didn't take that important second of imagining how my actions would affect him. I don't think he will ever forgive me for that one. (This episode might also have done a number on the trust my brother had that I would control my impulses!)

Boundaries are invisible protective lines around your feelings and your body that you create based on your experiences. Boundaries give you feedback on what you can tolerate in interactions with others—beginning even before you can talk. Can you ever remember your parents telling you that you *had to* hug your uncle with the scary beard, even though you didn't want to? Or scary-bearded uncle ignoring your frantic head shaking no and coming in for a big hug anyway? Classic lack of respect for a preverbal tot's boundaries. It's a well-intentioned attempt to demonstrate family affection, but if your clear messages about your own space and desire—or lack thereof—for contact are ignored, it can shape your attitudes toward physical touch in ways you don't even realize.

Healthy boundaries are what allow trust and compassion (and empathy) to coexist. Your boundaries keep you comfortable in your physical body and also help protect your individual identity by allowing you to remain present but in control when you are exposed to the feelings and experiences of others. It is perfectly normal, and even important, for you to test and define and redefine your boundaries. But be aware: if your boundaries are wobbly, when another person expresses strong feelings, your brain can react as if those are *your own* feelings and experiences. **You'll be perfectly fine, and then someone with drama comes into your life, and if your boundaries are not strong, the next thing you know you're dragged down with them. Someone else's strong feelings can break through weak boundaries, putting you at risk of catching those feelings—like an emotional flu.**

TCB IN ACTION

Knowing how something is supposed to work and seeing it in action can be two different things. Let's take a look at how using TCB can help in even the most awkward situations.

Alex and Mia were really good friends until the night Mia kissed Alex's boyfriend at a house party. To Mia, it meant nothing because she was totally drunk and thought Alex would understand. Mia doesn't even like Alex's boyfriend, and everyone knows that she gets super affectionate with everyone when she is partying. Mia would never consciously do anything to hurt Alex. But now Alex won't even text her back.

QUIZ
TCB: True or False

1. Alex and Mia have a trust issue.

2. Alex and her boyfriend have a trust issue.

3. Alex should have some compassion for her friend's mistake.

4. Mia has a boundary problem.

   BONUS QUESTION: Did Alex's boyfriend have Mia's consent to kiss her?

ANSWERS: 1. True, 2. True, 3. True (but this is hard!), 4. Also true. Bonus question: **He did not!** You can't get consent from someone who is under the influence.

How'd you do in your first TCB quiz? For some of you, the answers may have been obvious. Others may be wondering why Mia and Alex are making such a big deal of things. There's no denying their friendship has been affected. So, what can be done to get TCB back in this friendship? First of all, Mia needs to quickly take responsibility for her actions. It's hard, but it's the only way to begin to regain Alex's **trust**. And Mia needs to be patient as her friend works her way toward beginning to trust her again. Being honest does not mean there will be no consequences. There could be some sustained gossip (but that will die down soon). But taking responsibility will put Mia back in the position of ownership of what is happening.

Should Alex have **compassion** for Mia? She might try to understand what happened by asking herself why her friend behaved the way she did. And Alex should have compassion for herself. She might be angry or embarrassed or sad, and she is entitled to her feelings. She doesn't have to play it off as if this breaking of trust doesn't mean anything. If the friendship is worth anything to Alex, she will find a way to not stay angry.

As for boundaries, we don't know who initiated the kiss, but I can guarantee that both Mia *and* Alex's boyfriend need work on holding healthy boundaries.

Partying played a role here too. I suspect if Mia had not been drinking, she never would have crossed this line. Mia needs to think about her relationship to alcohol. (For more on this, see how you can TCB in your relationship to substances in chapter 14.) Alcohol (and other substances) can really mess with TCB. Being under the influence weakens boundaries and impairs decision-making. And it's hard to trust a person who can't take responsibility for their actions.

FRIENDS HELP FRIENDS REMEMBER TO TCB

Not being able to access TCB is a major reason why someone who is under the influence cannot reliably give consent. If you are ever in a situation where you see something like this happening with one of your friends, don't be a bystander. If your stomach drops when you see something: do something. Don't assume that someone else will take care of it, because it's likely that everyone else is also assuming the same thing. Tap your friend on the shoulder and ask, "How are you doing?" when you think they're in danger of crossing a line. Lean on your capacity to practice TCB when you feel like someone else can't. Maybe then you can help guide your friends into making fewer damaging choices.

STAY NEUTRAL:
DON'T PICK SIDES

Being able to recognize where TCB is out of balance doesn't just apply to crushes, hookups, boyfriends, girlfriends, or any sort of romance. If you look carefully, you'll notice it in all of your relationships. Let's see if you can tell how it's working (or not) in this friendship:

> *Lauren and Jane are getting into huge blowout fights in the halls in front of the lockers where everyone can see, and now they are making every girl in the class take sides. Sianalee's not involved, and she doesn't want to be involved, but when Jane asks her whose side she's on, she takes Jane's side—because she's better friends with Jane. And when Lauren asks to talk with her about what's going on, Sianalee feels like she has to act like Lauren's done something wrong. This leaves Sianalee feeling bad.*

Some of you may be thinking, "Of course I would take my friend's side! I'm a loyal friend!" Whereas others don't get why it should even be an issue—fights happen. However, this is a prime example in seeing how the boundaries in TCB can get wishy-washy. School is hard enough alone, but then you add the social aspect: WHAMMO! It's even more complicated. But let's take this scenario step-by-step to see where the problem lies.

The primary problem is between Lauren and Jane. They do not trust each other, they do not have compassion for each other, and they are definitely not respecting each other's boundaries. But even though the problem is between them, they are making it everyone else's problem. The best solution would be for the two of them to work it out. **They might not be able to see the real issues. But the fact is that people who have trusting, compassionate, and respectful relationships don't tend to get into screaming matches in public. So, agreed, Lauren and Jane should work out the problem on their own. If they can't? They should go to an adult they trust for help.**

It was unfair of Jane to ask Sianalee to pick sides—it was a massive violation of Sianalee's boundaries. **Sianalee needs to know that she does not have to take sides. (You never have to take sides.)** In fact, it is smartest to remove yourself from situations that are chaotic and do not involve you, even if it involves someone you have trust and compassion for. If Sianalee had checked in with TCB, she would have asked herself: Is my friendship with Jane strong enough to survive without publicly "taking her side"? Can I feel compassion for both people involved? Are my own boundaries strong enough that I can choose to not get involved?

And finally, Sianalee should have compassion for Lauren. Sianalee could have told Jane that, even though she understood that Jane and Lauren had issues, and even though she supports Jane, she doesn't feel right taking sides in public. She could have said that since Lauren asked her what was going on, maybe Lauren feels bad about the way things are. She could tell Jane that while neither of them have to be friends with Lauren, they don't have to treat her badly either. Even if you don't like a person, you should practice having compassion for them, because everyone deserves to be treated with compassion, no matter who they are. I'm sure you've heard it before,

but you should treat others how you want to be treated. We're trying to build a better world, right? It starts here.

#GOALS: TCB IN BALANCE

What happens when you approach situations with TCB in mind? Let's look at an example of TCB working to the benefit of everyone involved.

> *Taladega and Scorpion have been friends since the third grade, and Scorpion has been secretly in love with Taladega ever since. Now a sophomore in high school, Scorpion can't take it anymore and needs to tell Taladega how they feel. Scorpion texts Taladega to ask, "Hey, I want to tell you something. Is now a good time?" and Taladega responds back, "Absolutely." So they decide to meet after school. When they finally do talk, it turns out that Taladega does not have reciprocal feelings—unfortunately for Scorpion. Scorp is obviously devastated, but they are glad that they got their feelings off their chest. Taladega tells Scorpion that they need a little space to process what just happened, and Scorpion agrees. They don't talk for two months.*

This example shows something important: practicing TCB is hard work. Even though the situation was painful, the two teens were able to communicate their feelings to each other without attacking or actively trying to hurt each other. Scorpion did the right thing by telling Taladega their true feelings about them. Instead of holding them in and feeling like they were going to go crazy, they took a risk for the betterment of their friendship. Texting Taladega and asking if they were ready to receive heavy info was incredibly compassionate. (It's also a great example of asking for consent!)

If you're interested in someone, it might seem easier to text a slurry of drippy, gooey feelings. You might think it's easier to say how you feel without having to experience the other person's reaction in real time. But more times than not, if you're feeling that way, it's because you suspect that the expression of your feelings might feel awkward for the other person. And just dumping your feelings on someone else assumes that their boundaries are strong enough to handle what you are sending their way. Considering how your announcement might be received *before* you say it is having compassion for the person who is on the receiving end.

Even though Taladega does not have mutual feelings, they definitely have good boundaries. They did not make Scorpion feel uncomfortable or undesirable. They made it obvious that they valued the friendship, and it was mature to ask for space to process the new information. Taladega could have ghosted, but they were willing to tell their friend what they needed. Allowing your friend to know what's going on internally is a kindness.

The open line of communication between Scorpion and Taladega allows them to interact with each other while practicing TCB. Even though it didn't end in a new romance, the two were able to grow through interacting with each other while practicing TCB. If they've been friends since the third grade, that means that they've been friends for eight whole years! That's a long time! And that history doesn't just dissolve when you don't physically see each other. If your friend moved across the country and they no longer live in your neighborhood, that doesn't mean they are no longer your friend. Sure, you'll have experiences without them, and grow a few inches, and maybe kiss somebody before you see them again, but you will always have the friendship that you had.

Read on to see how **consent is a way of constantly testing how TCB is holding up at any given moment in your interaction with someone else.** When things start to feel a little blurry, it is wise to check for whether you trust the other person, whether you are practicing compassion, and whether you are respecting their boundaries. But more importantly: Do you trust yourself? Do you have compassion for yourself? And are your boundaries intact? Checking in with TCB helps us learn more about ourselves while interacting with each other. It's a long, difficult road, but we are gonna break it down for you, step-by-step.

TOP THREE
TAKEAWAYS FOR TCB

1 Balancing trust, compassion, and boundaries (TCB) is key to healthy relationships.

2 You need to look at TCB from both sides—yours and the other person's.

3 Practicing TCB in *any* relationship turns awkward encounters into a meaningful moment.

chapter 2

C-O-N-S-E-N-T

Oh! A little consent. Just a little bit, a little consent.

Elvis, the king of rock-and-roll, may have been Paulina's inspiration for TCB, but when it comes to talking about consent, I'm inspired by the queen of soul! **All right, old man.** So with all due R-E-S-P-E-C-T to Aretha Franklin, we're talking about C-O-N-S-E-N-T. **Doesn't roll off the tongue in quite the same way, but you get the idea: take care, TCB.**

Seriously, we assume you've heard about consent, but whether you have or haven't, you should check out UpRoot, a website dedicated to all things about consent (it's in our Resources and Recommended Reading section at the back of the book). When it comes to relationships and sex, it's likely that someone has talked to you about the legal, ethical, or moral reasons that "no means NO." Before we jump into our theory about consent and TCB, let's review these three areas where the concept of consent may have very specific repercussions:

LEGAL: There are individual guidelines, usually state laws, that cover various settings for consent (medical, interpersonal, mental health, surgical, etc.). There is a legal age when a person can consent to a sexual relationship; if you are under that age, your consent is not legally valid. If you have sex with someone under that age, even if they want to have sex with you, their consent is not legally valid and will be disregarded in a court of law.

ETHICAL: Ethics are rules made by external sources to regulate behavior. To convince or coerce a person who is drunk, or high, or otherwise incapacitated to participate in a sexual encounter is not ethical. That person cannot freely consent to a sexual encounter. **Remember Mia from chapter 1? She admitted she was drunk enough to cross the line and kiss her friend's boyfriend. So even if he asked for a kiss, and she said yes, he's still on shaky ethical ground when it comes to consent.**

MORAL: Morals are guiding principles that help us discern right from wrong. You probably get these kinds of messages about what is "good" or "bad" from your parents, religious leaders, or other respected adults. But research is starting to show that instinctive moral feelings are fundamentally present in your brain. This means that, if you can listen carefully, you'll learn to hear an internal voice that can guide you in confusing situations. These guiding feelings can also be refined and reinforced by family and culture. But, at the end of the day, these feelings about what is good or bad, right or wrong, belong to you. **By the way, if you don't conform to the majority of people around you, that doesn't make you a monster (even if people try to make you feel like one). However, it does mean that you have to be very clear about what core values you want to choose to guide your actions—and be confident in sharing those values with others.**

These three areas offer a good place to start thinking about consent. But we think the concept is much more complicated—just like real life can be. What's missing here is a discussion of **consent as a complex emotional and psychological negotiation** that involves how you see yourself in different relationships, and whether you are actually balancing trust, compassion, and boundaries in those relationships. **That's why we're here: to help cut through the confusion that surrounds how you feel and act with all kinds of people in your life. If you understand consent, and are aware of the balance of TCB, you will be able to confidently and consciously consent (or not). Maintaining TCB and being conscious of consent creates the foundation for healthy relating.**

While this book focuses on consent between individuals in all kinds of relationships, it is also important to think about a bigger picture of consent. For example, you have the power of consent in relation to the institutions you are part of. From your school to your government, there are structures that impart institutionalized beliefs. Looking at the practices and assumptions of these social structures using the lens of trust, compassion, and boundaries can help you figure out whether or not you believe what you are being told about yourself and others.

You may have attended protests or consider yourself an activist already—which means you are actively standing up for what you believe. We want you to know that it's okay not to consent to the status quo. Just because things are the way they are does not mean you have to be complicit. When it comes to consenting to taking part in the world around you, follow TCB: Educate yourself before you trust what you're being told. Be compassionate as you learn about how others view the world. And examine where boundaries apply—are they different for you than they are for other people? If you don't consent to being part of a practice or particular belief system, speak out! Ask questions of and listen to what people with different perspectives have to say. Learning how to raise your voice is a part of making change.

As a doctor, I ask for consent all the time. "May I take a look at that injury?" "Is it okay if I give you a shot?" "I'd like to run this test, is that okay with you?" Almost without exception (unless they're unconscious), patients have to sign documents saying they give consent for a particular procedure or treatment. There are legal reasons, of course. Different actions may involve different levels of risk. And no one can be forced to submit to a treatment or a medication if they don't want it. So, I work hard to reassure the people in my care (**trust**). I know that being sick or hurt can be scary or make people anxious (**compassion**) and I know that when I treat them, I am going to need to touch them (**boundary**). For the medical relationship (a thing unique to the patient and me—that third cocreated factor) to be successful, my patient must be a willing participant in that relationship. This process of giving another person the freedom to make these informed decisions, and then respecting what they decide, is what we mean when we talk about **consent.**

Lucky for me, my dad has always given me a lot of freedom to choose what I do or do not want to do. But I did not really connect my freedom of choice to my right to consent. That's because I have always been taught about consent in legal terms—which I suspect is how people attempt to emphasize its importance when they are trying to make sure teenagers limit the dangerous or stupid mistakes they make. But when I think about my experience in how consent is asked for, or given, it is often in a sexual context. "Wanna make out?" "Can I touch you there?" "Want to hook up?" "Do you like it if I do this?"

CONSENT TRANSLATOR

What if you're not sure of how to verbalize consent? It's vulnerable to say those things out loud! Well, lucky for you, we have a consent translator. More than one of these things can be happening in the same encounter, in any order. And remember, if it feels like you can't say anything at all, you need to pause the action and figure out what you want.

WHAT YOU WANT	WHAT YOU CAN SAY
Someone to stop touching you, talking to you, or pressuring you to do something	"No!" (Literally, this is all you have to say.)
To stop the action, but keep the vibe going	"I like you, but I don't want to do this."
You're not really sure. Might feel good; might not (emotionally or physically)	"I'm not sure how I'm feeling about this." "I need a minute."
Exactly what is happening to keep on happening	"Yes!" "Nice!" "Don't stop!"

You should understand that, in all kinds of ways, asking for consent is a good thing. The problem starts when people do not ask for, or give, their consent. Beginning in middle school, I was taught that consent was a tool to protect myself from unwanted attention from boys (stereotypical assumption, if I do say so myself). And boys were told to ask for consent to avoid facing false legal allegations. Which doesn't happen as often as you think it does, by the way. RAINN, the nation's largest anti-

WHAT YOU SHOULD DO IF YOU HEAR THIS

Stop! Cease what you are doing! Give the other person some personal space and check in with them and see if they are all right. Talk about what should happen next.

Stop! Check in with them: What *would* they like to do? Then shift gears and proceed. (If you like it too.)

Immediately take a pause in the action and check in: "Do you want to keep going?" "Can I try something else?" "What *does* feel good for you?" "Did you like what I was doing before?" "Should we slow down?"

Keep doing exactly what you are doing!

sexual violence organization, estimates that three out of four sexual assaults go unreported. Reporting an assault is one of the hardest things anyone will ever have to do. **So to assume a false accusation will come your way may speak more to your moral character than to the supposed nefariousness of wily, gold-digging girls.**

Later, and through some personal trial and error, I came to learn that consent is more complicated than knowing how to stop unwanted acts or attention. Consent requires that both participants know how to interpret (and respect) their own needs and those of their partner. I've learned that both friendships and romantic relationships are healthier when I start from a place of really knowing and trusting myself. When you are able to exercise trust and compassion because you know where your boundaries lie, you will do exactly what you want to do, and you will not give your consent if you, at your very core, do not want to.

CONSENT IS MORE THAN JUST SAYING YES OR NO

For many years I toured colleges and gave lectures about sex and relationships. I'd be in a big lecture hall full of students who I knew all had many of the same questions but were often too embarrassed to admit they weren't "sexperts" themselves. However, one question that always got a reaction was when I asked, "If hooking up is such a big part of social life on campus—and commonly accepted as something that a lot of people do—why are you usually drinking when hookups happen?"

The guys were usually the first to respond: "Liquid confidence," they'd explain. "I'm nervous about approaching girls." "I won't care so much if I get rejected." Then I'd ask the girls. The room would be quiet for a while. Then someone would share her truth. "If I'm drunk, I won't have feelings about it."

If you asked this group if they were practicing consent, they'd assert they were. The guys were asking. The girls were saying yes. In their minds, it was consensual. But was this good consent? Did they know how to TCB? Denying your feelings and instincts is the opposite of practicing effective TCB. And of course, using any substance until your boundaries get blurred makes it hard, if not impossible, to respect your own feelings. No one was having compassion for themselves. And possibly not for the other person involved, either.

From my perspective, hookups weren't fun or sexy or empowering. They were just physical encounters, lacking all the emotion and vulnerability that makes having sex a way of intimately and intensely connecting with another person. If only these college students had started learning about TCB and consent earlier!

I did not learn about consent until college. At college orientation, I was told that "consent is sexy" and that "yes means yes, and no means no." These messages were simple, but not nuanced. It felt like the punch line of a joke, rather than information that I needed. At eighteen, I could legally buy cigarettes and porn, but I didn't know that a million nos that turn into a reluctant yes is coercion and is not consensual sex; I didn't listen when I was told that I couldn't fully consent if I was heavily intoxicated; I didn't see the red flag that I had to drink in order to have the courage to have sex; I didn't know that I could revoke consent at any point in a sexual encounter.

College is too late to have your first real discussion about consent.

RED LIGHT, YELLOW LIGHT, GREEN LIGHT: SIGNALS FOR CONSENT

When it comes to sex specifically, consent happens on a continuum. It can be hard to say exactly what you want, and when you want it. Not everyone feels comfortable just putting it out there. And you may not even know what you want to do until you get to each point. And that's all okay.

If you've got your driver's license—or even been a passenger in a car—you already know this: a red light means "stop"; a light that is flashing yellow means "proceed with caution"; and green means "keep going."

Now it's time for a relationship version that can help you figure out where a potential romantic encounter is headed. These key verbal and nonverbal signals can help you and the other person navigate.

In some cases, a "yellow light" will turn "red" or a "green" will blink "yellow" and you'll need to slow down to see what comes next. You must look out for these cues. For example, eye contact and a smile may lead to physical touch (green lights all the way). Or quality time will lead to saying how you are feeling, which might lead to physical touch (yellow to green). By the same token, it's possible to not pay attention and not stop right away if the light turns red. If you are asking for what you want and your partner begins to seem anxious or embarrassed, or pulls away (yellow light turns red), you need to slow down, or stop, and ask how they are feeling.

Check in with yourself as well as your partner. After all, you're on this journey together! If you aren't making eye contact or smiling, or showing that what you're doing is what you want to be doing, you need to ask yourself: "Do I actually want this? Do I feel comfortable saying I don't like what's happening? Am I okay with stopping if they say they don't like what I'm doing? Can I ask them to do something different? Will I be okay if they ask me to change what I'm doing?" If the answer, for either of you, is no—use the language from our handy consent translator to call things off. *Remember: You can take back your consent at any point during an encounter. And never, ever let someone talk you into anything you do not enthusiastically want to experience.*

GREEN LIGHT, YELLOW LIGHT, RED LIGHT

Green light/Keep going:

- *You are both easily making eye contact.* You trust one another.
- *You are both smiling, laughing, or expressing positive emotion.* You're on the same page with what you're feeling and how you're expressing it.
- *You feel comfortable when they touch you, in both big and small ways* (and you feel like you want to touch them). You're exploring boundaries and trusting that your partner respects yours. Whether it's a high-five or a hug, everything feels comfortable for both people.

Flashing yellow light/Proceed with care:

- *You are platonically spending time together.* Keep moving forward but make sure you enjoy one another as people.

- *You can say what you feel, but you don't know if the other person has feelings for you.* Communication is key. Even if you don't know if they have romantic intentions, make sure you trust that your partner will hear and respect your part of the experience.

- *You can ask for what you want, and you can listen when your partner asks for what they want.* Having compassion for one another makes this a good experience for the both of you.

Red light/Stop!

- *You feel anxious or embarrassed or something just doesn't feel right.* Trust your instincts. You are not comfortable with that person.

- *Your partner is looking away, is suddenly silent, or seems distant.* The connection between both of you is severed.

- *Anyone—at any time—says they want to stop.* And so you stop. Breathe. And take time to reevaluate.

SAYING IT WITHOUT SAYING IT

Nonverbal communication is communication between people without words. **A nod to say hello as you're walking across the street or flashing a look at your best friend when someone says something outrageous are examples of nonverbal communication that many of us do without even thinking.** There's a lot that can be said through how you look at someone, the expressions you make, how close or far from them you keep your body, sounds that you make, and the ways that you touch them. **Your body is, in fact, speaking for you, whether you're aware of it or not. Rolling your eyes and crossing your arms is as loud as saying, "I think you're an idiot."** But, in fact, in almost all circumstances, nonverbal communication should be the signal that you need to clarify verbally where anyone is at.

Don't be shy about asking questions to help you understand what someone is trying to express without words. This is an important reminder for a lot of us. For many different reasons, a lot of people have trouble interpreting nonverbal cues. **When in doubt, shout it out! Remember, verbal cues are much clearer than nonverbal cues.** So even if someone is smiling, or nodding yes, or hugging you, or gazing deeply into your eyes, without saying a word, find a moment to check in and verbally confirm that they feel good about the way things are going **(and maybe let them know that you do, too, because they might be having trouble reading *your* nonverbal cues!).**

TOP THREE TAKEAWAYS FOR CONSENT

1 You cannot consent if you are not practicing TCB. Trust, compassion, and boundaries are the foundation of healthy consent.

2 Consent is not a transaction. There is a lot that can happen between asking and a yes or no. So slow down, tune in to what the other person is saying or doing, and check in if you're not sure.

3 No is a full answer. No explanation or apology needed. If you don't like what is happening—or even think you don't like what is happening—you have every right to tell the other person to stop.

PART 2

MIRROR, MIRROR, ON THE WALL

In order to even think about engaging in a relationship with another person, you must have a relationship with yourself—because as RuPaul says, "If you can't love yourself, how in the hell you gonna love somebody else?" Claiming your own identity means you have a clear sense of who you are, allowing you to accurately represent yourself to others, and making it easier for the world to see you as you see yourself. In other words, your relationship with yourself has a ton to do with how you feel in relationships with other people.

There are so many ways that you can tell yourself and others who you are. You can show parts of yourself by the fashion you love, the way you wear your hair, the music you listen to, the sports you play. Any of these things can reflect how you think of yourself and how you present yourself to others. In this section, we'll help you think about the things that make you uniquely you. There's a lot that goes into the mix that makes up your authentic self, including biological, social, and cultural forces. To feel comfortable and happy in relationships, you need to have a strong sense of personal identity. You need to understand, embrace, and love yourself if you are going to ask anyone else to do the same.

chapter 3

ME, MYSELF, AND I(DENTITY)

One of the biggest questions everyone grapples with (and at multiple times in their lives) is "Who am I?" And while there are as many answers as there are people in the world, there are a few basic things that are true for everyone. In every way, your earliest self is the result of a relationship. Your genetic characteristics are due to a reproductive relationship (egg, meet sperm). **It's wild to think about what we all share if we start from the very beginning: sperm + egg = zygote. Zygote + uterus = baby. Two components come together to create something larger than itself. (Sound familiar? Hint: 1 + 1 = 3. It's relationship math!)**

Your earliest sense of self begins to develop in relationship to another person (usually, but not always, your birth mother). Think about it: a human is the only creature that is born completely dependent on another human for survival. Evolutionary biologists would say that's because, relative to other mammals, humans have extra-large skulls (to house extra-large brains), so in order for our big heads to get out, we are born before the rest of our body is self-sufficient. **Have you ever held a baby? Their necks aren't strong enough to** hold up their own heads. Now, if you can, go thank the person who birthed you. Because your head was not easy to squeeze out.

Almost every other creature can walk, or run, or climb, within moments of being born. They have fur or feathers to keep them warm; they are born with teeth so they can chew. It's a matter of survival. But human babies are helpless. Without other humans to provide food, or warmth, or safety, we couldn't survive.

There's another important way your sense of self is determined by your earliest relationships. As a baby, you start to define your personality and identity in relation to the people who are taking care of you. In an ideal situation, you learn what it is like to feel safe, loved, and valued. And you learn how to communicate what you need. When my kids were born, I was always amazed how their mom seemed to know exactly what each cry meant. She knew what they needed without words. It was harder for me to make that preverbal connection. **Thank you, Mom, for hearing my cries and knowing what they meant. I'm happy to have survived this far.** But as children grow, they learn whether they need to be loud to be heard, what behaviors are rewarded, and what character traits their family values.

You're not supposed to suddenly wake up one day with a crystal-clear perception about your most authentic self. It takes some work to figure out who you are, especially in your teens and early twenties. You don't yet have a career that defines you. You may have things you try on for size—like leadership positions, or membership in clubs, or new groups of friends. **As you grow older, the pool of people you are relating to gets bigger and more varied, and things become a lot more complex. You likely were not aware of how your** early circumstances were shaping you, but now the stakes in figuring out who you are in relation to others can feel high. And they are. Because you can't have good relationships with other people without having a good relationship with yourself first.

A TALE ABOUT IDENTITY

You'd think I'd know everything about sex, and health, and relationships, because my dad is Dr. Drew—but no, we did not talk about sex at the dinner table every night. Still, even though I'm not a doctor or a Certified Sexpert, I am pretty knowledgeable on the topic because of my research, education, and lived experience. And I feel comfortable sharing what I know with you, not because I am a doctor, but because I am a writer.

I haven't always known that I was a writer. After graduating from high school, I moved to New York City to attend Barnard College, where I got my undergraduate degree in American studies with a concentration in media and popular culture. I did student musical theater and played rugby, which is to say: I had no idea what I was doing and what I wanted to do. My junior year, my friend asked me to write a piece for my college newspaper. "Get Your Teeth Checked" explored incredibly difficult topics: bulimia, eating disorder recovery, and the complications of the mother-daughter relationship. Lucky for me, it was celebrated within my college community. It was the first time I was seen for who I was: a writer. But I still didn't see myself that way.

After I graduated from college, I wanted to become a comedian.

I didn't want to handle difficult topics anymore, I just wanted to make people laugh. In 2015, I moved to Chicago to study at the Second City Conservatory. At Second City, I honed my improvisational and sketch comedy skills, so I am always quick to make a joke (consider yourself warned). There, I learned how to play to the height of my intelligence. What does that mean? Playing to the height of my intelligence means I always make the smartest joke possible: no racism, sexism, or homophobia. Do better, be smarter.

But then it hit me: I'm a writer, and I have to pursue the truth. Storytelling has the capacity to heal people—just like doctors. And who said I can't make people laugh along the way? The year after Second City, I found my way back to New York to pursue my master's of fine arts in nonfiction creative writing at Columbia University. Throughout my coursework, I learned how to fully express myself and how to tell my story. Now, I have command over my written voice. And I have an appreciation for how everything is cumulative, meaning that everything you learn and feel and experience serves a larger goal: the future you. Because of everything past Paulina experienced, I am confident in what I say and how I say it. I am proud to be a writer.

WRITE YOUR OWN IDENTITY STORY

Our identities are the stories we learn about who we are, which allow us to develop into our authentic selves. Being comfortable with who you are means that you can share your story with other folks, and their reactions may support or challenge what you believe to be true about yourself, helping you learn more about who you really, truly are. Discovering your authentic self is a journey, and you should expect to go down different paths of self-expression over your lifetime.

Obviously, figuring out your entire identity isn't as simple as taking a quiz—you very well may have already found out what type of dessert and which Disney Princess you are. That is very important information. But as someone who knows that she'd be a pint of Ben & Jerry's Milk & Cookies ice cream and Mulan, I feel as though we can dive a little bit deeper. Settle in, take your time, think about your answers. Bonus tip: use a journal and retake this test at different times so future you can look back and appreciate the path you've taken.

Are you ready? Let's go!

What is your name? _____

_____

Do you know the story of your name? _____

_____

Where do you live? _____

_____

How old are you? _____

_____

How many siblings do you have? _____

_____

Where do your ancestors come from? _____

_____

Which religion do you practice? (If any at all) _____

_____

What gender do you identify as? _____

    (This might feel like a complicated question. If you are
    unsure, please leave it blank until after you read chapter 4.)

How would you describe your racial identity? _____

_____

What are your extracurricular(s)? _____

_____

What is your favorite song? _____

_____

What is your favorite food? _____

_____

What careers are you interested in? _____

_____

What is your favorite thing to do alone? _____

_____

What is your favorite thing to do with other people? _____

_____

What about where you are from are you proud about? _____

_____

Do you define yourself by what music you listen to? _____

    Why or why not? _____

_____

Do you sometimes act differently depending on what
    friends you are with? _____

_____

What about you do you think will remain the same in
    five years? In ten? _____

_____

What do you think will change? _____

_____

How do you think you did on the quiz? Lucky for you, there's no real way to grade it. This ain't school! But that doesn't mean it isn't important. The quiz does teach you something: how you identify yourself. More than anything, we are starting to inspire self-reflection. The best thing you can do to get to know yourself is to think seriously about what makes you *you!*

RACIAL AND ETHNIC PRIDE

All of these facets come together in different ways at different times as you define your identity. Do not be afraid to be who you are: you are fantastic. You are the sole person who is privileged enough to experience everything, from birth to death, from your very own point of view. Go back to the quiz and put a star next to the characteristics that feel permanent. Which parts of your identity are temporary and which parts of who you are will last forever?

Some of the things you listed may shift over time, like where you live, and what kind of job you want to have. On the other hand, you might have said that where your ancestors came from or your racial identity are things that are fixed forever. For some of you, that is true. For others, you might also be surprised to learn that racial and ethnic identity can shift over time. Psychologists who study how cultural and racial identity develops confirm that these processes are especially dynamic during adolescence. **(Even though identity development is a lifelong process!)**

Your physical appearance is based in biology—in other words, it's a gift from your ancestors. But *race* is a social construct, meaning it is a flexible way in which a society puts people into groups based on appearance. Your *racial identity* is shaped as you navigate through social structures. Psychologist William Cross identifies four *statuses* of racial identity. Any one of these statuses may feel accurate to you in explaining how you are feeling about how your race fits into your identity:

Pre-encounter—Your race doesn't feel like the part of your identity that has the most impact on your life. This is especially true if you are in an environment where most people look like you. So a white teen living in a predominantly white community might not even consider race as a primary part of their identity. But a Black, Indigenous, or person of color (BIPOC) teen living in the same community is likely to have an awareness that becomes a bigger part of their self-identification.

Encounter—You become aware of your race through an experience. For nonwhite teens, this is often a negative encounter where they experience racism for the first time.

Immersion—You want to know more about your racial identity; you actively want to learn and spend time with people like you. This is a particularly important status for nonwhite teens. If you are in a community where you can't find a lot of peers or mentors, you may have to get creative in seeking out others who have shared your experiences. Research cultural groups within your community that you can find identification within. If you share the same racial identity with your parents, they may also be a great resource. And, if not, there's always the internet!

Internalization and commitment—You feel secure and proud of your racial identity. You are as confident socializing with your own community as you are with people who don't look like you and haven't shared your experiences. This, my friends, is the goal.

Internalizing one's own racial identity is a conscious journey. As a white person, I can't say that understanding my own racial identity was all that complicated or painful. But that can't be said for my BIPOC peers. In middle and high school, I never would have thought to ask my Black or Brown friends what it was like for them (the very definition of privilege—I know). But thankfully, I woke up and started to ask questions. So, to learn more, I talked to a friend who is about a decade younger than I am. Here's what they said:

Avery remembers the first time they noticed race. "I was maybe four or five and I would look for families like mine. I remember telling my mother, 'That family is like ours, only the mom is Black instead of the dad!'" But Avery didn't connect their desire to find similar-looking families to their racial identity, until they hit grade school. When a classmate asked, in all sincerity, "Why would your mom marry your dad, anyway?" the hurt Avery felt was connected to the color of their dad's skin. And by extension to their own. Things continued to be complicated through junior high. Avery had transferred to a different school, a few towns over, in a mostly white, conservative community. "I still remember I was one of three nonwhite kids in the whole school, but the other two girls had darker skin. I'm light-skinned, and they knew my privilege. I didn't fit anywhere." Avery eventually started to feel more confident in their identity in high school. They had changed schools again, and while classmates were still mostly white, the school was arts focused and the inclusive community allowed Avery "to become proud of my Blackness" because it was as much a recognized part of them as their musical talent and love of theater. Now, when people ask Avery "what they are," Avery chooses to reply they are "mixed." They explain, "Even though I would not choose white as a primary part of my identity, when people look at me they see lighter skin. When I say I am mixed, it gives me an opening to talk about my Blackness." As complicated as defining their racial identity has been, Avery also knows they have the privilege that comes with lighter skin. "I feel safer than some of my friends. People don't make assumptions. I've never had to fight against a stereotype."

In addition to your race, you may also have an ethnic identity. This can be represented by the music you listen to, the language you speak, the way you dress, the beliefs of your family and community, and certain holidays or traditions you practice. Race and ethnicity can blend and blur. At different times one or the other may feel primary to your identity. From thinking about your answers to the quiz above, you should realize that it's perfectly normal to change your perception of who you feel you are.

Ultimately, it's okay to want to show different parts of yourself. But it can be challenging to feel confident in your identity when people prejudge your behavior or ascribe certain attitudes to how you express yourself, or make assumptions about you based on appearance. If you are struggling with how to make sense of your identity, one approach is to contact someone you admire and question them about these issues and what their struggles might have been. This could be a teacher, a family member, or even someone in your community. Don't be afraid to reach out and ask questions.

But all in all, your identity is for you and you alone to define. Sure, some people will try to shove you into a box based on what they think they know about you. But it is your right to bust out of any box and proudly say exactly who you are.

DEALING WITH "ISMS"

No one single aspect of your life has to define you, although you may give some more weight than others. We want to acknowledge here that if you're a BIPOC teen reading this book, you have less control than white teens when it comes to people forming instant impressions about you. That's racism.

Any time people make assumptions based on your appearance and treat you differently because of your appearance—that's discrimination. This is also true if you have a visible disability. It can be frustrating when hardware (like a wheelchair) or a helper (like a service animal) causes people to make assumptions about you. This kind of judgment is called ableism.

The other important thing to remember is that not all of our differences are visible. If you've got an invisible condition—a psychological or developmental challenge, a learning difference, or hearing or vision challenges, for example—that part of your identity may not be apparent to someone looking at you, but you may still face real "isms" and discrimination. At times, you may feel like you are the only person in the world who has to deal with this part of your identity. **But what others may see as a challenge, you may claim as a positive part of your identity.** That's true. No one looking at me would know that I struggle with anxiety and obsessive/compulsive traits. I've come to see these characteristics as a positive part of my identity as a doctor. My compulsion to check and recheck made me a good medical student and an extra careful physician.

All kinds of "isms" and "whatever-phobias" (sexism, racism, ableism, sizeism, classism, transphobia, homophobia, etc.) lead to discrimination and can take root in society, leading to oppression of large groups of people. **If you are against one kind of discrimination, it makes sense for you to be against all kinds. (Go to page 131 to learn how you can stand up and be an ally!)**

It is emphatically not fair when people judge you without knowing you. But it can still be hard to stay strong and confident in your identity in the face of discrimination and oppression. **Luckily, you are TCB strong! Trust** that advocating for yourself doesn't make you selfish. Be **compassionate** with yourself. Don't internalize any negativity that is reflected at you. Seek out those people who positively reinforce the part of your identity that is being judged. And then turn that compassion outward to evoke it in others. If you feel like confronting the "ism," say "Ouch, that hurt." And then tell them why.

And remember, it is on those other people, the ones who are making assumptions—*and not on you*—to change. So hold those boundaries firm. Even if you have a history together, you don't have to stay friends with someone who hurts or demeans you.

If you're feeling like your journey to be confident in your identity has more roadblocks than some of your peers, know that you can find people who will cheer you on so you can feel good about showing the world the real you. As you live through struggles day to day, take pride in your strength and in the strength of your ancestors. Honor what they faced, and what they've come through. You carry on their legacy. You are stronger than those people making judgments know. **Be proud. Be brave. Claim your identity. Not only are there a lot of people who are like you, there is also space for every single one of us to confidently express our individuality in this big ol' world.**

THE EVOLUTION OF YOU

It's not just the first impressions people form that can impact your developing self-identity. Your environment—where you are and who you are with—can also play a big role in how you see yourself. You need to pay attention to this, because the fact is that the reflected version of you becomes yet another part of your full sense of self. In other words, your identity isn't totally formed from the inside out. Part of knowing yourself is acknowledging the powerful influence of outside factors, which can make you act a certain way or define yourself in relation to the situations you find yourself in.

As an adult, I've had a lot of time to think about how my own identity has evolved. In high school, I really struggled to define who I was. It took until my senior year before I had the confidence to ask out a girl, try out for a sport, and take on a leadership role in my class. And even though I was suddenly "successful" at all three, I still didn't feel 100 percent comfortable in my own skin. What made it worse was that I felt a tremendous amount of pressure to live up to that image of success. So when it was time for college, I traded my identity as a Southern California guy for being a preppy college student in New England. I felt like I had landed in a foreign country. There was no beach. I'd never been so cold. I didn't even have a winter coat. My family, friends, and girlfriend were three thousand miles away. I was adrift. Everyone thought I was successful (in all the ways that mattered as a teen). Everyone, that is, but me. I didn't trust that I could be successful. I had no compassion for myself—only criticism. I had no good emotional boundaries to contain all of my chaotic feelings, and I started having panic attacks.

I withdrew from school and went back home. Now my identity was "that guy who didn't make it." I hung out with friends at the beach and took a few courses at a local university. I was already anxious about the grade I would receive for my first paper, and when the professor called me in, I thought, "Oh crap, this is going to be bad." Instead he said it was the best paper in the class. But what was weird was that instead of feeling like, "This is it. I can coast through college without even trying," I suddenly felt like writing the B-minus papers at the school I had left would be better for me than getting A-pluses without any effort. The professor was telling me I was smart, but I felt like a fake because I wasn't making an effort. In that moment I learned something important about myself. I didn't just want people to see me as a good student, I actually wanted to learn.

I realized that to learn more, I needed to keep challenging

myself. I went back to the East Coast and back to the college I had left. I recommitted to my studies in science and found a passion for biology. I started to feel like what I was doing had meaning. Don't misunderstand, it wasn't an easy transition. I had a huge task ahead to catch up with my science training, but I got to it. I embraced the nerd culture and I made new friends who saw me as a smart and curious individual and validated my identity as a scientist.

But I still wasn't treating myself with trust or compassion (it's truly a lifelong journey), and my boundaries were still a little wobbly. I jumped into my medical training and early career as if it was the only thing that mattered. I didn't trust that my identity could expand to include things other than being the best doctor. I believed the work I was doing was so very important that I couldn't have compassion for myself when I was exhausted or overwhelmed. What mattered was that people saw me as I saw myself: a tireless healer. And what happened? My job crashed right through my boundaries and I became a workaholic.

I didn't know all of that. Well, I knew the workaholic part. But not the rest of it. It's nice to know that I'm not the only one who has struggled. Sometimes, it is easy to think that our parents have it all figured out. But they were young once, too.

I really had to work at it. When Paulina's brother needed brain surgery when he was just a one-year-old, my anxiety spiraled like never before. Even in a crisis, my workaholism was so strong that I just couldn't be fully present for my family. Finally, what happened was that my wife, who was taking care of three babies, told me emphatically that I needed to get professional help to deal with it. I took her seriously, found a therapist, and focused on learning to connect with my emotions and to create boundaries. I accepted that it was okay to not be perfect (even as a doctor). I started to pay attention to other parts of myself and try new things. I figured out how to be more compassionate to myself, and how to set boundaries in my relationship to my work.

The more I worked at all these things, the more my identity began to expand. I felt more confident. I advocated to government officials and wrote books. I said yes to trying TV shows and podcasts. I let people see that I loved to sing. I've learned to trust that I can be successful in other ways and to go easy on self-criticism when I don't achieve my goals, and—if I'm being totally honest—I still have to work really hard at holding those boundaries that keep work from becoming all-consuming. And even though I'm so far ahead of where you are in your identity journey, I know I still have room to grow and change.

Yes, yes, you do. But then again, so do I. Who doesn't?

MIRROR, MIRROR, ON THE SCREEN

The key to feeling comfortable in your identity is making sure that your internal and external selves agree. The more authentically you can show on the outside what you know to be true about yourself on the inside, the more comfortably you can live in your evolving sense of self. But you have a twist on your search for your identity that I never encountered. I had to meet people in person for them to form an opinion about me. Thanks to social media, you can project your image out into the world, choosing what to reveal—or manipulate—about how people see you. And that's not always good news for your emerging identity.

It's hard to practice good TCB online. I'd dare to say it's almost impossible, unless you actively (and consistently) think about it. Acting in a way that's fake (even if it's online) is not good for you. If you are carefully crafting your emotions in texts or online in order to make others feel some kind of way, you are not being authentic about your insides. If you are curating your image on your Instagram, you are probably not being truthful about your outside. If you consistently project an image that is inauthentic, you risk becoming disconnected from yourself. After a while, it can start to feel like you are just performing for people, and that's no way to let people get to know the real you.

Putting yourself out there as an overproduced, carefully curated "brand" violates every part of TCB. It might feel like your ticket to online popularity, but it's also a ticket to feeling miserable. Research has proven that social comparison—focusing on things that happen online, thinking about what you're going to post, thinking about how good everyone's lives look and how yours could look better—is more than a waste of time. It can suck the happiness out of your life.

PUT YOUR BEST FEED FORWARD

Ask yourself before you post:

- What do I want people to think when they see this picture? Why does that matter?
- Am I showing who I really am? Why or why not?

- And if you're commenting: Do I know how it will affect the other person?

Consider before following:

- Do I know this person in real life? If I don't know them in real life, where do I know them from?
- Do they inspire me? If so, why?
- Am I comparing my life to theirs? Does it make me feel worse about mine?

We appreciate how hard it can be to truly be yourself online. From puberty through adolescence (and even beyond), you can feel like you are waking up in a different body every day. Some of you might not like the body you are living in. You might feel self-conscious, confused, shy about the changes in your body, or physically awkward. Teasing or comments on your appearance might make you feel an intense pressure to take control of your body—even at the expense of your health. At the same time, you are bombarded with media messages about how you should ideally look.

Here's the thing: You can control some things about your image, like how you dress or cut your hair. But your body will forever be changing. So ditch the idea that you have to control what your body looks like to fit some societal ideal. Your obligation to yourself is to keep your body healthy. And healthy bodies look different for different people. (You can thank your genetics for just another way of making you uniquely you.)

I know that you're thinking, "What about all those celebrities or influencers who are perfect-looking and have perfect lives/houses/children/clothes?" Here's the real truth: I have worked in the entertainment business for more than thirty years, and I am not exaggerating when I tell you that nearly everyone on TV (and tons of people on Instagram) has a real life entirely different from the one they show on camera. It's okay to admire things about these people without wanting to be them. But you have to know that you're not seeing the real person.

Let's make one thing clear: the people who you think you want to be like most likely don't accept themselves as *they* are. They are so consumed with constantly scrambling after being relevant that there is **no way** that they are invested in being themselves. And isn't that the point of this whole thing called life? Figuring out who you want to be, rather than trying to be like someone else?

Trying to look a certain way or have a certain car can create a lot of noise in your life, and there's only one way to truly transcend all that: radical self-acceptance. What does radical self-acceptance mean? Well, if you feel as though you are lacking something because you are who you are, it is a "radical" idea to think that you could possibly be totally cool exactly the way you are. Yes, you! Without having the haircut you're dreaming of or the outfit you've got saved in an online shopping cart, you can simply accept yourself. Pretty out-there idea, I know. But I can say that I practice radical self-acceptance because I've learned to love my body as it is. No diets, no clothes, and no celebrity idol is going to change who I am and how I view myself.

In other words, start from the inside and work your way out. So, why not take the first step toward accepting yourself as the person you feel you are? Even if you can't hang on to a positive feeling every day, that doesn't mean that you can't work toward accepting yourself one day at a time. When you feel good about yourself as a person, you can choose healthy ways to sync your inside and outside appearance to show others the real you.

TOP THREE TAKEAWAYS FOR FINDING YOUR IDENTITY

1 You can't have good relationships with other people without having a good relationship with yourself first.

2 Claiming your own identity means you have a clear sense of who you are, allowing you to accurately represent yourself to others and making it easier for the world to see you as you see yourself.

3 Don't let likes drive how you show yourself to others. Healthy relationships are built on a foundation of TCB, not on your "brand."

chapter 4

GENDER EXPRESSION: NAMING IS CLAIMING

GENDER IS COMPLICATED

If, when you were born, the doctor said, "It's a girl," and you feel like a girl: *that's great!*

If, when you were born, the doctor said, "It's a girl," and you feel like a boy: *you do you!*

If, when you were born, the doctor said, "It's a boy," and you feel like a girl: *that's awesome!*

If, when you were born, the doctor said, "It's a boy," and you feel like a boy: *fantastic!*

If you were born and, no matter what the doctors said, you don't quite know where you land: *that's rad, too!*

No matter your gender, just being you should be a cause for celebration!

Talking about gender can be complicated. It can be overwhelming. We recognize now that there are so many gender identities and variables in the world. But these variations are what make us beautiful. So stay with us while we break it down so you can see the beauty in it all, too.

LET'S TALK ABOUT SEX, BABY

Not that kind of sex. Biological sex.

When it comes to humans, biological sex is determined for the most part by something called our **sex chromosomes**. Humans have forty-six chromosomes, matched into twenty-three pairs. The first twenty-two pairs are the same for everyone. That's right: male and female humans differ by virtue of their twenty-third chromosome. Female humans have XX chromosomes, while males have XY. **So everyone has an X chromosome?** Yes. Actually, during fetal development we all start out female. But some babies have a Y sex chromosome that turns on a series of biological processes that diverts the fetus into a male.

Your **biological sex** has to do with whether you have XX or XY chromosomes, or whether your estrogen or testosterone develops as your dominant hormone to influence the physical characteristics of your body. Some things relating to your sex are visible (your genitals), some are not (chromosomes and hormones). **Your biological sex also determines the gender you are assigned at birth.** Based on what they saw when they looked at your genitalia when you were born, doctors announced to your parents "It's a girl!" or "It's a boy!" **It may seem unfair that you start life with a label, but the truth is that it unfortunately takes a while before you get a say in how you express your identity.**

Certain biological forces are at work regardless of someone's gender identity. I think there is a lot of confusion because of the sensational aspect of how those biological forces manifest: genitals. A lot of people assume that your genitals define your gender. Not necessarily! So how do you define your gender if you don't fit into a binary? Well, from a clinical standpoint, my understanding of gender is rooted in biology. For example, some individuals may have been born with a biological insensitivity to sex hormones or different combinations of sex chromosomes, like XXY or XO. Some people are born with genitalia that did not develop as male or female—a medical condition called "different sexual development" or DSD, which has historically been medically addressed shortly after birth. All of these biological variations may impact how an individual experiences their body. All proving that talking about gender can be confusing and that individual experiences are what we should focus on.

In the past, doctors checked the genetics of their patient before performing surgeries to conform their genitalia with their sex chromosomes. A rigidly binary approach—you're either a girl or you're a boy—caused doctors and parents to assign gender based purely on what they observed about a baby's biology at birth. **In recent years, intersex individuals have come out and spoken out against such gender assignment surgery. We now know that determining someone's gender is much more complex than deciding to match their genitals to their chromosomes. In fact, these surgeries can prove to be very painful and traumatic. Unless there is a pressing medical need to correct an imminent risk to health, some parents now choose to let their child grow up and decide their gender for themselves.**

That's why it's important to think about sex and biology in a nuanced way. Certain drives and behaviors are encoded in our biology; they can be influenced by society and shaped or redirected by external forces, but to deny them entirely can cause confusion and pain as you grapple with your gender identity. **In other words, physical biology plays a role in informing your sex, but it's not the only (or even the strongest) influence on your gender. That's why you might feel like you don't have a lot of control over your internal battle to claim your gender identity—at least in the beginning.**

GENDER EVOLUTION

When you are born—or even before, if they have done an ultrasound—the doctor looks at your genitals and makes a call: boy or girl. And based on this long-established medical observation, many people believe that gender can be only one of those two things (what's called a *binary choice*: this or that; male or female). But the reality is that **gender exists on a spectrum.** Navajo and Hawaiian cultures recognize individuals they consider as embodying both male and female spirits. Indonesia, Albania, and India all have cultures that recognize a spectrum of gender expression. As complex as biological sex can be, our experience of gender adds another layer of complexity. Think of gender as being the degree to which you feel and experience your identity, which may encompass different aspects of traditional masculinity and femininity to varying degrees.

Environmental experiences may impact how you think about your gender identity, which is usually dictated by a combination of your biological sex and your culture. Often in the United States, girls are dressed in pink, given dolls, and shown princess movies, while boys wear blue, are given a baseball, and are taught the names of construction vehicles. But why should any particular culture be able to tell boys and girls who we are? Girls like makeup, boys like sports. Girls are soft, boys are rough. Girls can cry, boys can't. The list goes on and on.

The constructs of gender can be deployed to reinforce characteristics of biological sex. This can make some people feel uncomfortable with gender expression, because they may feel like they are a different gender from their biological sex. **We see you kids who don't conform to rigid gender stereotypes!**

GENDER: LEARN THE LINGO

There are so many gender ID options. These are the most mainstream. You can find a more comprehensive list online at PLFAG.org. *(PFLAG is the first and largest organization for lesbian, gay, bisexual, transgender, and queer [LGBTQ+] people, their parents and families, and allies.)*

CISGENDER: In Latin, cis means "same"—so if your sex at birth matches your gender expression, you are cisgender.

Cis man: A cis man is an individual who was **assigned male at birth** (AMAB). This person's gender identity matches his assigned sex. This person identifies as a man.

Cis woman: A cis woman is **assigned female at birth** (AFAB). This person's gender identity matches her assigned sex. This person identifies as a woman.

TRANSGENDER: In Latin, trans means "opposite side." If your gender identity does not match the sex you were assigned at birth, that makes you **transgender.**

Trans woman/Trans girl: This individual was **assigned male at birth** (AMAB). The assigned sex at birth does not align with their affirmed gender. This person **identifies as a woman or girl.**

Trans man/Trans boy: This individual was **assigned female at birth** (AFAB). The assigned sex at birth does not align with their affirmed gender. This person **identifies as a man or boy.**

NONBINARY OR GENDERQUEER: Nonbinary, or gender-queer, individuals may be assigned female or male at birth. However, these terms encapsulate many different gender experiences. There are people who experience two or three different genders (**bigender** or **trigender**). **Agender**, **nongendered**, **genderless**, **genderfree**, or **neutrois** people experience no gender, whereas **genderqueer** people slide between multiple gender identities.

HOW GENDER ID DEVELOPS

Your gender identity is different from your biology and comes from how you are socialized and the roles you take on. It's important to understand that **your sex doesn't determine your gender, and your gender doesn't determine who you will be attracted to** (you can read more about attraction in chapter 5). Gender is how you feel—and you can feel different from the sex you were assigned at birth. Your gender expression is how you show others a part of your identity. **Gender can be expressed in the clothes we wear, how we style our hair, and the ways we behave. Being seen the way we want to be seen can be hard because gender roles are entirely con-**

structed, and often reinforced, by society—starting with babies: girls are dressed in pink and boys are dressed in blue.

Your gender identity is not something you decide so much as something that you become increasingly aware of. You may begin to make a series of conscious choices that take you in a particular direction in your appearance. Or you may feel a spontaneous urge to express your authentic self. **Yes! It can be hard to articulate gender because it is something that evolves over time. When you hit puberty and grow breasts, or start to have facial hair, you may begin to have strong feelings about whether the way you look on the outside matches how you feel on the inside.** That's why sometimes gender roles feel just right—and sometimes they can make you feel like you're trapped by how others see you.

QUIZ
The Gender of Adjectives

How do we define who we are? Let's start from a simple place.

List seven adjectives that describe who you are. **For example, mine would be: kind, thoughtful, funny, smart, sensual, vibrant, outgoing.**

1. _____
2. _____
3. _____
4. _____
5. _____
6. _____
7. _____

Next to each quality, write down whether you think it is masculine, feminine, or neither.

Count the masculine. Count the feminine. Count the nonbinary.

Results: You might have found that it's a mix—you've got a little bit of everything. If not, totally okay! It is okay to see yourself as masculine, it is okay to see yourself as feminine, it is okay to be nothing at all! But after everything is said and done, ask yourself why you feel that these qualities have a gender. Is it based on your experience, or is it based on what you've been told? Because characteristics like being kind or being honest are not tied to any one gender. They are tied to being a good person!

Casey is very involved in the high school theater department and is the most respected and efficient stage manager. Casey is creative, empathetic, organized, and kind of shy. Casey likes to dress in practical clothes: jeans, T-shirts, sneakers. Casey's quiet, but gets stuff done. In fall of senior year, Casey told teachers and classmates that their correct pronoun was "they." Even though Casey at first felt nervous about what people would think, guess what? They are still creative, empathetic, organized, and kind of shy. They still wear mostly jeans and T-shirts. They are still quiet and they are still respected by theater casts and crews! They are just no longer identifying in the binary of "girl" or "boy."

Gender is just one piece of your identity. Changing how you express your gender does not mean you are changing your personality or other qualities that are part of who you are. **Which is to say: if someone transitions, they are still the same person at their core. They may just express themselves a bit differently. And, probably, more confidently.**

A+ ALLY

There's another important word you should know: *ally*. Anyone can be an ally. An ally is a person who, while not part of a specific community, supports and speaks up for the rights of the people in that community. If you are an ally, you make an effort to understand the struggle of people who do not have the same privilege you do. (You can read more about being an ally on page 131.) When you notice injustice or oppression and support your LGBTQ+ and BIPOC friends by standing up and speaking out, you are being an ally. How do you start? Share what you learned in this book with those you love! That, my friend, would make you an excellent ally.

EXPRESS YOURSELF: PRONOUNS

One way people can express their gender identity is to use a pronoun that aligns with their chosen identity. If a friend tells you their pronoun is different than it was before, spend some time that day practicing by talking to yourself about them using their new pronouns—it'll help. If you mess up your friend's pronouns, don't panic. Apologize and quickly move on. If you're afraid you'll make a mistake, use your friend's name. Realize that using the wrong pronouns can make your friend feel even more awkward than you do (particularly if they are trans). If you feel like your friend gets impatient with you, be compassionate. Imagine how you would feel if people constantly forgot important info about how you wanted to be known.

Just as it feels awesome and oh so right when your friends and teachers use your correct pronouns, it can feel frustrating (or even hurtful) as others may struggle to get your pronouns right. You might feel like these people are doing it on purpose, or that they don't really see you when they misgender you, but give them room to learn, especially if they are making a sincere effort. Remember that what feels comfortable to you may feel unfamiliar to even a close friend.

PRONOUNS AND IDENTITY

GENDER IDENTITY	PRONOUNS
Cis woman	she/her/hers
Cis man	he/him/his
Trans woman	she/her/hers (sometimes they/them/theirs)
Trans man	he/him/his (sometimes they/them/theirs)
Nonbinary or Genderqueer	they/them/theirs ze/hir co/cos No pronoun xe/xem/xyr hy/hym/hys

If you are changing your gender pronouns at school, you can ask the administration to send an email to your teachers to let them know your correct pronouns. Tell your friends in person—or send a group text if that feels easier. Realize that it might be particularly hard for your friends' parents or other people who have called you by one particular pronoun to make the switch at first. Not everyone is equally fluent in gender-speak yet!

HOW TO USE THEM

She likes her friend's haircut.

He chews his gum loudly.

Her brother is my friend.

He didn't do his homework.

They went to watch Netflix in their room.
Ze left hir coat on the bus.
Co left cos red coat on.
Use person's name: _____ feels tired.
Xe just went to find xyr computer.
Hy is making it clear what hys pronouns are.

CHANGING YOUR BODY: TRANSITION AND TRANSGENDER

Choosing a gender identity that is different from the one that you were assigned at birth can be liberating, but it also can be terrifying. For people who live in open-minded communities, gender transition may be accepted more readily. People who live in closed-minded communities will most likely have a harder time. When it comes to gender identity, "transitioning" refers to any physical, mental, or emotional change that a person makes in order to better reflect the gender they feel they are. Gender transition can be social (changing your pronouns, your clothing, or your hair), legal (changing your name), or medical (taking hormones and/or having surgery), or may include all of the above. Not all transgender people transition. Some may transition only socially. Some may choose selected medical procedures. No matter whether, or how, someone chooses to transition, all transgender people should have their choices respected.

There are a number of ways—some permanent, some not—to change one's gender appearance. Nonpermanent changes can include clothing, makeup, binding breasts, tucking (hiding external genitalia), prosthetic breasts, pronouns, and name. Hormone therapy is more permanent but can still be reversed. It can be administered by injection, gel, or patch. Some of the effects of taking testosterone for a masculine transition will include increased muscle mass, decreased breast size, and deepened voice. Taking estrogen for feminine transitioning will cause effects including some breast development and a loss of muscle mass. Taking hormones may affect one's mood and, because hormones are metabolized in the liver, people using hormones long term need to have their physician regularly check their liver function. Surgical procedures are more serious and should be considered carefully. The risks and benefits depend on many factors and will be an individual decision between you, your doctor, and ideally your family. If you want to learn more about transitioning and transgender health, both Planned Parenthood (plannedparent hood.org) and the American College of Obstetricians and Gynecologists (acog.org) offer good resources. Search for "transgender teens."

GENDER IDENTITY AND EXPRESSION Q&A

IF I'M A GUY WHO WEARS NAIL POLISH, OR A GIRL WHO HATES DRESSES, DOES THAT MEAN I'M TRANS?

First of all, step away from the binary! Style doesn't have to be just for girls or just for guys. How you choose to dress or decorate your body shouldn't completely define how you express your gender. The fact that you like wearing nail polish or hate wearing dresses means that you like color on your nails or hate wearing dresses. Your fashion choices can help convey your gender identity, but your gender identity is your gender identity no matter how you present.

In fact, I have a buzz cut (and I'm a cis woman) and I also have a lot of adult cis men friends who wear nail polish. I constantly play with how I dress. Sometimes I want to appear more masculine, and sometimes I want to appear more feminine. I strive for androgyny most of the time. But that doesn't make me any less of a woman. In fact, because I am confident in my gender identity, I don't worry about how I look. This, of course, is a privilege.

I CAN'T GET MY DAD TO RESPECT MY FEMALE PRONOUNS. HE HAS A HARD TIME WITH THE FACT THAT I'M TRANS, BUT I CAN'T STOP BEING WHO I AM.

It's true. You can't stop being who you are. We hear and see you. You're a girl, you've always felt like a girl, and you will always be a girl. And, of course, you should be able to expect support from your dad. While you are waiting for your dad to come to terms with the new family dynamic and learn to respect your choice, it's helpful to cultivate a support system—which might include someone your age, or an adult who has been through something similar with their family. If your community or school has specialized resources for support, by all means take advantage of that.

I hope you can trust me (as a dad myself) when I say you need to give your dad time. Although this may not be what you want to hear, he is going through a transition too. He understood he had a son. (Remember, the doctor likely said, "Congratulations, it's a boy!" when you were born.) And now he has a daughter. But if you keep checking in with TCB (for him and for you), then, hopefully, he'll realize that you're still his child. You're just more yourself than ever. But no matter how your dad (or anyone else) feels or acts, that doesn't mean your gender identity is not valid. You deserve to be respected. At the same time, compassion means you give people time to evolve, grow, and make mistakes.

However, if you feel like your family's reaction puts you in danger, or you can't find a trusted someone to talk to, that is an entirely different story. Call 877-565-8860 to be connected with Trans Lifeline. Don't feel embarrassed or shy about reaching out. We guarantee they have heard other stories like yours, so you don't have to feel so alone or afraid.

I GO TO A SCHOOL WHERE WE WEAR UNIFORMS, AND I HATE IT! HOW CAN I EXPRESS MYSELF IF THE DRESS CODE IS COMPLETELY BINARY?

Some schools believe that it's important to eliminate distractions—like fashion, which can be distracting. It can also be a marker for how much money someone has. So in order to make everyone feel like they belong, they have everyone wear the same thing. Still, there is one big way you can express yourself: use your words. If you can come up with a solid case for why you think there shouldn't be uniforms, write it out. Then, start a petition and have your classmates sign. There is always a chance that you won't get what you want. But use the one thing you have at your disposal: your voice.

I had to wear a uniform in high school and I always thought it was particularly sexist because the rules were so much stricter for the girls. Back then, it wasn't even part of the conversation whether or not it was unfair to enforce a binary dress code. But today that is a perfectly legitimate issue to address. The answer might not be in undoing your dress code; it might be in petitioning the school to create a gender-neutral dress code or allowing students to choose which uniform they would rather wear.

I TRIED TO EXPRESS MYSELF, BUT THE BULLYING WAS UNBEARABLE.

First of all, I'm proud of you for trying to express yourself. That requires bravery, strength, and courage. I am so sorry that you are being bullied. Being bullied is isolating, demoralizing, and frightening. But know this: you will get through it. All of the people that I respect in my life express themselves fully. Sure, people may not understand them. But they understand themselves. Rather than looking for the acceptance of your peers, strive to be your most authentic self. Trust that time will pass and you will be out of school soon. Have compassion for those who don't know how to interact with difference.

Bullying violates your boundaries, so first and most important, figure out what you need to do to be safe. Are your parents supportive? Your friends? Is there a counselor at school, or can you get an appointment with your doctor? Then, with your backup in place, do everything you can to assert your boundaries. Verbalize them. Let the bully know that you feel attacked. If, after speaking up, your boundaries are still not being respected, pull in your allies to help. Think TCB. Trust someone to help you, trust that you have properly assessed the situation, have compassion for the bully, try to avoid aggression, and maintain your boundaries.

MY PARENTS MAKE FUN OF HOW I LOOK AND SAY THIS IS JUST A PHASE. HOW CAN I GET THEM TO SEE THE REAL ME?

I can't even imagine how you feel. How painful. I am so sorry that your parents are reacting in this way. I am sure it is because they don't know what to do. They don't understand what you are expressing and probably feel that it is easier to make jokes and chalk it all up to a phase. **But your parents' reaction doesn't change who you are or make you any less valuable as a person to be loved and respected.**

You can try to educate your family—because how else are they gonna know what's up? It's a nuisance, and it's exhausting, and they could just go and do the research themselves. But you've got TCB on your side and you can show them that you trust them enough to explain this part of your life to them, offer them compassion as they catch up to where you are, and hold your boundaries if they push back.

Have you watched *Queer Eye*? It's a show where five queer people are on a mission to improve the lives (and grooming) of all kinds of people. If you're a fan, you know that often, the makeover candidates express some degree of discomfort about being around queer people. Before they meet the *Queer Eye* squad, they don't have compassion for people who seem so unlike them. Yet by the end of the show, they come to understand that queer people are just people, too. Sometimes, people need a living, breathing example. **And you, my friend, can choose to be the example to your community of someone who moves through the world with trust, compassion, and a strong sense of boundaries.** You can be the change you wish to see.

Lead by example, and then educate those around you along the way. Or, if you're over being a role model, you can share links that send people on their way to educational materials. (Start with the ones in our Resources and Recommended Reading section in the back!)

HOW CAN I EASE INTO EXPERIMENTING WITH MY GENDER EXPRESSION?

Trust your instincts. What are you drawn to? Do you want to try wearing nail polish? Lipstick? Or are you more interested in seeing how you'd look with a crew cut? There are ways to make yourself appear more feminine, masculine, or nonbinary. Should you find yourself interested in exploring, you can. Play with makeup, how you style your hair, and the clothing you wear. You can bind your breasts. Make sure you are doing it in a healthy way: don't use Ace bandages or duct tape. Do use a sports bra or compression binder. Don't wear a binder for more than eight hours a day, or overnight. Don't exercise while wearing one. FtM Essentials and Point of Pride offer free and low-cost binders to trans teens. On the other end of the spectrum, you can stuff a bra with just about anything: tissues, cotton balls, socks . . . Just keep experimenting until you feel your reflection in the mirror matches how you feel inside. Once you know what you are interested in, you can keep playing with your look! You can start by trying these things out in your bedroom. And if they feel uncomfortable (which they might), by all means take them off, and try them again later if you want. But if they feel amazing? Then you know!

Remember, how you naturally look does not define your gender identity. It is convenient when your gender identity matches up to your gender presentation, but there are people who present more masculine and there are people who present more feminine, and that doesn't make them any less of a man or woman or however they identify.

I LOVE THE ANDROGYNOUS LOOK BUT HATE IT WHEN PEOPLE GET MY PRONOUNS WRONG.

People are bound to mess up. The first time they make a mistake, give them a chance to correct themselves. The next time they get it wrong, just gently remind them, "My pronouns are _____." If they continue to use the wrong pronouns, you can say, "Those are not my pronouns, and it really feels like you don't respect who I am." And if they are moving forward with good intentions, trust that they're trying. But, of course, there are people who are not moving forward with good intentions. Do your best to exert your boundaries. There will always be people who don't understand. That doesn't mean you are doing anything wrong. No matter how people treat you, you should feel proud of who you are. Try treating those who don't understand you with compassion. Give them space and time to catch up. And if you come to believe they don't care enough to try? That says more about them and doesn't make you any less of who you are.

TOP THREE TAKEAWAYS ABOUT GENDER IDENTITY

1 Biology generally determines your sexual organs and external genitalia, which is how your gender is assigned at birth. However, gender identity and expression are determined by how you feel, and they evolve along with you.

2 Gender is a spectrum.

3 How someone else expresses their gender is up to them. If someone else's gender identity challenges your worldview, maybe it's time to challenge your own thoughts, feelings, and ideas. A cis person will never know what it's like to feel their gender is different from what was assigned at birth. But you don't have to understand someone's gender experience to have compassion for them and to respect and support them. What's most important is being a supportive friend, and keeping TCB front and center in your relationships.

chapter 5

SEXUAL ATTRACTION: HE'S HOT. SHE'S HOT. THEY'RE HOT. YOU'RE HOT!

So you think you are good (for now) with your gender identity (or not) and now you're ready to start acting on your attractions. And we are here for that! To get you started, let's consider: What is attraction?

When I think about defining attraction, I think about how it feels like you have Pop Rocks in your stomach. Or fifteen tennis balls. Your limbs can go numb or they can light on fire. For some reason that person is all you see, but you don't feel like you're staring. But you are. You'll find any excuse to be in the same room as them, even if it makes no sense. All of a sudden, you're joining clubs you

don't care about or reading books you've never heard of—just to be around them.

Sexual attraction is part of your **sexual orientation**—it's where sex (biology) and gender (identity) meet . . . and meet others. It's your body and brain's way of signaling to you that you are physically, emotionally, and romantically interested in another person. That's why we talk about having chemistry with someone. **You come in contact with someone and there's a reaction—or not. Whether it's "Boom!" or "Fizz . . ." depends on your sexual attraction.** Whether you act on your attractions can be influenced by environmental and cultural forces that can sometimes try to tell us who we are supposed to be attracted to, and why.

THE GREAT SEXUAL ATTRACTION EXPERIMENT

Between 1938 and his death in 1956, Dr. Alfred C. Kinsey and his research team conducted more than seventeen thousand face-to-face interviews with a diverse group of people—college students, sex workers, and also incarcerated folks—about their sexual experiences and histories. Their research showed that sexual behavior, thoughts, and feelings toward the same or opposite sex were not always consistent across time. Instead of assigning people to three categories—heterosexual, bisexual, and homosexual—the team used a seven-point scale, ranging from zero (exclusively heterosexual) to six (exclusively homosexual), with an additional category of X (asexual). We imagine that if Kinsey were to make his scale today, it would look very different. The full gender spectrum means there are unlimited ways for people to be attracted to one another.

PINSKY SCALE

In the spirit of Dr. Kinsey, we offer you (ta-da!) the Pinsky Scale. There is no way to score this quiz. More than anything, it is just to get you thinking. Be honest with yourself! There is no harm in knowing who you are.

1. Who do you find attractive?
   a. I think boys are cute.
   b. I think girls are cute.
   c. I find everyone attractive, no matter their gender.
   d. Eh, not really into anyone at all.

2. Who do you fantasize about smooching?
   a. Not a single soul on this earth.
   b. I'd love to smooch a boy.
   c. I'd love to smooch a girl.
   d. I'd love to smooch anyone of any gender.

3. Who have you kissed?
   a. Yuck! Nobody.
   b. *Sigh* Nobody.
   c. Only boys!
   d. Only girls!
   e. I don't discriminate ;)

4. With whom do you form strong emotional bonds?

   a. Not a single soul.

   b. Only boys!

   c. Only girls!

   d. Everybody!

5. With whom do you form friendships?

   a. I don't have many friends.

   b. I'm only friends with girls.

   c. I'm only friends with boys.

   d. I'm friends with people of all genders.

6. How would your friends identify?

   a. Not sure, never thought about it.

   b. They're all super straight.

   c. They're all super gay.

   d. I've got a mix.

   e. They don't like labels.

7. What do you think your sexuality is?

   a. I haven't thought about it much.

   b. I am very, very straight.

   c. I'm straight but I'm open.

   d. I'm straight but there are exceptions.

   e. I'm bisexual.

   f. I am very, very gay.

   g. I'm gay but I'm open.

   h. I'm gay but there are exceptions.

   i. I'm not interested in anyone at all.

As you can see, there's a lot to attraction. Kinsey may have assigned a score to someone's sexuality, but we believe our scale is more flexible and sexuality can't be assigned a score. **Also, there are more than just three types of attraction.** As we saw in chapter 4, there is a wide spectrum of identities. **For some of you, this all will be extremely clear, for others, a bit confusing. And that's okay! Sexuality is a lifelong exploration.**

DON'T I NEED TO LOOK HOT TO ATTRACT A BOYFRIEND/GIRLFRIEND?

Everyone finds different things attractive. Despite what popular culture and the media are telling you, one size does not fit all. **Preach it! Just because you're being told to like a certain body type or a certain hair color doesn't mean that you have to. And if you do, question why you find it attractive. Are you attracted to the person as a person, or are you treating them like an object?** Treating a person like an object means reducing the value of the whole person to their body parts, a process called **objectification**. When you can't see the subject of your attraction as a person with thoughts and feelings, it's easy to feel entitled to do whatever you want with your desire. And trust, compassion, and boundaries cannot exist in a relationship where a person is little more than an object.

When you focus on "looking hot," you are sexualizing attraction. And being attracted to someone isn't the same as just wanting to have sex. But when so much social media, television, and advertising

both online and on TV shows mostly women (but some men, too) getting attention for sexualizing themselves, why wouldn't you do the same?

There are some very real reasons why presenting yourself as a sex object can be dangerous for you—and for others. A psychologist who specializes in how social media affects kids told me about a client who posted sexy pictures of herself on Instagram. She had over five hundred thousand followers. As a result, seven people have gone to jail—because, guess what? She's twelve. And when those men tried to go beyond just looking at her pictures by contacting her, they were soliciting sex from a minor. The girl, by the way, said she loved the attention, and more disturbingly, the power, that "looking sexy" brought her. Do you imagine that she will grow up to have a healthy relationship based on trust, compassion, and appropriate boundaries?

QUIZ
Hot? or Not?

It's important to expand our ideas about what is attractive. Step out of the mainstream culture and define for yourself what makes someone "hot."

I'll start us off. Here's a list of things that I find hot:

- Emotional intelligence
- Kindness
- Authenticity
- Playfulness
- A sense of humor
- A strong moral compass
- Laughter
- Honesty
- Commitment
- Consistency

You may have noticed that none of these things that are "hot" are physical. So why do we, as a culture, focus so much on physical beauty? Take the time to define what is attractive to you for yourself. Write a list of five (nonphysical) things that make someone compelling to you:

1. _____
2. _____
3. _____
4. _____
5. _____

ATTRACTION AND ITS MANY FORMS

You do not have to actively practice your sexuality in order to be that sexuality. Who you are attracted to may be different than who you are having sex with. And guess what: everything can change. You are currently in the process of figuring out who you are, and as time passes, things shift. Embrace the journey!

We're covering only the most basic and mainstream definitions here; if you don't recognize yourself, we don't mean to exclude you. Check out the awesome videos and glossary at the It Gets Better Project (itgetsbetter.org) for a comprehensive list of terms having to do with sexuality and gender expression.

Heterosexual. *Hetero* is Greek for "other." And heterosexuality is exactly that—an attraction to the opposite sex. People who identify as heterosexual may also call themselves "straight."

Homosexual. *Homos* is the Greek word that means "the same." And so, obviously, homosexuality is an attraction to people of the same gender. People who identify as homosexual may also use the term "gay." Women who are attracted to women may consider themselves lesbians.

Bisexual. *Bi* comes from the Latin word for "two," and bisexuality is mainly used in the context of being attracted to both men and women. People who identify as bisexual give themselves the freedom to be attracted to people of either sex, not in any particular time, not in any particular way, and maybe not even to the same degree. Bisexual attraction is all about possibility.

Pansexual. The Greek word *pan* means "all," and pansexuality, or omnisexuality, is attraction to individuals regardless of their sex or gender identification. People who identify as pansexual may be attracted to others based on personality, or appearance, rather than gender or sex. Being pan is about having *all* of your options open.

Asexual and Aromantic. Like other sexual orientations, asexuality can exist on a spectrum. Generally speaking, an asexual person is not drawn to others in a sexual way, and an aromantic person isn't interested in romance. Both can exist on a spectrum, and a person can identify as one, the other, or both. People who identify as asexual may have romantic feelings for other people, but they do not feel compelled to pursue sex in their relationships. People who are asexual sometimes refer to themselves as "ace." People who are aromantic ("aro") can be attracted to someone and sexually interested without desiring a relationship based in conventional notions of romantic love.

It's important to note that it's perfectly valid to be anywhere on the spectrum of asexual and aromantic. Just because you don't want to have sex or be romantic doesn't mean there is something wrong with you! The Oxford University LGBTQ+ website (oulgbtq .org) has a great section on busting the myths about ace and aro individuals.

However, because I am a doctor, I would be remiss if I didn't tell you that, if you have noticed **a significant change** in your sex drive, you shouldn't immediately decide you have an asexual identity. You might, in fact, be asexual, but in *some* people, lack of sexual desire can be the result of an underlying physical issue. So if you notice a **change** in your sex drive that concerns you, discuss it with your doctor. (Doctor/patient confidentiality varies from state to state. If you are under eighteen, make sure you are aware whether your doctor can keep your conversation private if you don't wish to share information with your parents.)

And here's one more important thing to know: **sexual orientation is not contagious.** It is not transmitted by peer pressure, and hanging around with someone of a different sexual orientation than yours doesn't mean that you'll suddenly find yourself attracted to the same kinds of people they are. **In other words, when it comes to sexual orientation, *trust* that your attractions are valid; have *compassion* and develop understanding and tolerance for people whose orientations are different from yours; and know that your own *boundaries* allow you to *consent* or *not consent* when anyone signals they find you attractive!**

WHAT'S MY QUEER IDENTITY?

Max is a trans man who is dating Katie. Before Max transitioned, he was an out and proud lesbian. He did not consider himself queer before—just a lesbian. Now, he is still out and proud, but he's no longer a lesbian woman. He is a man. He's still dating Katie, but now they present as a hetero, instead of lesbian, couple, and Max chooses to identify as queer.

Queerness generally has to do with sexual orientation rather than your gender identity. Let's break it down:

Max was assigned female at birth.

Max (at first) presented as a woman.

Max was sexually attracted to women.

Max chose "lesbian" as a sexual orientation label.

But Max then gender-identified as a man.

Max transitioned and now presents as a man.

Max is still sexually attracted to women.

Max now chooses "queer" as a sexual orientation label. (If he wanted to, Max could also choose to identify as "straight" since he is a man in a relationship with a woman.)

The way you identify in your relationship could be the same or different from how you identify personally. If you are a straight cis man and have a straight cis woman partner, you can call your partnership a "straight" one. If one of the partners is bisexual or queer, then you can identify it as a queer partnership. **Queer is a term that describes various LGBTQ+ identities. You and your partner are the ones who get to label** your relationship, no matter what other people think—if you even want to label your relationship or yourself. You don't have to!

That being said, if you find yourself in a situation where someone doesn't see you as a "real" man or woman, that is transphobia. To say that Max and Katie aren't part of a straight partnership because Max wasn't born with a penis is transphobia. News flash! *People who identify as men can have vaginas and people who identify as women can have penises.*

Remember from chapter 4: Your sex does not define your gender. Queer or straight, pan or ace: your sexuality and how you choose to express it is your right. There may be people who disagree or vehemently don't believe it—but that doesn't make your sexual orientation any less true. **Sexuality is just one dimension of your self-expression based on who you feel tingly around. And whoever makes you hot and bothered doesn't make you anything less or anything more: it's just fact. Trust your attractions. Have compassion for those who are not being accepted for who they are. And set a boundary with people who are homophobic or sex-shaming. When it comes to sex and attraction, treating yourself and others with TCB may change the world.**

"COMING OUT"

In Eve Kosofsky Sedgwick's foundational queer theoretical text, *The Epistemology of the Closet,* she writes about the idea of "the closet" and how it represents the public and private lives of gay people. When the door is closed, one's identity is concealed. When it is open, the public has access to what lies inside. Before someone comes out, or publicly expresses their sexual orientation, they are seen as being "in the closet."

"Coming out" means you are choosing to be open and honest with everyone around you about your sexual orientation. It can happen slowly, or all at once. You might decide to tell your mom or your best friend before you tell your dad and your grandpa. It is all dependent on your own experience and who you feel safe telling. It may be something you keep doing throughout your life as you continue to meet people who may assume you're straight.

When making any decisions about sharing your sexual orientation with others, it is important to be realistic about your family and your environment. A lot of people who call in to talk to me on the radio have the same story: "I'm gay and I don't know if I should tell anyone." I say to them, "There's nothing to be ashamed of. Why wouldn't you tell people?" And that's when they share their fears: They're afraid of the reactions of their family, or their community, or their friends. They're afraid of being physically hurt, of finding themselves homeless, of being rejected, or of disappointing people they love and who love them. Unfortunately, for some people, these fears can be grounded in the reality of their situations. But many people who choose to come out find loving, accepting communities where they thrive.

It can be a great relief to come out and share who you are and who you love! Take Olivia and Leah, for example.

Leah and Olivia have been inseparable since the seventh grade, when they met in a community youth group through their church. When Leah came out in high school, her parents, her best friend, and even her church community were unbelievably supportive and accepting. But then things got weird between the two friends. Leah felt like Olivia was distant, not saying what was on her mind. Leah worried that the fact that she was gay made Olivia uncomfortable. That theory was quickly proven wrong when, one fateful night in the Sonic parking lot after the Friday night football game, Olivia told Leah she was in love with her—and had been since the seventh grade. Leah admitted she felt the same. (Of course, they kissed.)

It took a while for Olivia to work up the nerve to tell her parents she was gay. But her mom and dad had been so accepting of Leah that she wanted to get it all out in the open. Olivia worried that her parents would think it was okay for someone else to be gay—just not their daughter. But her mom and dad hugged her and told her they loved her no matter what. So she dropped the bigger bomb: that she and Leah had kissed. That news was even more exciting for her parents because they loved Leah—she had been a polite and hilarious house guest for years. And wouldn't you know? Leah and Olivia have been dating ever since.

START THE CONVO

When it comes to sexual attraction, the only person you really have to come out to is the person you are attracted to! We hope you can tell where your friends stand on LGBTQ+ issues—or at least that you feel comfortable asking them about their views. If you're not sure about how your parents would react to a discussion about your dating life, you can test the waters in a few ways:

> Comment on something you see on TV that is a good springboard for discussion.

> Ask your parents for advice about what you can tell a "friend" in a similar situation.

> Start with open-ended questions about their own life as a young person and who they were attracted to and why.

The bottom line is that you do not have to tell anyone anything about your sexuality until you are comfortable doing so. If you have a loving and supportive relationship with your parents, it can be a great relief to let them in on your love life. Pretending to be someone you are not can take a toll on your mental and emotional health. That's why it's important to be able to share parts of yourself with family and close friends. Other people feel like coming out is not even necessary. Still others reject the idea of coming out as an unwarranted nod to heteronormativity. **Yeah! Why do only gay people have to come out? Why is heterosexuality the norm? If gay people have to announce their sexuality, then straight people should have to announce it too!**

We believe that everyone should be respected for whatever their orientation, especially as they move through adolescence. **Yeah! Love is love, y'all.** But we also acknowledge that for some people there can be a lack of acceptance and support of different sexual orientations.

I want to encourage you to express yourself, to be embraced for who you are. *And* I want you to be safe. And so the only responsible thing I can say is, if you feel you will be in danger (emotionally or physically) by expressing your sexual orientation, then, as hard as it is, hold on. Wait. Make sure you are safe. Search out local LGBTQ+ youth centers where you can find support and counseling on strategies for coming out. It may be the harder, but safer, choice to choose to keep your sexual orientation to yourself as you build a community of your own.

Choose to come out when you can:

1. Trust that your safety will not be compromised.
2. Practice compassion for yourself if you stray out of hetero norms.
3. Establish a boundary between what you feel and what other people think.

All in all, the choice to come out is up to you. Let TCB be your guide here: Who do you *trust*? Can you anticipate *compassion*? Are your *boundaries* up for the challenge?

KIRA'S COMING-OUT STORY

Coming out is a difficult decision. What if you're not accepted for who you are? What if something really bad happens? For some people it's a process. But their desire to live their life authentically is so powerful that they persist. Let me share a story about my friend Kira, who came out to her parents in college.

The first time Kira came out, in her first year of college, her family was vocal in their lack of acceptance because they did not understand. "Truth be told, there was a lot I was still trying to understand too," Kira admits. "My parents had never heard the word queer before, and I didn't really know what my queerness looked like yet. And so, yes, their reaction was painful and quite homophobic, but looking back, I now understand it as confusion." Kira's culture and religion played a part in her challenges with coming out, but ultimately it was more nuanced than that. "The reality is my parents came to me with questions about queerness that I was not able to answer, and so they cast it off as a phase and used our culture and religion to back themselves up."

Kira told her parents about her second girlfriend on the day of her college graduation, and it actually went better that time. "Of course, it's not an on-and-off switch. It never is," Kira explained. As a result, a lot of unresolved homophobia leaked into her new relationship. But that relationship also suffered from its own unique set of challenges, and when it ended, it was as a result of all of those things. "To say 'my parents were not happy, and then my relationship ended' feels inadequate. The truth is my parents began to try to understand, that second time, but it wasn't fast enough. And then the relationship I was in ended for other reasons."

A few years after she graduated, Kira started dating a man. He is also queer and from the same culture as she is, so they found a common ground in both their sexual orientation and their culture. Kira's parents are happy that she's dating a man. But Kira still wants them to know that she considers herself queer, and out. For Kira, queerness is a lifelong identity no matter who her partner is at the time.

WHAT DO I DO IF PEOPLE ARE NOT ACCEPTING?

Kira's parents were not accepting. Her mother used to write her letters about how disappointed she was in her decisions. When Kira made coming out the topic of her college thesis, she ended up using those letters from her mom, cutting and pasting them together as part of her thesis work. Unintentionally, her mother's lack of acceptance helped Kira create something beautiful and thought-provoking.

Through writing her thesis, Kira found healing. But she also found a good therapist and talked (a lot) about how she felt. We know that there are people who will be disowned or kicked out of their homes for being LGBTQ+. You can't control who accepts you. But we accept you. And one of the bravest and most important things that you can do is to accept yourself. **Make time to express yourself, whether publicly or privately. Make art. Paint, draw, write, sing, or dance about how you feel. And celebrate what makes you uniquely you. I know this seems like corny advice. But it works. So if you have to hide in your room and sing into a hairbrush or write poetry in a journal that you hide under your mattress, just do it! The worst thing you can do is push your authentic self away.**

WHAT DO I DO IF PEOPLE MAKE FUN OF ME?

Here's where friends really matter. If you don't think you have any friends who will support your choices, go online and search for LGBTQ youth resources. **Whether you find local gay and lesbian youth centers or an online support network online, seek out or follow people who are actively out and thriving. If you take the time to look for them, you can find role models and meet people who are actively grappling with the same things you are.**

Also, try to hold on to compassion and perspective. The people who are making fun of you right now are absolutely insecure themselves. It's likely that—for whatever personal reasons—they feel threatened by the fact that you have chosen to live authentically. And we can't stress this enough: if things are bad enough, especially if you feel like your safety is threatened, talk to a trusted adult.

WHAT DO I DO IF THERE IS GOSSIP ABOUT ME?

This is a concern for everyone—always. No one likes being talked about behind their back. **But haters gonna hate. I see gossip as a form of prejudice, and like other forms of prejudice, having contact with the person who is spreading rumors or talking trash about you might help.** Realize that your peers are much more concerned with themselves than anyone else. **Go back and read that sentence again! Gossip serves to make other people feel better or more**

powerful when they themselves are feeling insecure.

When it comes to gossip, you need the B of TCB most. Focus on your **boundaries** and realize that while their words may sting, the fact that they are gossiping has little or nothing to do with you and everything to do with them and their ignorance. Know who your real friends are and **trust** that they will be there for you—and that they will help set the record straight. Have **compassion** for yourself. Your feelings are real, and gossip can be painful. If gossip crosses over into bullying, go to chapter 7 for some strategies and to know when to call in outside help.

TOP THREE TAKEAWAYS FOR SEXUAL ORIENTATION AND ATTRACTION

1 Sexuality is a spectrum. It isn't as simple as being straight or gay. It can be nothing and everything in between.

2 No matter what you have been told, sexuality cannot be changed, nor is it contagious.

3 Be realistic about your family and your environment. If it is unsafe for you to come out, hold on. Wait until you can do so safely. And in the meantime, find your people.

PART 3

YOU AND ME AND TCB

It's time to take everything you learned about trust, compassion, boundaries, consent, and your authentic self in the first five chapters of this book and make that knowledge part of your everyday life. In the chapters that follow, we'll help you figure out how TCB can help you have stronger friendships, navigate the excitement (and pain) of making and losing friends, and protect your self-esteem from bullies. You'll see what TCB looks like with your parents and other adults and learn what consent looks like in a world where other people have a lot to say about what you do and don't have to do.

In the chapters about identity, you learned that who you are and how you see yourself is, in part, shaped by your family and friends, community and culture. That's why taking a look at how trust, compassion, and boundaries are balanced (or not) in all of these kinds of relationships is important: how you feel about yourself can determine what you do and who you hang around, and the people you interact with most often can influence how you feel about yourself.

chapter 6

FRIENDSHIPS: MAKING THEM, KEEPING THEM, LETTING THEM GO

Two thousand years ago, Aristotle, a Greek philosopher, was already thinking about TCB and consent and how they applied to friendships. He said any friendship could be put into one of three categories: utilitarian, pleasurable, and virtuous.

In the first type, *utilitarian,* people form relationships based on usefulness. For example, I wanted to become friends with the smartest girl in my AP Bio class, Calliope, because she understood the material better than I did. She was really nice, and our time spent studying together after school actually made the entire process of digesting a mountain of information almost enjoyable. But in the end, we were more like study buddies than hang-out-on-the-weekend friends, probably because the initial reason I was friendly to her was in hopes of getting better grades. And that is the problem with these kinds of self-serving relationships: they often end when their objective is reached.

Pleasurable friendships are self-centered too. You hang around with someone because they make you feel some kind of way about yourself that you enjoy. **Like the dude from college who I would study with every night, not because I wanted to study, but because I had a massive crush on him and would use any excuse to be around him. This, of course, led to some kissing (which was definitely pleasurable), usually when we were very, very drunk (so not very utilitarian for a study session, and considering the drinking, not practicing healthy consent either!).** But again, if that pleasurable feeling goes away, often the friendship does too. **With this guy, the fire went out quickly, and the friendship went out with it.**

What Aristotle called *virtuous* friendships are the kind where both people successfully balance trust, compassion, and boundaries. These friendships are collaborative and supportive: each of you recognizes what is good in the other person, and you want the best for them because it will be good for *them*—not because it will benefit you. If you don't have a lot of these friendships, don't panic! One or two is all you need. Aristotle didn't judge the other kinds of friendships (and we don't either). **I like to say that I collect friends. From each phase of my life or from each place that I've lived, I collect one virtuous friend. They're the ones I call when I'm crying so hard I can't breathe, the ones that call me when they don't know what to say. These friendships are rare, deep, and life-altering. Not all friendships are of this caliber.**

It's not just philosophers who tell us we need friends. Science tells us that friendships are important, too. People who have strong friendship networks have better mental health, less depression, feel a sense of belonging, and have positive feelings about their relationships with others. **A healthy friendship is a two-way street. You give what you get, and you get what you give.**

FRIENDSHIP: IN AND OUT AND BACK IN AGAIN

Cleo and Jackie seemed to have everything in common. In middle school they were both crazy about horses and spent all their time at the riding stable near their homes. By eighth grade, when people asked Jackie if she was going to the Olympics, she always responded, "No, I'm going to go to college and be a vet." But Cleo—she had Olympic ambitions. She was a better rider than Jackie at the time, and her parents invested a ton of money in horses and lessons. Also, Cleo was fiercely competitive, and, to be honest, Jackie was more interested in eating hot fudge sundaes after she was done competing.

But by sophomore year in high school, the pressure Cleo put on herself started to affect the friendship. Their friendly competition was not always so friendly anymore. Cleo went around the school telling everyone who would listen she was going to the Olympics, but that Jackie wasn't good enough. Deep down, Jackie agreed, but still, it was painful to hear her classmates agree with Cleo. And despite all the time and effort Jackie spent on her equestrian identity, it was Cleo who was treated like the future champion. So, Jackie began to compete against Cleo in other areas—getting better grades, kissing the boy she knew Cleo liked, throwing herself into a ton of school activities. There was so much tension between them that Jackie and Cleo didn't even think of themselves as friends anymore.

And yet . . . Jackie and Cleo did eventually set aside their differences. By senior year of high school, they were talking a lot. Cleo had burned out on riding and left the sport. She joined the cheer team and Jackie was captain, and they started hanging out after school. They again realized how much they shared: they'd had the same coaches, the same difficult relationship with their changing bodies, and felt the same pressure to excel. Though they went to different colleges, they are still friends. Jackie knows she can text Cleo when she needs advice about a guy she likes, and Cleo knows she can complain to Jackie when her mother is driving her crazy. They stay in touch, hang out when they are home on breaks, and refer to each other as "my best friend from high school."

A friend is someone you can **trust**, someone who you feel **compassion** for, and someone whose **boundaries** you respect—and who feels and acts the same way toward you. But the fact is that, in a long friendship, these three key elements can go in and out of balance over the years. Keeping a relationship strong takes awareness and effort, and using TCB as a checklist for what's weak and what's strong in your friendship can help you see the areas that need attention.

Sometimes, it can be difficult to tell what's gone out of balance in a friendship. How can the same person make you feel good and then turn around and make you feel terrible? For Cleo and Jackie, at some point, **compassion** went missing in the friendship. Cleo couldn't recognize how hard Jackie was working. Aristotle would have said that if Cleo was a real friend, she would have wanted Jackie to go to the Olympics, too. And in a chain reaction, **trust** was damaged. Because how could Jackie trust a friend who didn't have her back?

When the two former friends found space for **compassion**, they were able to rebuild **trust**, and realized it was okay to have **boundaries** and to want different things. They were able to appreciate that they were two different people with equally admirable strengths and weaknesses. Their shared history actually became a bonding agent, rather than something that pushed them apart.

MAKING NEW BUDDIES

Potential friends are everywhere—at school, on teams, in your community, even in other friends' social circles—but it can feel hard to know how to take the first steps toward finding them. **It helps to start with the attitude that everyone you meet has the potential to be a friend. It's not so intimidating to approach people if you think of them as "not-yet" friends instead of strangers.** Then be willing to really get to know someone. A study published in the *Journal of Social and Personal Relationships* recently calculated that, on average, it takes about fifty hours of time with someone before you consider them a casual friend, ninety hours before you become real friends, and about two hundred hours to become close friends. **So, in other words, slowly and patiently!**

*Eva was nervous before she started the eighth grade at a new
school. Her dad got a new job overseas and she found herself in
a new city, in a new country, where how she looked made her
stand out in a crowd, where her clothes didn't look right, and
where everything just felt so strange. The first day of school,
she was assigned a buddy. The moment she met Johann, she
started to feel better because he smiled and said, "I love your
accent. Want to sit together at lunch?" Eva relaxed. Maybe it
was going to be okay to be different.*

There's one more important thing to keep in mind when
making new friends, and you don't have to move to a different
country to put it to use: **spend time with people who are different
from you and have ideas that don't necessarily align
with yours.** Building empathy can be a challenging process.
That's because we all carry internalized ideas and expectations
for ourselves and others. Sometimes these ideas are so subtle that
we don't even realize we have them. Such a block is also called
"implicit" or "unconscious" bias. There are ways of checking
your own biases; try taking a test from ProjectImplicit (implicit
.harvard.edu/implicit).

Once you have an idea of your personal biases, it's a good idea
to check in with someone you trust so you can safely work on them.
For example, my friend Dr. Adolph Brown is a psychologist and
psychoanalyst whose work centers around diversity, equity, and
inclusion. My conversations with him help me take a perspective
that is not necessarily part of my everyday experience. Here's what
I've learned from him about working on my own biases:

1. Look in the mirror: are you really ready to admit there are views you hold that may be hurtful or harmful to others?

2. Test the conversations at home. Question beliefs or "truths" that your family may hold. Get comfortable with asking why it is okay to assume things about people you don't know.

3. Let your friends know you're open to listening to their experiences without judgment (even if their negative experiences involve encounters with people who look like you or hold the same beliefs as you).

4. It can be tempting to argue your points in these conversations. Remember you are there to **listen and learn**. When you find yourself wanting to disagree, try one of these responses instead:

   - I never thought of it like that before.
   - I don't know enough about this to respond. Let me find out more and we can keep talking.
   - What I hear you saying is [repeat what they said]. Can you say more about that?
   - Thank you for being willing to have this conversation; I'm learning a lot.

You are part of the most beautiful ethnically and racially diverse generation in history. Instead of looking for people and relationships that feel familiar, challenge yourself to ask questions, listen to other life experiences, and welcome the viewpoints of people who are different from you. It's how you exercise your empathy muscle. Push yourself outside of your comfort zone; it's worth it.

WHERE TO BEGIN?

You can feel vulnerable when you go to talk to someone new. Think about how you would want someone to approach you—with a smile and good intentions.

Find a common interest: "Hey, I love the band on your T-shirt. Have you listened to their new album?"

Compliment them: "Your outfit is amazing. Where did you get it?"

Find common ground: "I also tried the mystery meat at lunch. Wasn't it nasty?"

Ask a question: "Where can I get the best iced latte around here?"

Make an observation: "You run fast."

Come right out with it: "I want to be your friend. We should be friends."

IF YOU WANT TO MOVE FROM NOT-YET FRIENDS TO FRIENDS

1. **START FROM A PLACE OF KINDNESS.** You've heard it before: treat others how you would like to be treated. And isn't it nice to be treated kindly?

2. **BE YOURSELF.** Pretending to be someone else won't get you the kind of friends you really want. Fitting in is over-rated. Move through the world in a way that feels authentic to you. Your friends will love you for who you are.

3. **REMEMBER THAT TRUST IS EARNED, NOT GIVEN.**

It is easy to try to serve up every single thought, feeling, and secret to someone who you have a new connection with. But if you act on that impulse, it actually shows that you have poor boundaries. **Sometimes, saying a bunch of things that are personal feels like it creates instant closeness. But what really creates closeness is trust, and you shouldn't immediately trust someone you just met.**

4. **ACCEPT THAT NOT EVERYONE IS GOING TO BE YOUR FRIEND.** Accept that not everyone is going to like you and that you're not going to like everyone else. **There are so many people in this world, it quite frankly is impossible to be friends with everyone.** And that's okay.

5. **DON'T BE A JERK. This ties back to number 1: start from a place of kindness. If you act like a jerk, then you're inviting people to be a jerk to you.** And if someone else treats you like a jerk? Well, they're probably hurting more than you can possibly imagine.

FROM ONLINE TO IN PERSON

Horace and Summer met in an art history course in college. They would sit together in class. They might say hi if they passed one another on campus, but they didn't hang out. After graduation, they started following one another on Instagram. After liking and commenting on the other's selfies, they switched to texting. And then after that, they got dinner. And then after that, they started hanging out more.

Even though Horace felt really attracted to Summer, it wasn't until they met in person that he found out she was in a relationship with a girl but hadn't told her parents. At dinner, Summer learned that, despite Horace's wild Instagram posts, he was sober—and had been since high school. They learned they both had lost a relative to drug abuse, and that their shared art history class had inspired them so that they still loved going to museums. They both wanted to get a master's degree and teach middle school. When Summer and her girlfriend had a fight, she called Horace. When he felt depressed, she took him to look at art. Horace and Summer are a true twenty-first-century friendship. If social media and texting didn't exist, they wouldn't have gotten as close.

Maybe you're talking to someone online or via text and you already feel like friends. But here's the thing to keep in mind: you don't know if you can trust them yet, though you may have compassion for what you know about their situation. So it's important to move a friendship forward in person. **Your body will give you a lot of information if you let it. But it's impossible to listen to your internal instincts when there's a screen between you and the other person. It's hard to register whether or not they deserve to be trusted, they can't feel your compassion, and—literally—you are looking at them through the boundary of technology.**

You remember relationship math from the introduction, right? (Hint: 1 + 1 = 3.) So what happens when you introduce a device? A whole new problem: 2 + 1(screen) = 2. In other words, there's no co-created experience when you are separated by a boundary. So rather than a truly shared phenomenon that belongs to both of you equally, you are each having an independent version of the relationship.

Introducing a device changes TCB. In the same way that a filter changes a picture, a screen gets in the way of getting to know someone. Suddenly it's not 100 percent authentic. Sure, your words may be true. But how can someone truly understand what you're saying in a text when they can't hear the tone of your voice? Or see the expression on your face? **Emoji are fine, but they're not a replacement for your body picking up signals from theirs.** Without that awareness of feeling things in your body, it can be hard to know if you are getting what you need from a relationship—and that makes it tough, if not impossible, to practice healthy consent.

KEEPING 'EM CLOSE

So now you understand that friendships are fluid and can exist on a spectrum from "acquaintance" (the person you feel comfortable asking for notes when you've missed class) to BFF (your one and only ride or die; the first person you call in big life moments—good or bad). The kids I played recess games with in grammar and secondary school became teammates in high school. The guys I hung around with in college remain some of my closest friends to this day. As busy as we have been with families and careers, we might only see one another once a decade. But that doesn't matter. We pick up where we left off, no matter how much time has passed. Having history together can help cement friendships. As you move through different phases of life, you'll make (and lose) friends. From middle school to summer camp, from college to career, people will move in and out of your life with varying degrees of intensity and closeness. The friends you want to keep, the ones who last, check all the boxes for TCB. They make you feel safe, seen, and respected.

A BEST FRIEND IS FOREVER . . . RIGHT?

You might think that once you attain best friend status, it will last forever, but I would suggest that the idea of "keeping" a best friend is flawed. In fact, a 2009 Dutch study found that the average friendship lasts seven years. Good friendships take work. Clinging desperately to a friend who needs space is not an effective strategy for ensuring a lifelong bond. I find my strongest friendships are the ones that can withstand space and time. You know, when you haven't seen them for a long time, but when you do see them, it feels like no time has passed at all? Those are the true BFFs. Otherwise, let time take them away. There will be more friends.

KEEPING FRIENDSHIPS TCB STRONG

- Check your T: Be trustworthy. Show up when you say you will. Don't overpromise.
- Amp up the C: Ask open-ended questions. Practice empathy by really listening to the answer and imagining how your friend might feel. Treat your friend like you would want to be treated.
- Respect the B: Check in, but don't be stalkerish. You don't need to keep showing up everywhere you know they'll be, or constantly text with the expectation that they'll reply right away. A good friend will always be there when you really need them!

- Keep the lines of communication open. This is especially important when you have a misunderstanding with a friend. Don't wait for things to get better on their own. Make the first move. Pull your friend aside after school or send a simple text: "I understand if you need space, but I want you to know that I'm here whenever you are ready to talk."

WHEN FRIENDS GROW APART

Sometimes people can try to keep a friendship going past the point where it's good for either person. Let's take Sam and Ben as an example:

The two have been friends since the third grade. They've had joint birthday parties and sleepovers and have even gone on vacation with one another's families. But there's one problem: Sam always has to be in charge, and it's gotten worse. They're in high school now and Sam still won't let Ben make any decisions. Sam decides what clothes are cool. When they go to Ben's house, Sam decides what snacks they eat. If they have a crush on the same person? Sam wins. If they're hanging around in a group, Sam has to be the center of attention—even if it means making fun of Ben to get a laugh. They've been best friends forever, but Ben is starting to feel like he's nothing but Sam's shadow. And every time he tries to assert himself, Sam gets mad, accuses Ben of not being a good friend, and stops talking to him until Ben gets lonely enough to apologize.

Sam and Ben very clearly have known each other for a really long time, but it doesn't sound like it's a relationship that is mutually beneficial—meaning it doesn't seem like the relationship is helping them both grow as people. Healthy friendships that are grounded in TCB always have room for multiple, and even changing, points of view. In a mutually beneficial relationship, the two people should each take turns making decisions.

Some compassionate communication might help get this friendship back on track. It's possible that Sam doesn't know that his teasing feels like criticism. But is he supposed to know that Ben is feeling diminished if Ben doesn't speak up and tell him? If he can take the compassionate view that maybe his friend is unaware of the dynamic, Ben can try to break this communication block. And if Sam is really a good friend, he'll apologize and try to do better.

QUIZ
Can Your Friendship Grow with You?

It is always our hope that our friendships grow along with us, but sometimes things can crash and burn. A fight, a misunderstanding, a falling out. Your values and sense of yourself change as you develop. As a result you may experience your friends from a different point of view. Be honest with yourself about these feelings. If this is a good friend, you can certainly bring these issues up. Do you and your BFF have what it takes to withstand the test of time? Answer these yes-or-no questions to check in with where y'all are at.

1. Would they keep your biggest secret? **Y/N**
2. Can you cut them some slack when they're not at their best? **Y/N**
3. Is it easy to tell them when you need space? **Y/N**
4. Do you have their back, even if there's a social cost? **Y/N**
5. Are they someone who doesn't make you feel bad when you mess up? **Y/N**
6. Are you still best friends if they don't tell you every single thing? **Y/N**
7. Do you (mostly) share the same values? **Y/N**

If you answered mostly (ideally all) YES, then you are in good shape! Pay attention to where you answered NO. Are these things you feel like you could talk about with your friend? Do you think they would react in a good way?

TAKE WHAT YOU NEED

If you and a friend have had an awkward moment, think about having an honest conversation about taking a little time apart. Taking space is a sign of a healthy friendship. Some friendships die from time apart, but the ones that are meant to last only grow stronger. Being 100 percent honest and respectful isn't always easy, and any friendship can hit a bump. It is okay to ask for what you really need. And if the other person cares about you, they will respect your wishes and want to do what is best for you.

TALK IT OUT

Friendships naturally morph, change, and often drift apart. You don't need to feel guilty if your friendships change. **But if you think a friendship is worth saving, it's time to start talking.** If you really want to build friendships that stand the test of time, you need to be able to be open about both good things and not-so-good things and be ready for real talk. **Friendships that thrive have an open dialogue.** Once you are ready to talk, here are some good lines to open with if the situation is not tense:

- I miss you! Can we hang?
- Remember when we _____? That was fun. We should do that this weekend!
- I saw that you did _____ on Insta. I loved your caption. Tell me about _____!
- Are you busy tonight? We should _____.
- *How are you?* (Then listen.)

If things are tense and you have to address the situation head-on:

- Things have felt different since _____. Can we talk about it?
- I've noticed things are different. Is there anything I need to know?
- I appreciate and love you as a friend, but I've noticed _____. Do you want to talk about it?
- Is something wrong? If so, I really want to listen.

- I feel like we are drifting apart and it is breaking my heart. I am unsure of what went wrong, but I want to know. Will you tell me?

There are two ways these kinds of conversations can go down: your friend opens up and shares with you . . . or they deny, deny, deny. **No matter the reaction, you must listen to what your friend says. If they are open and honest with you, be receptive. Don't allow your defenses to come up, don't immediately shut down, don't start screaming. Listen with your whole body. You've got this!**

However, if your friend is denying that something is wrong, but your gut tells you otherwise, you need to both listen to what your friend is saying **and** trust what you are feeling. This is where boundaries can help get a friendship back on track by allowing for a little space. **If your friend is** *saying* **that nothing is wrong, but** *acting* **like something is, it is time to give them space. They may just need some time to get their feelings and thoughts together. Or, you may have to accept the painful fact that the friendship is fizzling out.**

BEING A FRIEND CAN BE EASY. BEING AN ALLY CAN TAKE WORK

Sometimes, despite all of your best intentions, you can take your friends for granted. You might assume that because you have a great friendship, you and your friend are more alike than you are different. So you might feel shocked—and maybe even a little defensive—if a friend who is of a different gender identity, race, religion, ability, or socioeconomic background says to you, "You have no idea what my life is like!" When a friend trusts you enough to share that their life experiences are different from yours, they are inviting you to be a friend *and* an ally.

It's important to remember it is not your friend's job to educate you on how to be a good ally—they've got enough going on! To become a better ally to your friend, you must **MOTIVATE,** then **ACTIVATE:**

Make time to educate yourself and reflect.

Open your ears, open your mind, and listen deeply.

Treat yourself with compassion if you make a
   mistake. Apologize.

Initiate a conversation with a trusted person; ask questions;
   be willing to learn.

Venture into uncharted territory; it's okay to
   feel uncomfortable.

Alter your perception; check your biases.

Target what you don't understand. And then
   seek knowledge.

Evolve the way you think based on what you've learned.

Now take the work you've done on yourself and get to work being a good ally! Here's how you can translate your good intentions into tangible action.

Actively listen. Realize that you don't know everything about your friend's experience; when they talk to you, really listen.

Communicate with compassion. If you hear someone say something that is racist (or sexist or homophobic, etc.) about one of your friends, make it personal. Don't label them by saying "You're a racist!" (or a sexist or a homophobe). Instead tell them, "That's a hurtful thing to say and I don't think you would want to hurt so-and-so." Try to help them see why they don't need certain language in their vocabulary.

Teach others what you've learned. If you hear someone say something racist (or sexist or homophobic, etc.) about someone else, don't immediately shame them. Try to educate first.

Inspire others. Hold yourself accountable to your own beliefs.

Volunteer. Organize in support of a cause.

Amplify. Use your privilege to let others be heard. Sometimes this means making space for other voices. Sometimes it means using your voice to reinforce a message. Sometimes it means gathering as a group with a common cause.

Turn up. Be there for your friends. If your friend is organizing a food drive, support them. If you know they're anxious about a particular situation, let them know you've got their back.

Expand your circle. Direct your energy toward making friends who are different from you.

TOXIC FRIENDSHIPS

Luke and Jared would say they were friends. They're both on the basketball team, they usually meet online for gaming, and they are both obsessed with Brittany. When Luke tells Jared that he's going to ask Brittany to prom, Jared doesn't say anything. The next day at school, Jared tells Brittany he needs to talk to her. "Luke really likes you," he tells her. "But so do I. Will you go to prom with me?" Brittany says yes and Luke, of course, is furious.

This feels less like a friendship and more like the toxic fallout of a classic male situation. As a scientist, I'm going to tell you that in some ways, we have not successfully evolved from our original biology. Since cave-dweller times, men have been genetically programmed to aggressively compete (especially for sexual partners). The urge was hardwired in early human brains to ensure the human species continued with the strongest gene pool. We like to think we've evolved over the past several thousand years, but every now and then the inner caveman can come out.

Clearly cavemen didn't know the first thing about TCB. But that doesn't mean guys are off the hook. Let's break it down: **Trust,** where is the trust? Jared went behind Luke's back and did what he wanted because of the "best man wins" mentality. But what about their friendship? Poor Luke trusted Jared. If he was a real friend, Jared would have admitted that he also had a crush on Brittany. From there, they could have discussed a strategy for how to cope. Maybe they would have said, "best man wins." And maybe the outcome would have been the same. But at least the trust between the two guys would not have been destroyed.

If Jared and Luke had **compassion** for one another at the start—if they had talked about it and agreed that neither would move on a girl the other liked, or that since Luke said something first, he could ask Brittany first—there would have been an explicit **boundary** that would have kept them from getting into this mess. **And honestly, when all is said and done, Brittany (who is not an object to be fought over) gets to say who she wants to go to prom with, and then do as she pleases. Because ultimately, the choice is up to Brittany.**

It's not always easy to see that a friendship is toxic. If you are questioning whether a friendship is healthy, ask yourself these questions about your friend:

1. Do they make jokes at your expense? Target specific things about you for a laugh?
2. Do they deliberately exclude you?
3. Do they make you feel uncomfortable for saying what you think?
4. Have you ever found out they are talking behind your back?
5. Do they pressure you to do things you don't want to (drugs, drinking, risky behavior)?
6. Are they jealous when someone pays attention to you when you're together?
7. Are they happy for you, even if things aren't working out for them?

8. Do you find yourself talking about them when they're not there?

9. Do you feel good after you spend time together?

SORRY, BUT IT'S OVER: ENDING FRIENDSHIPS WITH TCB

I wish that someone had told me about friendship breakups. In my experience, they are more painful than romantic breakups because you don't go into them thinking they might end. (Which maybe says more about my approach to romantic relationships than friendships!) But friendships can end. Sometimes for no reason, sometimes because the two participants are better off without each other.

After I graduated from college, my best friend ghosted me. Even when I think about it now, it's immensely painful. Losing that friend was probably the biggest heartbreak of my life. I don't have closure, but I think she was having trouble saying goodbye to me (I was moving to another city) and I think the friendship itself wasn't viable.

Ending a friendship is never easy. No matter how long you've seen it coming, it can be devastating. However, there is a way to do it without ruining everyone's year. With the guideposts of trust, compassion, and boundaries, you can do what needs to be done.

Here are important things to remind yourself before starting a friend breakup:

1. Be kind. Don't let things get heated. Choose your words wisely.
2. Make space for both of you to say what needs to be said.
3. Take responsibility.

Here are some things to say that may help you feel closure. Remember, these are all phrases to use with someone you trust (or, at least, trusted at one time) and someone who you feel compassion for (even if you feel they have wronged you). Set a boundary by using your words.

- I want to discuss what happened between us. Can we?
- I want to express this so that you understand why I feel _____. It really hurt me when you _____.
- I hear you.
- I understand.
- I am sorry.
- I heard when you said _____. I am sorry that I made you feel _____.

Don't be afraid to express gratitude for what you had! This person was, at one point, someone you cared about.

. . . IT'S COMPLICATED

I'M CAUGHT BETWEEN FRIENDS

It can feel awful when your friends are not getting along. And maybe your first instinct is to try to make things better. That's not always wrong. When two people you like are in fight or at a standoff, both want their own version of events to be heard. And being a good friend might mean listening to both versions. But here's the most important thing to know: You do not ever have to take sides. You can listen, you can sympathize, but don't get caught in the middle by carrying messages or trying to make one person feel bad about how they acted. In fact, the more you remove yourself from their drama, the better. (Remember: boundaries!)

You can still talk to both friends, but make sure you let them each know where you stand. If they can't sit in the same room, then talk to them separately and explain: I will not get in the middle of this. I trust you, I have compassion for you, however this is not something I can get mixed up with. It will be difficult. And your friend(s) may not like it, but you need to protect yourself before you take care of anyone else. In order to help your friends, you must exercise a boundary. Because they shouldn't be pulling people into their drama! That only creates more drama.

HOW CAN I BE FRIENDS WITH SOMEONE WHO IS NOT LIKE ME?

First of all, you need to be secure in your sense of who *you* are. That's so true. Insecurity is never a good basis for a friendship. But don't let your own discomfort keep you from trying to get to know someone who could become a good friend. **Preach!** If you continue to feel nervous about interacting with someone who is different from you, you need to examine carefully why that might be. Is it prejudice that you were exposed to in your family or community of origin? Are these truly your beliefs? **Or are they the beliefs of everyone around you? Just because other people believe something doesn't mean you have to.** Ask yourself why this person intimidates you. What about the difference between you makes you uncomfortable? If you are clear on who you are, then you should have some capacity for C: compassion. Being present and sensitive to people different from you should only be interesting to you as a way of expanding your sense of the world. If your boundaries are sound, why would you feel intimidated? **Plus, they're probably really freakin' cool. Give 'em a chance. Maybe they'll take a chance on you, too.**

MY FRIEND REALLY LET ME DOWN

It's inevitable that you will find yourself in a situation where you feel like a friend has let you down. Maybe you told them something personal and they told someone you didn't want them to. Maybe they knew something would hurt you—but did it anyway. Maybe you were assuming they would act one way, but they acted in the opposite way. You might be disappointed, or hurt, or embarrassed. But what happens next is up to you. Is what they did worth ending a friendship over? What does it take to forgive them and move on? Here's where evaluating TCB can really help. First take a look at the relationship—from both sides:

Has the trust been severed? If so, take a second to gut check: trust has to be cultivated, it should not be automatically granted.

Exercise compassion for yourself. You're disappointed, but you have to be realistic. What does this feel like? Does it really hurt? Go ahead. Take the time to nurse your wounds. You can't force someone to be someone they are not. Rather than pretending that it didn't happen or pretending that they are a glorious, faultless person, be realistic.

Finally, think about friendship boundaries: What do you need? Do you need space? Do you need to talk? Do you need to pull in a counselor or trusted adult to help you figure out where the boundaries should be?

Now go a little deeper—using TCB to decide your course of action:

Can you trust in your gut feeling that you deserve more than your friend is giving?

Do you feel that you are worthy of better treatment?

Are you ready to be clear and firm in the result you want from a conversation?

If the answer is yes, when the time is right, you can talk to them about it. **But you have to make sure you know what you want and that you are in a good place. Only then can you operate from a place of integrity, rather than heightened emotions and faulty reasoning.** You can ask, "Why did you _____?" You can say, "I feel _____."

Ultimately, you have to remember: When someone has let you down, it's not you, it's them. And all you can do is evaluate that balance of TCB. And if the **trust** can be recultivated (over time), or maybe you hear something that makes you feel **compassion** and gives you insight into why your friend acted like they did, or you are able to establish new **boundaries** that give you both space to grow, after which you can consider restarting the friendship. **If not? Do what you need to do to feel closure.**

I'M WORRIED FOR MY FRIEND

Sage told Harley that she didn't want to be alive anymore and that if she could just take a handful of pills and disappear, she would. Harley wasn't sure what to do; they had never heard Sage say anything like that before. And it wasn't like she seemed super depressed. She was always helping out with the community service club and checking in to see how other people were doing. Sage wasn't the most popular person at school, but she wasn't an outsider either. It seemed so weird and out of character for her that Harley laughed and said, "What are you talking about?" Sage just said, "Don't tell anyone!" and walked away. Harley thought about following Sage but wasn't certain of what to do. So they didn't do anything, and when Sage wasn't at school the next day Harley felt sick with worry.

Trust can be a confusing issue to navigate when you know something about a friend that is concerning. Are you violating the trust in that relationship if you tell someone what's going on? It's possible your friend could feel betrayed, but generally the foundation of a real relationship is based on a genuine caring for the well-being of that person. **I think you need to hear that again: *the foundation of a real relationship is based on a genuine caring for the well-being of that person.***

If you are worried about a friend, you can also ask an adult close to them—like a school counselor or a teacher you know they trust—to check in with them. (The adult does not have to say who tipped them off.) Suicidal thinking *and especially having a plan* is a medical emergency and should be treated like one. **You must do something. And thinking about getting a handful of pills is having a plan.** If your friend fell down a flight of stairs and broke their leg, you'd go get help. If a friend talks about killing themselves, don't judge them. Tell them you love them, and want to help, and then stay with them until you can figure out how to get an adult on the scene. Or you can ask your friend if they will go with you to talk to an adult to get help. You are not in a position to judge whether or not your friend is being serious about their intentions. And by the way, my advice is the same if you have a friend who is cutting or self-harming. Don't be afraid to ask a friend if they are okay. If they say they are, but you're still worried, don't hesitate to let a trusted adult know about your concerns.

That kind of dedication to one another's well-being is what makes the relationship safe and allows for real trust. Are you looking out for your friend by maintaining secrecy? Not usually, and you may contribute to the harm of someone you care about. Your friend may initially be angry with you, but that is a small price for showing that you really care. If they tell you they are angry, explain that you did what you did because you were worried for them and wanted them to be safe. Don't let a friend's potential indignation stop you from acting when their well-being hangs in the balance. **We repeat: this is too big for you to handle alone. A good friend gets help for their friend. The National Suicide Prevention Lifeline is 800-273-8255. Sometimes talking to a stranger can be an easier way to get started talking about suicidal feelings and they can help you figure out what to say to a parent, teacher, or counselor.**

TOP THREE TAKEAWAYS FOR FRIENDSHIPS WITH TCB

1. Shout-out to Aristotle and TCB: there are all kinds of friendships; the best are those where both people successfully balance trust, compassion, and boundaries.

2. You can find potential friends almost anywhere, even online. But the healthiest friendships are those that develop in person and over time.

3. Toxic friendships can be hard to identify when you are in one. It takes effort, clear communication, and balanced TCB to sustain a healthy friendship. If your friendship feels lacking in any of these areas, it's time to reevaluate.

chapter 7

THE BIG BAD ONES: BULLIES AND ENEMIES

WHAT IS A BULLY?

We all know the classic bully narrative:

You're at your locker when, all of a sudden, you hear him before you see him. He's banging on lockers, his posse hooting and hollering behind him. Suddenly you know: you're doomed. You try to run, but he's behind you before you can even catch your breath. Before you know it, he has you pinned up against your locker and he's yelling, "Give me your lunch money!" You squeak out, "Please put me down!" He screams, louder this time, "Cough up the change, nerd!" You do as you're told. He lets go and you fall to the ground. His friends laugh before spitting on you. And in a flash, he's gone.

Is it that simple? It can be. But more times than not, it's a bit more complicated. It can be as subtle as people whispering and laughing—but stopping as soon as you walk into the room. Bullies disregard the rules, they disregard TCB, and they feel bigger when they make you feel small. Seeing you cower in fear makes them feel like they are powerful.

According to StopBullying.gov, bullying actions are defined by two things: power imbalance and repetition. **Bullies want you to believe they have power.** Power imbalance can manifest in different ways: Bullies can attack you physically or socially. They might threaten you—saying they'll beat you up or that they'll spread rumors that can ruin your reputation. Shoving someone into their locker and stealing their lunch money is bullying; telling someone not to be friends with someone else is bullying. So is using embarrassing information about someone as blackmail. Verbally tearing someone down or deliberately not inviting someone to a party (even though you're posting about it and everyone can see) can be just as painful as a punch to your face.

It's possible, even likely, that someone you consider a friend will cross a line and do something hurtful, like gossip about you, make a mean joke where you're the punch line, or even lose their temper and shove you. People use poor judgment and lose their tempers. But a friend will apologize and never do it again. They have **compassion** for you. They can appreciate the pain they caused you and they never want to repeat that behavior. *Bullies repeatedly target their victims.* If someone acts in a way that is hurtful to you, and does it more than once, that person is bullying you. So, when you see *that* someone walking toward you, or hear "Voldemort's" name and your stomach drops, it's time to take some action. Bullies exist at school, but they can also live in your house, or be your boss, or create chaos in your online life. One thing unites all bullies: the fear and terror they strike in the heart of their victims. And three things can help you deal with them . . . read on!

TCB AND BULLIES

Here's how we want you to look for bullies: Instead of **trust**, do they trigger fear, anxiety, or frustration whenever they approach you? Do they lack **compassion**, cutting you down in front of others? Do they disregard **boundaries**, invading your physical, emotional, or cyber spaces? If you are working on recognizing and using TCB in all of your personal interactions, a bully can really test your skills. And if you're not making sure trust, compassion, and boundaries are present in how you deal with everyone in your life, you might need to ask yourself: Am I the bully?

Your body recognizes a bully before the rest of you does. Since bullies can lurk in every corner of your daily life—school, work, friend groups—you need to learn to *trust* your internal "bully radar" in order to secure your *boundaries*. But what about the C of TCB: *compassion*? Having compassion for a bully can be a way to protect yourself from their negative energy. Usually, bullies have been bullied themselves or have other issues: problems at home, abuse, or trauma. They may be feeling angry or vulnerable, which makes them act out. You may not be the target for any reason other than that you are in their path. Sometimes, showing a bully a bit of humanity can be life-altering. However, there are situations where the bully is a ticking time bomb and they're about to go off, compassion be damned.

There's not much you can do for a bully who can't be reasoned with except for going to an adult.

After Jada was systematically bullied by Morgan, they had to talk to a school counselor because they were having trouble focusing in school, felt socially isolated, and didn't know what to do. The counselor, thankfully, was good at his job. He brought Morgan in separately, too. He talked to her about what was going on in her life. Turns out, Morgan was struggling at home with an alcoholic abusive father. It wasn't like Jada and Morgan ever became friends, but Morgan stopped attacking Jada when she started to understand more about why she was lashing out.

Use your judgment. If the bully has proven to be unreasonable, confide in a trusted adult. If you think they could use a bit of compassion, be bold. Be brave. **And don't be afraid to say, "Are you okay?"**

CYBER BULLYING

When you don't have to look someone in the face, it is easy to say things you don't mean. In this way, trolls reign supreme. When it comes to cyberbullying, we've seen it from both sides. As someone who is on television and has many social media accounts, I've definitely experienced my share of bullying. People on Twitter routinely attack my character, my motivation, or my professional abilities. There's something about this kind of anonymous forum where people behave in ways they never would in person. It's almost as if they can't see me as a real person. **They don't. First, they're literally only seeing you on a screen. But second, "celebrities" or public figures are seen as immortal. Or immune. Or just, other.**

I can say firsthand that it feels terrible when someone repeatedly attacks my personality, integrity, or professional skill. The reason I know that this is bullying is how it makes me feel—helpless. There is no way for me to respond, no way to engage in a discussion with the person to try to defend myself. My professional ethics and discipline don't let me respond angrily. **I'll take care of them *puts fists up* . . . NO! AH! Fists down. See, I'm learning too. Let's try to understand rather than fight.**

Codirectors of the Cyberbullying Research Center Justin Patchin and Sameer Hinduja define online bullying as "willful and repeated harm inflicted through the use of computers, cell phones, and other electronic devices." Cyber expert and author Nancy Willard breaks cyberbullying into seven specific categories:

1. **FLAMING:** Sending angry, rude, vulgar messages directed at a person or persons privately or to an online group. Go through the comments section on any platform, and that's where you can see some of the most hateful, rude, and vulgar messages. But it can be more personal: a text or even a subtweet. It doesn't have to be directed at the person to do damage.

2. **DENIGRATION (PUT-DOWNS):** Sending or posting harmful, untrue, or cruel statements about a person to the person or other people. It can be as easy as talking

about someone in a group chat with your friends or as complicated as photoshopping someone's head on a vulgar image and texting it around the school.

3. **ONLINE HARASSMENT:** Repeatedly sending a person offensive messages. These messages can be direct: DM or text or Snap. Or they can be public, on Instagram or Twitter.

4. **CYBERSTALKING:** Harassment that includes threats of harm or is highly intimidating. Even if it is online, your threats still stand. Saying you're going to "kill" someone or telling them you're going to "reveal their secret to the whole school" is a threat. You don't have to stand face-to-face to intimidate someone. Especially if you make the threat more than once.

5. **OUTING:** Sending or posting material about a person that contains sensitive, private, or embarrassing information, including forwarding private messages or images. Tricking someone into giving up embarrassing information, which is then made public. Screenshotting a personal conversation and sending it to someone else. Telling anyone that someone is gay before they've decided to come out. Sending around someone's nudes after they were sent to you is outing (not to mention illegal!).

6. **MASQUERADE:** Pretending to be someone else and sending or posting material that makes that person look bad or places that person in potential danger. When you've got your friend's password and you think it's funny to text that guy she likes and ask for a sext

back. Or making a fake Twitter account in order to spread rumors.

7. **EXCLUSION:** Actions that specifically and intentionally exclude a person from an online group. The group text about the party that everyone in the group is at . . . except that one person.

SEE A BULLY, BLOCK A BULLY

Cyberbullies say things that they never, ever would have the nerve to say in person. And that can make it seem hard to challenge online bullies, since it can feel like nothing you can do will make a difference. Parents and teachers, too, can dismiss the stress of being bullied online. **But you do not have to stand for it. If you are being bullied on a platform that allows you to report someone, then report them! Let me say it again—three times, so it sticks—Report. Report. Report. And then? Block. Report, then block, got it?**

Rainn tweeted something they thought was funny. Within minutes, a rando replied, "ur an idiot." Rather than engaging with a reply, Rainn hit Report. Then blocked. Before anything could even happen, Rainn nipped a potential problem in the bud.

When it comes to online bullying, you must always report it. Likely you'll keep someone else from getting bullied, and do good for the larger community. **But what do you do if it isn't just a random person? What if, instead, it's someone who you know?**

Tucker opened up Instagram to see that his former best friend, Calvin, had commented, "u try too hard. stop embarrassing urself sweetie" on one of his posts. As a "former" best friend, Calvin knows this is an insecurity of Tucker's. Uncertain as to why Calvin would do that, Tucker DMed him and asked, "Did I do something wrong?" To which Calvin replied, "You know what you did." But Tucker didn't know what he had done. He spent the rest of the night crying, worried that everyone could see how hard he was trying to be cool.

If there's any hope for Tucker to feel better about himself, it's through bringing TCB into play. He needs to check in with himself, so he can trust that he's posting content that feels authentic. Calvin's comments have shaken his self-esteem, and even though Tucker is the victim in the situation, we have discussed how showing **compassion** for a bully can be a way to defuse their anger. **Additionally, those who say horrible things to others are often saying worse things to themselves.** So, if Tucker replies, "Are you okay?" and Calvin backs off, then Tucker has successfully restored a boundary. But if Calvin attacks again and says something like "The problem isn't me it's you!" Tucker needs to amp up his boundary-building and protect himself by documenting the bullying. Take a screenshot. Exit the app. Go tell a parent. And, if things get bad enough, and Calvin begins bullying him in person, Tucker should bring the evidence to school and show the proper adult.

If this topic is making you uncomfortable because you've engaged in this kind of behavior, you need to take a hard look at your online use—**and you probably owe a friend an apology.** And if a friend has done any of this to you, you need to check whether they deserve a second chance. You will need to explain that they have lost some of your **trust**, and how they can rebuild it. Exercise **compassion**. Any one of us can occasionally cross a line. It's how we discover where lines are. And if you haven't figured out what comes next . . . those "lines" are your **boundaries** (and you get to decide where your boundaries are). Remember that the definition of "bullying" is that it is *willful and repeated*. If someone continues this behavior after you confront them and ask for it to stop, you need to bring a trusted adult into the conversation.

IF YOU ARE BEING BULLIED

If you feel like you are being bullied, you probably are. In a 2018 Pew Research report, 59 percent of teens said that they had experienced some form of cyberbullying, including being the subject of false rumors, being called offensive names, being sent sexually explicit images they didn't ask for, or having sexually explicit images of them shared without their consent. Others reported being constantly asked (by someone other than a parent) where they were and what they were doing and/or receiving physical threats. If you are being bullied, you must take steps to protect yourself and your self-esteem. You may worry about facing social embarrassment, or increased bullying, but the long-term damage of silently suffering these kinds of assaults will affect your behavior, self-esteem, and confidence in the future. **You are capable of protecting yourself. You** are capable of finding a way to solve the problem. You are going to get through this by calling on TCB:

> **Trust** that you have the ability to stand up to a bully.

> Have **compassion** for yourself—you are not what any bully says you are. Think about what you would do if you witnessed someone else in your situation. You'd probably want to help.

> Pay attention to physical **boundaries**, including withdrawing from the bully to a safer environment, whether that means moving to a different room or location, or putting down your phone or blocking or muting them on social.

WHAT IF YOU'RE THE BULLY?

Bullying is being identified and called out more these days. So if you are examining your behavior and are worried that you have bullied someone, we are proud of you for asking the right questions. We also encourage you to go back and read the first part of the book. As you think about how you treat others, think about how you define yourself. It may be that there is something in your own identity story that can help you understand why you are lashing out to hurt others.

At the same time, have compassion for yourself. We all have times when we have behaved in ways we are not proud of. Like, I'm not super proud of the fact that I threw a remote control at my brother in the fifth grade. But what you can do is acknowledge your misdeed moving forward and vow to not repeat the hurtful behavior. We've said it before and we'll say it again: no one is perfect, and it is important to learn from our mistakes.

Consider whether there is a culture of bullying at your school or in your friend group that has sucked you in. If so, is there someone like a trusted friend, your parents, or a teacher that you can talk to? Were you bullied yourself and felt justified in bullying back? There's even a name for people who display this behavior: bully-victims, referring to people who are both bullies as well as victims themselves. As we learned earlier in the chapter, bullies are often the victims of bullying, trauma, or abuse. And so the cycle is perpetuated. The bullied becomes the bully.

Is there a history of bullying within your family? How do your parents speak to each other? Your siblings? For me, I was much meaner at home than I was at school. Mostly that was because I felt powerless in so many other areas of my life that having power over my brothers made me feel stronger. Looking back, I'm not proud of it, but I think it's more important to be honest than it is to hide from the truth.

Ask yourself why you feel the need to tear people down. If you feel small or insecure yourself, it may be tempting to try to bring others down to your level. Finally: are you willing to change? Just because you were a bully does not mean that you have to continue being a bully. People change. A simple aphorism: treat others how you would like to be treated. How do you start to do that? Turn back to the beginning of the book for a refresher. When you understand how powerful the trio of trust, compassion, and boundaries is when turned inward, you can start thinking about how to treat others with TCB.

WHAT IF I SEE SOMEONE BEING BULLIED?

When someone is being bullied, there are typically several relationships manifesting simultaneously. There is the bully and their victim, but there are also the witnesses who may be allies or bystanders, and there are the friends or peers who may step in after the bullying to provide emotional support. Planning ahead can help you be a good ally when you see someone being bullied. Think about what you would want someone to do if it was happening to you. Your willingness to act can make a difference. According to StopBullying.gov, when bystanders intervene, bullying stops within ten seconds, 57 percent of the time. You can choose to step in to support the victim of bullying, whether online or in real life. You can also rally support from other bystanders. Bullies rarely continue their behavior in the face of a crowd.

SEE A BULLY; BE AN ALLY

Here are some nonaggressive things you can say to make a bully stop and think:

"Hey! What's going on?"

If they don't respond, assert yourself from a safe distance.

"Cut it out. That's not cool."

"Imagine if someone did that to you."

"Hey, that's over the line."

"Wow, that's really messed up."

"Do I need to get a teacher?"

And if they can't be reasoned with?

"Stop!"

"I'm getting an adult!"

Bullying can be physical, but you can still be an ally. In order to de-escalate a bully, you must be mentally ready to be assertive without being aggressive. Think about what it feels like to have someone in your corner. You can choose to be an active, rather than passive, bystander.

A crowd is starting to gather, some of the boys are shouting, "Fight! Fight! Fight!" Amy is screaming in Margeaux's face when their mutual friend Petunia walks up to see what the commotion is about. Petunia is careful to keep a safe distance, but as soon as she hears what Amy is saying, she loudly exclaims: "Wow! That's not cool!" Amy yanks Margeaux's ponytail, which makes Petunia yell, "Stop it or I'm getting a teacher!" Amy freezes and lets go. Petunia looks at the crowd and announces, "Nothing to see here! Move along!" The crowd melts away. Amy and Margeaux go their separate ways. And, because Petunia is smart, she immediately goes and tells a trusted adult what went down.

What did Petunia do right?

1. She made sure she was a safe distance from the altercation.
2. She made declarative statements in a strong, clear voice.
3. She asserted a boundary that Margeaux couldn't.
4. She showed compassion for Margeaux by saying something.
5. When her statement was ignored, she upped the ante and made it clear that she would find an adult to intervene.

Petunia successfully used declarative statements that caught the attention of the bully. Through her assertion of boundaries, Petunia was able to help Margeaux in their time of need.

All of this is to say, you can still use TCB to be an active bystander. *Trust* your own sense of what is right and wrong. Have *compassion* for the person under attack. And finally, assert a *boundary* between the participants. And if that boundary is violated? Immediately go get a trusted adult for help.

WHEN WORDS DON'T STOP A BULLY

Before you try to push back with words, make sure that you are not in physical danger. If someone *is* hurting you, your priority is to get them to stop. Make as much noise as possible and get the attention of as many people as you can. "Help!" "Stop!" Scream at the top of your lungs.

TRUTH? OR BULLYING?

Kelly and Barda are best friends. Kelly always comments on what Barda wears. Yesterday, Kelly told Barda that she "shouldn't wear that skirt." When Barda asked why, Kelly replied, "Because

blue is a bad color on you, and you look like a fat blueberry."
Barda burst into tears and ran into the bathroom.

Sometimes, friends can be bullies, even if they don't mean to be. Kelly may feel as though they are helping their friend out, but there are ways to tell people what we think without hurting their feelings. It's important not to confuse bullying with assertiveness. A bully will make a declaration that belittles you, like "You look stupid when you do that." However, you can be assertive without being aggressive, threatening, or disregarding others' boundaries or values. A declarative statement like "When you do that, it makes me feel uncomfortable" is much more effective and leaves the other person's integrity intact. **In fact, that would have been a great statement for Barda to make to Kelly. We can assert boundaries with our words, even when we are under the attack of a bully.**

FUNNY? OR BULLY?

As someone who teaches improvisational and sketch comedy, I have just three rules about how to deploy humor:

1. *Don't be a jerk.*
2. *Play to the height of your intelligence.* Assume that your audience is as smart as you. Play to the smartest person in the room. They're not going to be impressed by easy jokes. They'll get the stuff that you get.
3. *Punch up, not down.* Think about how you can make

commentary on power structures, not character or appearance. Who are you making jokes about? Are they higher up in society than you? A president? A teacher? Rather than making a joke about them personally, think about the joke you can make that takes aim at their power. That's punching up. If someone holds less power in society or school, making jokes at their expense is punching down. That's why you should avoid making jokes about things like race, ability, religion, gender, or sexual orientation.

If you stick to these rules, you will actually be funnier than someone who makes easy jokes. Pointing out someone's difference is not funny. It's straight-up lazy.

MY BULLY IS IN MY FAMILY

Full transparency: I have experience with bullying—on both the giving and receiving end. My brother has horror stories about how much I bullied him as a kid.

However, Jay has a brother who screams in their face, punches walls, and actively makes Jay feel afraid. This is not normal behavior, nor should it be tolerated—by Jay or by their parents. Bullying does happen in families (as you just admitted), and chronic, repetitive, threatening behavior is abusive and traumatizing. A damaging traumatic response begins at any point where the victim feels truly powerless, or feels that their physical safety is being threatened.

If the bully is within your own family, rely on TCB to protect yourself:

TRUST YOUR INSTINCTS. If you feel like you are in danger, do anything and everything you can to get yourself to safety. For some that may mean walking to another room, for others it may mean living in a different house.

EXERCISE COMPASSION FOR YOURSELF. What you are experiencing is debilitating and scary. Do what you need to do to keep yourself safe and sane.

KNOW YOUR BOUNDARIES. Understand what you can and can't tolerate. And if you can't tolerate any more bullying, circle back to number 1: Trust your instincts.

BULLYING CAN BE DEADLY SERIOUS

If you are being bullied and feel like no one is listening or believe the only way out is to not exist, put this book down and immediately call the National Suicide Prevention Lifeline at 800-273-8255. Someone will answer 24/7 and they will offer free and confidential support, including resources near you. You matter. You are important. You are worthwhile. Don't let the bullies tell you otherwise.

BEYOND BULLYING— SWORN ENEMIES

A sworn enemy is someone whose name cannot be uttered without feeling like you're going to burst into flames. Harry Potter and Voldemort, Alexander Hamilton and Aaron Burr, cats and dogs . . . **Enemies can also be known as haters. And as we all know, haters gonna hate, hate, hate.** Your sworn enemy may have something you want. Or, they could be an enemy for historical reasons—you seek revenge or vindication because they wronged you, or your family, or your friend, and you want them to pay. Or, even worse, they could have been a friend, or a romance, and they broke your heart.

> *Quinn and Jaime have known each other since middle school. From the moment they met, they could not stand each other. They competed for the attention of friends, battled over the lead role in the play, and tried to outdo each other academically. And for the next six years—until the end of high school—they were (unspoken) sworn enemies. "It's just something you feel in your soul," Quinn explained. "The way Jaime behaved, the things he believed . . . I wanted to be exactly the opposite." And when people gave Jaime praise or attention, Quinn felt it implied that he wasn't as worthwhile. Eventually, the only way Quinn could feel he was succeeding was if it was at Jaime's expense. But such victories stopped feeling good. Quinn wasn't achieving things because it was what he wanted. His only goal was to take those things away from Jaime. This way of thinking was toxic to Quinn's self-identity. Instead of learning more*

about what made him happy, Quinn went down the path of defining personal success according to someone else's goals. And, of course, Jaime noticed that Quinn was personally targeting him. In return, he acted in the same way: going after whatever he thought Quinn wanted, just to take it away from him.

Sworn enemies may be antagonistic, their behavior may border on bullying, but ultimately, if you're being truthful, you want to see them fail. **Not because you get a sick pleasure out of seeing others in pain, but for toxic competitive reasons—you believe that if they fall, you rise.**

Here's another important thing to reckon with: if you start a war with your enemy, then you become an enemy, too. **By having an enemy, you become an enemy. If you name someone your enemy, then they can name you their enemy.** It doesn't matter how "right" you are. There is no room to practice TCB with enemies. Once you act out of malice, you are being drawn to perform behaviors that you aren't proud of. This was definitely true for Quinn. When Quinn would trash-talk Jaime to mutual friends, or date someone—not because they liked them, but because they knew that Jaime did—they eventually began to feel they were betraying their own moral code.

DEALING WITH AN ENEMY

So you've got an enemy. What do you do? TCB seems far, far away. How do you establish trust with someone who doesn't deserve it? You don't. Never do anything that keeps you from practicing TCB.

If you are in a situation where you don't trust yourself, don't have compassion for yourself, and are violating your own boundaries, get out of there.

Which is why I'm here to pitch a radical idea: just ignore them. If you can, walk away. If you're trapped with them in a class, imagine you can't see them, can't hear them. They don't exist. Seems impossible, right? How do you walk away from someone who you feel burning hate for? Well, here is your chance to be the bigger person. As Michelle Obama said, "When they go low, we go high." Radically accept that that person will never be your friend. And in doing so, maybe you can find you have compassion for them. But ultimately, respect your boundaries by exiting the situation altogether. **Radical acceptance is the way out of this one, kids. Don't react, just be done. That way, you can be bigger than your enemy.**

NOT AN ENEMY, NOT A BULLY, BUT NOT A FRIEND

Now that we have enemies down, it's time to talk about adversaries. What is an adversary? An adversary is different from an enemy (who is always against you) in that their self-interest is different from yours, but only at a specific point in time. So an adversary might work against you at some point, but that might change. They don't actively cause you harm in the same way as a bully, and if their interests switch around and become aligned with your interests, they can become an ally.

Dylan and Lee are both seniors and they both want to be captain of the soccer team. However, there is only room for one. They have both demonstrated that they work hard, they both have strong leadership skills, and they both have dreamed of being captain their senior year. They aren't enemies; in fact, the only thing that's keeping them from becoming closer friends is that they are vying for the same position.

With an enemy, it is smart to walk away. But you might not want to walk away from an adversary. Like in the case of Dylan and Lee, this might be a time for both of them to step up for the challenge. Who will be captain? Do you want to walk away from your passions in order to maintain a friendship? Or do you want to compete, letting the best person win? And maybe even be happy for them?

QUIZ
Enemy or Adversary?

How do you differentiate between an enemy and an adversary? Here's a quiz to help you figure it out:

1. **Was there ever a time this person was on your side?**

   a. Yes

   b. No

   c. Sometimes

2. **Are you competing for the same thing?**

   a. Yes

   b. No

   c. Sometimes

3. **Do they have qualities that you admire?**

   a. Yes

   b. No

   c. Sometimes

4. **Is TCB present within the relationship?**

   a. Yes

   b. No

   c. Sometimes

If you responded YES for more than half of the questions, then you, my friend, have an adversary. They have qualities you admire, you're competing for similar things, they have been on your side before, and they can be on your side again.

If you responded NO to more than half of the questions, then you are stuck in enemy territory. Ask yourself: Can TCB be applied to our relationship? Is this a person that I trust? Can they trust me? Do I have compassion for them, and do they have compassion for me? And boundaries: Are they being respected?

If you responded SOMETIMES to more than one question, then you need to find some clarity. Is TCB accessible? If not, you may be in enemy territory. If you have compassion for the person and you both respect each other's boundaries, then maybe you've got an adversary on your hands.

This quiz can be clarifying. If you have an adversary, step up to the challenge. Fight your hardest to win out, but also be open to a friendship after all that is said and done. You can always hope to reason with an adversary. But an enemy? Do not waste time or social capital trying to turn enemies into friends. Focus on your allies.

TOP THREE TAKEAWAYS ABOUT BULLIES, ENEMIES, AND ADVERSARIES

1 Bullies aren't trustworthy, they don't have compassion, and they plow right through boundaries. In short—they have no respect for TCB.

2 If you have been a bully, you can work your way out of it by committing to bring TCB into your relationships. Chapters 1 through 6 will help you get realigned and on the right path.

3 An adversary is different from a sworn enemy. The first can be a motivating relationship and the second is not worth your social, emotional, or mental energy.

chapter 8

YOU'RE NOT THE BOSS OF ME: PARENTS AND OTHER ADULTS

Parents. What can I say? Some of you may have great relationships; some of you may feel like they're in your business too much. Like mine were. But I also know children who couldn't wait for the day when they got more attention. **Like me!** The dynamic between you and the people who are responsible for your health and well-being as you grow into an independent adult is a *relationship*. And like with any relationship, keeping trust, compassion, and boundaries at the forefront can keep both parties in sync and make challenges easier to navigate.

For the most part we want you to accept that your parents are doing the best that they can. **And it helps if you can appreciate that you both share a goal: to ensure you grow up into a capable, kind, independent person.** You may not always agree—you may even fight. But if you have been raised in a home where you feel safe and seen, I'd ask you to consider that many of the things that frustrate you about your relationship with your parents are coming from a place of loving responsibility.

There's a wide spectrum when it comes to the parental experience, and each parent/child relationship is unique. Young people today are living in a variety of family structures: with two parents, with one parent (often a single mother), with grandparents, with two parents of the same sex. Remember chapter 3? We talked about how your identity develops partly in relation to the people who are taking care of you. The short version is that, no matter what your family looks like, it's where you have your first experiences with relationships. Biological or adoptive, your parents' first duty is to care for you.

We know the world isn't perfect, and sometimes things are less than ideal, or even awful. Babies who are separated from—or have inconsistent—primary caregivers within their first year of development, or are raised in an environment where their parent is depressed or incapacitated by drugs and alcohol, can develop feelings of insecurity that stay with them as they grow from toddlers to teens to adults. **In an ideal situation, babies grow up surrounded by TCB and learn the fundamentals of consent. They learn what it is like to feel safe, loved, and valued. They learn that they have physical and emotional boundaries that others will respect. That's why your relationship with your parents is so important: If you can trust your parents, you learn how to trust others. If you have compassion for your parents, you can have compassion for others. If you can hold your boundaries because your parents have respected them, you can recognize, and respect, boundaries in others.**

A WORD TO PARENTS AND TRUSTED ADULTS

Parents and other trusted adults, here's my advice for you if a young person in your life brings you this book: I know that you want to protect them and shelter them from mistakes that could change the trajectory of their lives. And I'm guessing I'm a little ahead of you in the challenge of raising young adults (our triplets are in their late twenties as I write this book!). When a young person comes to you with a big life question, they are also likely bringing you their anxiety, maybe mixed with confusion. They are attempting to navigate complex terrain and they are telling you about their experience—not so you can tell them what to do, but so you can validate the fact they are wrestling with grown-up, real-world issues.

It's not your job to amplify or negate their emotions, but rather to receive information calmly. If your response is fueled by your own anxiety, the natural response for the young person will be to become defensive, push back, or shut down. Take a deep breath, and practice reflective listening: "So you'd like to get birth control . . . tell me more about why you think now is the right time for sex in your relationships." As the conversation goes on, you'll be able to offer other prompts: "Have you thought about what you'll do if _____ happens?" It's okay to offer concern: "I'm worried you could be hurt in this situation." And, of course, if someone is telling you they are contemplating something that could cause them real physical or psychological harm, you should take action. If you've been looking at this book—with or without a teen at your side—you'll already know that the foundation of a good relationship with anyone is **trust**, **compassion**, and **boundaries**. In short, if a young person you know is trying to open a difficult (or any) conversation with you, remember to listen with TCB:

TRUST: Don't attack, threaten, or judge; be a person who deserves trust. Show interest by not interrupting and using your reflective listening skills.

COMPASSION: Validate their experience by acknowledging their thoughts and feelings; but more importantly, have empathy by remembering what their experience *feels* like. (You were once young, after all.)

BOUNDARIES: Mind your own boundaries. Try to have an easy attitude; don't become caught up in the drama, or jump in to rescue them from their experience. And respect their boundaries: don't press them to say more than they are ready to say; be patient as they figure out what they want to share.

BEFORE BRINGING UP A SENSITIVE TOPIC, THINK ABOUT TCB

Okay, reader, back to you! If you decide that you feel safe in sharing something with your parents (or another adult), first take some time to think about how TCB can make the conversation easier for the both of you:

How is the trust between you and your parents? Do they have reason to doubt your motives or intent? Do you believe they have your best interests at heart?

Have compassion for yourself. Will the process of opening yourself up cause emotional distress? Can you expect to be received with compassion and can you maintain compassion for your parents if they react negatively? If you already know that this conversation will not be well received, it's important to think about why you want to have it in the first place. Even if you expect them to react negatively, is it more important for you to be fully known? Or is it more effective to keep the status quo?

Everyone has boundaries, which means that both you and your parents are entitled to have opinions. And learning to hear opinions that are different from yours, even from people you love, is an important part of developing compassion and empathy. Learning how to inform without insisting helps exercise your boundaries. Are the boundaries in your family stable enough for everyone to tolerate what you wish to say? Or are your parents going to reject your ideas, or superimpose their beliefs and feelings and marginalize yours? Will you be able to sustain your boundaries without shutting down or withdrawing?

HOW DO I ASK MY PARENTS ABOUT SEX?

I think it's important to talk to your parents about relationships of all kinds—even those that involve sex. Heck, I'm literally writing a book about consent with my dad. Did I ever think that I would be doing this? Absolutely not. But as an adult person who went her whole life without talking to her dad about it, I'm trying to make up for lost time. And if I can do it, you can try too.

The attitude your parents have toward relationships and sexuality is the attitude they'll want to pass down to you. If your parents are religious or conservative, it may be difficult (or impossible) to have a nuanced conversation about your life. Luckily, the internet exists. Luckily, we exist. Gently point your parents toward resources or topics—or leave this book lying around where they can pick it up. Perhaps your parents gave you this book and said, "Let's talk after you've read it all." **Or, your parents talk about sex all the time (like mine!) and you don't want to know anything else about it. You get it already!**

Whether your relationship to sex is open or apprehensive, it's okay to talk about it with your parents. Have compassion; this may be an awkward conversation for them too. But try to trust that they are going to do their best to help you through this confusing time.

Here are some prompts to start the conversation:

Talk about your "friend." This lifts the pressure off you, even if you are talking about yourself. This allows you to ask anything and everything.

- "My friend at school said _____. Is that true?"
- "My friend said that someone did _____. Is it safe to do that?"
- "I'm worried about my friend. They are doing _____. What do you think is the best way to help them make informed choices?"

If your parents have brought the topic up before:
- "Do you have time to talk?"
- "I wasn't ready to talk about sex before, but now I am. What is _____?"
- "Can you tell me more about _____?"

If you parents are super-duper open:
- "I know you've been waiting for this day. And it has come. Let's talk about sex. What do I need to know?"
- "You brought up _____, and I have more questions. Can we talk about it?"
- "Ugh, fine! Let's talk about sex."

If your parents are rigidly opposed to your way of thinking:

Soften them up:
- "I am incredibly grateful for all that you have given me."

- "I am so glad you're my parent."
- "I love you so much!"

Then, get to the meat of the matter:

- "I know that you believe _____. However, I feel like we need to explore the topic of sex so that I can be fully informed. I want to know more! And I trust you, so I need your input."
- "I need your help. School hasn't covered the topic of sex, and I really want to be informed on the topic. What do you know about _____?"
- "As you know, I have a boyfriend/girlfriend/partner. I know that you believe that abstinence is the only choice. I do too! However, I think it's important to talk about sex in a way that informs me of the reality of sex, so that when I am married I can make strong and informed choices."

And, if you're feeling extra bold:

- "I already know _____. However, I don't know about _____. Can we talk about it?"
- "I don't believe that abstinence is the only choice. Can we talk about it?"

All of these prompts are intended to ease the pressure on your parents. Whatever tactic you choose, depending on what you know about your parents, this will help open up the conversation. Even if it feels impossible, it is worth trying.

I DON'T WANT TO TELL MY PARENTS I'M HAVING SEX.

This is not an uncommon feeling. So let's check in with you first: Are you feeling good about your choice to be sexual with your partner? Or are you finding things confusing or emotionally painful? Are you at least sixteen years old? Most experts agree that prior to sixteen, our brains are not necessarily developed to the point that sexual activity can be navigated in a flexible and healthy manner. If you are older than sixteen, and in a good relationship (practicing TCB and consent), it is fine to keep the information about the sex you are having between you and your partner!

If you are not sure how you feel about where your relationship is going, reaching out to your parents (or another trusted adult) could be an opportunity to avoid making mistakes in your relationship. Not all parents will be comfortable with this conversation. Some parents may believe that just having this conversation gives you their permission to engage in behavior that they would rather you not. Or they may feel that they might give you bad advice or somehow send you astray. Some might try to put it off, some might send you to school or clergy for guidance. **Which parent do you think you can confide in? One of them? Both of them? Neither of them?**

Remember: your mom and your dad (or your moms or your dads) have been exactly where you are. That's right, there was a day when your parents were struggling with how to tackle the big question of sex with *their* parents. They went from being the kid with questions to the adult with some answers. And one day, you'll be the adult navigating difficult conversations as well. So start from a place of empathy: they want you to be safe and they want you

to be healthy. You can remind them that knowledge is power. The more information they can give you, the better prepared you are to tackle life.

As terrifying as it may feel, being open with your parents may save you from doing anything prematurely. (It might also make it easier to access birth control and reproductive health.) The older you are, the more equipped you are to make strong choices. Honestly, I've never heard anyone say, "I wish I had sex sooner." The more secure you are in your choice, the better.

MEET THE PARENTS

Whether it's pointing out your crush or introducing your partner, letting your parents in on your romantic life can be a learning opportunity. I can verify this statement. Every crush or boyfriend that's met my parents has taught me something new about my parents, my partner . . . and myself. Or, rather, about what I'm attracted to.

If your parents welcome home every single person you've ever flirted with, ask yourself if that's saying more about what they wish *for* you than *who* they wish to see you with. Your parents should have the space to get to know your partners as people, not just as a romantic accessory. They don't have to like everyone you like. If your parents are truly objecting to someone you are seeing, try to figure out what it is about your crush that your parents find objectionable. Is their opinion based on the way someone is treating you, or is it the way someone looks? How does that person behave when introduced to adults they don't know?

Sometimes, the "parent test" can pick up on future issues. Don't just write off a strong negative reaction. If your friends said the same thing, would you listen? Your parents' opinion, though you may not feel like it, can be as valuable as a best friend's take on your love interest. And though you may not like to hear what they say, keep TCB in mind and *trust* that they have your best interests at heart, have *compassion* for their instinct to protect you, and know that healthy *boundaries* can let parents express their opinion, while you make your own decision.

If your parents' objections to your love life come from rejecting someone because of different ethnicity/religion/sexual orientation, that's when you can disregard their comments. Though you may not have their approval, it is more important for you to explore what you are attracted to. As I noted, every introduction is a learning opportunity. And perhaps the learning opportunity extends to your parents opening their minds a little.

MY PARENTS WON'T STAY OUT OF MY BUSINESS.

It really depends what you mean by that. The very nature of good parenting means your business is their business. **NOT COOL. But true.** What I think you really mean is that you are having trouble maintaining good personal boundaries with your parents. You might want to address this straightforwardly with them to see if you can set any ground rules. Start the conversation by saying, "I know you are doing what you think is best for me, but I think we need to have a discussion about boundaries." or "I feel like you don't trust me. Can we talk about it?"

If you feel like you can't have this conversation, find a place where you can express yourself in private. **Diaries kept me connected to myself throughout my childhood—well, actually, my whole life. How you build out from your private conversations with yourself will be a negotiation.** Your parents are just trying to do what they believe is best for you. Introduce them to TCB—tell them that in order to make sound choices and grow as a person, you need to assert some boundaries. It may be a difficult conversation, but it's an important one.

Sometimes, for your safety and well-being, your parents have to override your boundaries. As your parent, your legal guardian, they get final say. Even if you are mad about it. For instance, if you are having a mental health issue or substance use problem, all bets are off until they get you to a professional. You may not want to go, but in order to protect your health in the long term, there may be new ground rules in order to keep you safe.

I'M EMBARRASSED BY MY PARENTS' VIEWS.

Whether you are perceiving your parents as homophobic, racist, classist, or simply intolerant, this problem can exist on a spectrum from being truly dangerous to merely being, well . . . ignorant. And I mean ignorant literally, in the sense that their life experience has never exposed them to people who are different from them. **This is important: Ignorance stems from not experiencing things. Sometimes, if you haven't experienced something yourself, you don't understand it. But it is the differences between ourselves and others that make life beautiful.**

The gentle way to help expose your parents to a bigger, more diverse world is through contact. The more time you (and they) spend with people who are different, the more comfortable everyone becomes with those differences. If this seems too hard to do in person, try asking your parents to watch a movie or a TV show that features the kind of people they are voicing their opinions about. **What's key in this approach is to not try to change your parents' mind in the moment. Just keep asking them to watch with you. You may start to see a change.**

Expose your parents to your friends. You can tell your friends that you worry your parents might express opinions or make comments that could be awkward. **Give them a briefing beforehand: "My parents don't know better, but I've got your back." And if your parents step out of line or say something wrong, sure, it's embarrassing. But your friend has been forewarned and you can remind them that you are working to educate your parents.**

Make sure your friendship has good TCB as well. Your friend needs to **trust** that you are not like your parents, be **compassionate** about helping someone learn how to spend time with people who are different from them, and have good **boundaries** so they don't become hurt. Over time you will likely find that your parents will start to see your friend as the person they are, rather than some representation of a group your parents excluded or were afraid of. Then trust that, with time, they will come around.

DON'T POKE THE BEAR

If your parents hold views that are violent or dangerous, you need to make a plan to get yourself to a safe place. Call one of the hotlines listed in the back of this book. While you are working with a trusted adult to create a plan, lie low and avoid provoking them to action. Your most important concern should be for your personal mental and physical safety and well-being.

BUT MY MOM IS MY BEST FRIEND . . .

Symphony and her mom are "best friends." Symphony tells her mom everything—who she's having sex with, and how often. Really. All the details. Her mom tells Symphony everything about her history as well: how many people she's slept with, what drugs she's tried, and what she thinks about everything Symphony has ever done. They go shopping together and like to hang out. Symphony's mom tells her she can't wait until they can hang out at her favorite wine bar together.

You know this is a boundary problem, right? **I do know that. And honestly, it freaks me out to see kids who are "best friends" with their parents. When you get older, sure. Parents can act and feel more like friends. But no matter how old you are, first and foremost, your parents are your parents. And with that certain dynamic comes certain boundaries.**

A lot of the time this extreme closeness is what your parents need in order to feel like a good parent, or the kind of parent they wish to be. But it is not what you need. **So, in short, it's about their ego more than it is about what you need.** It is very seductive to fall into this sort of a relationship with a parent because, like a best friend, they are interested in having a good time and avoiding conflict. But that means avoiding setting boundaries that are challenging, but good for your development. **Like we talked about earlier in this chapter, your interpersonal relationship with your parents is going to teach you about how to have relationships with other people throughout your whole life. Parents can be fun, sure. But they need to be there to guide you toward the larger goal: the development of you. And if it's a party all of the time, where is the push for growth?**

HOW CAN I GET MY PARENTS TO RESPECT MY BOUNDARIES?

It isn't easy. This is a navigation, not a one-time deal. Boundaries protect our physical integrity and our emotional landscapes, but they are not rigid, like the walls of a house. They stretch and change as you grow and explore, and you are entitled to determine where your boundary lines are.

Bodily boundaries must be respected. A good way to show this is not to have to kiss or hug a family member if you are uncomfortable for any reason. **In other words, you don't have to hug that creepy uncle or rub your mom's feet (though you may want to if she's on her feet all the time!).**

Emotional boundaries allow us to have separate needs, wants, and feelings from those of our family members. A sign that boundaries are loose is if you are responsible for others' feelings in your family, or if you feel guilt or are given unwarranted blame for something someone else is feeling. **For example, imagine you say that you want to go to college, but your mother starts to wail and cry because she can't imagine her baby leaving. So she forbids you from applying to schools outside of the state. That is an emotional boundary that she is crossing. You are not responsible for your mom's reaction.** Weak emotional boundaries can make it difficult to identify your own feelings or cause you to suppress your feelings and give priority to the feelings of others. You may find you have difficulty saying no if this is your family culture. **Like when grandma gives you more food when you are already gut-bustingly full.** On the other hand, overly rigid emotional boundaries can make you cold and closed off to others. **You might not show emotion to anyone under any circumstances.**

All of this is to say: assess your needs, wants, and feelings apart from those of your family members. **Once you figure out what you need, then you can use your words.**

SETTING BOUNDARIES WITH FAMILY

Setting boundaries is not always easy, especially when it comes to family. However, here are a couple of key phrases you can use to help establish a strong boundary:

- Calmly state your preference: "I like/I don't like/I prefer/ Yes/No."
- Tell the truth: "It really makes me uncomfortable when you _____."
- Take physical space: "I appreciate what you are saying, but I need to go out for a walk to clear my head."

- Take emotional space: "I can't hear you when you speak to me that way."
- Bring in another person: a guidance counselor, therapist, or religious leader may be a good person to have around to act as a buffer.

OTHER ADULTS

We hope that your strongest relationship is with your parents, but it is also good to have other trusted adults who are in your life. Among your teachers, spiritual leaders, coaches, doctors, and various other family members, you can find advocates and allies, mentors and cheerleaders. Sometimes, it's even easier to talk to these adults than it is to talk to your parents. As you develop relationships with adults outside your immediate family, make sure that you are balancing trust, compassion and, especially, boundaries.

This is important because, sometimes, these other adults *do not* have your best interests at heart. It can start small, like a dance teacher putting you in the back of a formation because you are bigger than the other girls, or it can be more obvious, like a teacher screaming in your face. In both of those scenarios, that adult is acting inappropriately. Any time an adult makes you feel targeted for your identity or body, or worse, afraid, that adult is violating a boundary. You are not the problem, they are.

HOW DO I TELL IF MY RELATIONSHIP WITH AN ADULT IS APPROPRIATE?

There are so many times when an adult's behavior can feel inappropriate, creepy, or dangerous. Sometimes it's clear when an adult is crossing the line. Sometimes those boundaries feel blurrier:

- That relative who insists on hugging you while making comments on your body
- A teacher who overshares about their personal life and tries to act more like a friend than a mentor
- A spiritual leader who tries to tell you that something that feels wrong to you is "right" in the context of particular beliefs
- The coach who picks on you to "toughen you up"
- Your doctor who makes negative comments about your weight

No matter the context, the most important thing you need to remember about relationships with other adults is that **you have the power of consent** (backed up by TCB). Now is a good time to go back to chapter 2 for a refresher on consent, because it can be difficult to tell when someone does not have your best interest as a priority. And adults who create toxic situations count on this confusion. Learn to listen carefully to your internal voice for guidance. If you feel uncomfortable with a particular adult, don't stay silent. **Tell someone. No matter what. Your words have power. You have power.**

In the beginning, the attention you receive may feel very positive. Maybe an adult you admire begins singling you out for special praise, or one-on-one attention. **This treatment can be particularly powerful if you are going through an emotional time, or feel particularly lonely.** However, the power dynamic distorts your sense of trust, compassion, and boundaries, making it difficult to see the inappropriate nature of the interaction. You've got to trust your instincts here. If an action or conversation initiated by an adult feels inappropriate—it probably is! Assume that adults can look out for themselves, and do not feel that you have to protect them. Do not feel embarrassed or ashamed to tell someone what is going on. **Flip TCB and think about boundaries first, and you can choose to do so compassionately if the relationship is still appropriate.** Most importantly, trust *your* instincts. Do not second-guess yourself; there are no consequences if you are misunderstanding. Safety first.

RED FLAGS!

It can feel good to be recognized by an adult! However, not all attention is good attention. Here are things that are inappropriate in any and all circumstances:

- Inappropriate touching, meaning any kind of touch anywhere on your body that makes you feel uncomfortable
- Asking about things that they have no business knowing
- Asking for sexual favors or kisses
- Giving gifts for no reason (not your birthday or other celebration)
- Asking to meet in private environments
- Discussing sexual topics (it's okay for your parents or your doctor to bring up this topic; and it's okay for you to ask for information from a trusted adult)

THINGS TO SAY TO AN ADULT WHO MAKES YOU UNCOMFORTABLE

If you feel you are in a situation where you can't tell if what an adult is saying or doing is inappropriate—but it's making you uncomfortable in any way—use this three-level approach to assert yourself and give yourself the power of consent over the behavior:

TALKING ABOUT YOUR BODY (MORE GRAPHICALLY THAN YOU WOULD LIKE):

Level 1: "I'm not really cool with you saying that."

Level 2: "Please, don't talk about my body."

TOUCHING YOU IN A WAY YOU THAT YOU DON'T LIKE (LIKE TICKLING):

Level 1: "Stop!"

Level 2: There is no level 2 when it comes to physical boundary violations. Move directly to level 3 (below).

REPEATEDLY AND HARSHLY GIVING NEGATIVE CRITICISM:

Level 1: "How could I do this better?" (Try to find out if they think they are offering constructive criticism.)

Level 2: "I need more guidance, can you help me?" (If they say you're beyond help, then that is showing a total lack of compassion and you need to move to level 3.)

MAKING "JOKES" AT YOUR EXPENSE, ESPECIALLY IN FRONT OF OTHERS:

Level 1: "Ouch, that hurt."

Level 2: "That's just not funny. You need to stop."

TELLING YOU SOMETHING YOU THINK IS WRONG IS "RIGHT":

Level 1: "Can you tell me why you think that?" (Test whether you should try to have an open mind in a particular situation.)

Level 2: "That's not what I believe." (It's okay to stand up for yourself.)

TAKING PLEASURE IN "SCARING" YOU (EVEN IF THEY SAY THEY ARE JOKING):

Level 1: "I don't like that."

Level 2: "I need you to stop."

LEVEL 3 IS ALWAYS: TELL SOMEONE YOU TRUST AND ASK THEM TO HELP YOU MANAGE THE SITUATION

Remember, **you** have a say in how you are treated. You have power to **consent** to participating in behaviors or patterns of behavior. If the behavior escalates or intensifies after you get to level 2, you are being bullied or victimized, and you need to go to level 3.

Pro tip: These Levels don't just work with adults. Try them out on your peers!

HOW DO I KNOW I CAN TRUST THIS ADULT?

Let me get this out of the way right up front: If you have met, and are communicating with, this adult online, you cannot automatically trust them. If the adult is someone you know well, share your thoughts and questions about the interaction with your friends. And ideally tell another adult you feel comfortable with and get their take on it. Other people you trust should have trust for this person—your siblings, parents, other teachers, your friends. **Even if someone feels trustworthy, pay attention to what your gut is telling you. Most people get a certain feeling of discomfort when their boundaries are being violated. Listen to that and trust it.**

As for the adults you know in real life, ideally they are coming from a place of wanting to guide you to learn to make your own decisions. No one should dictate how you should live your life—unless you are doing something dangerous or are in need of medical care. So when adults in your life tell you what to do, take in the information, trust that they are looking out for you, and take your time assessing the information they have given you. **The one thing that is true for the rest of your life is that you will receive (and probably give) both good and bad advice. TCB can help you learn to listen while trusting your gut, giving consideration to the experience of the person sharing their advice, and knowing what works—or doesn't—for you as you navigate through life and become an adult who gives advice yourself!**

TOP THREE TAKEAWAYS FOR RELATING TO PARENTS AND OTHER ADULTS

1 For better or worse, your relationship to your parents will inform the rest of the relationships you have in your life.

2 You can (and should) talk about sex and other personal topics with your parents, even if it is uncomfortable. However, don't reveal any information that puts you at risk.

3 Trust your instincts: if a relationship with an adult feels wrong, say something. (If you can't talk to your parents or another trusted adult, see our Resources and Recommended Reading section for some places to go for help.)

PART 4

KISS, KISS— SMOOCH, SMOOCH

Okay. We've walked you through some pretty sophisticated stuff to give you some tools for understanding who you are and how you got that way. And we're not going to lie, no matter how good you're feeling about yourself, you'll likely hit some bumps. **Those bumps don't have to take you down. You can turn speed bumps into fist pumps, when you have the confidence to keep your balance.** Keeping your sense of self strong and thriving is a lifelong project. Still, we've armed you with some pretty powerful knowledge in the earlier chapters, and so if you're feeling ready to do IT—to jump into a romantic relationship, feel all your feelings, and have (or not have) sex, here's what we want you to know.

There is a theory that says love is made up of three components: intimacy, passion, and commitment. Psychologist Robert Sternberg, who developed this theory, identifies seven types of love, made up of different combinations of these three elements:

- Infatuation (passion)
- Liking (intimacy)
- Empty love (commitment)
- Fatuous love (commitment + passion)
- Romantic love (passion + intimacy)

- Companionate love (intimacy + commitment)
- Consummate love (passion + intimacy + commitment)

Man, when you put it into those terms, it sounds so simple. Just like the relationship math that says 1 + 1 = 3 . . . So how come romance can feel so very complicated? In the next few chapters, we'll tackle your most common questions about love and romance. And show you how TCB can help you navigate crushes, dating, committed relationships, and sex.

chapter 9

AWOOOOOGA! CRUSHES!

August 5, 2003

  Dear Diary,

Now I have a crush on:

  1. Jack

  2. Kevin

  I tell everyone I have a little crush on Kevin but I have a huge crush on him. Jack's sexy. Kevin's cute.

  Written by,

  Paulina

True entry from my third-grade journal: One day I had a crush on Jack, other days I had a crush on Kevin, and some days I hated both of their guts! I was very temperamental when it came to who I gave my heart to—I've had over a million crushes, and let me tell you, I've learned a lot over the course of my short lifetime (trust me, you will also be twenty-seven before you even know it).

THE BEST AND WORST OF CRUSHING ON SOMEONE . . .

Crushes can feel like:

- You've being irresistibly pulled toward someone—like a moth to a flame
- A loop-de-loop on a terrifying roller coaster, exciting and scary
- 25 percent butterflies, 5 percent hope, 50 percent what if it crashes and burns, and 20 percent nausea

And sometimes, crushes feel:

- Frustrating
- Uncomfortable
- Paralyzing

Ultimately: Crushes are nice when they're mutual, horrible if not. If you've got a crush, remember to approach the person in a way that shows good TCB.

SO WHAT IS A CRUSH, ANYWAY?

Crushes are the result of a biological storm that begins—but doesn't end—in puberty. In the list at the beginning of this section, crushes would fall into the first two categories: most often, infatuation, and sometimes, liking. **Infatuation is a powerful force that can override reason.** When you're infatuated with someone, your feelings seem extra urgent. Your thoughts, or actions, might be reckless. You might ignore that tiny voice in your head, or that feeling in your gut, that tells you "This is a bad idea." Thinking about, or being around, your crush can trigger strong physical sensations, making you feel excited—or anxious.

"Liking" is an attraction that drives us toward intimacy with a person. Intimacy doesn't mean being close physically. It means deeply knowing another person, and feeling deeply known yourself. Healthy intimacy requires honesty, vulnerability, and excellent TCB. When you're "in like" with someone, you want to become closer to them through sharing your thoughts and feelings, and you are honestly interested in understanding theirs. You want to learn if your values align. You may or may not feel a physical attraction to them.

I have felt so much infatuation in my life. Just a burning in my chest whenever THAT person was in the room. I am the crush queen—I've like liked so many people in my life. It always starts small: my hands sweat, my mouth feels dry, my cheeks get red. And then before I know it, I have used every excuse in the book to get myself in the same room as them.

Both infatuation and liking have an important role in helping you learn about romantic relationships. It is just as important to take a risk and talk to a crush as it is to spend time with people you think you might like. It helps you figure out what that "third thing" you're going to create with them should feel like. Oh man, that sounds nerve-racking. I never did that. I always spent my days obsessing about someone I didn't know, blowing them up in my head into something that they could never measure up to. You really can't know if your crush is valid unless you spend time with them. Unfortunately, a lot of young people feel too anxious to put themselves out there and risk misstepping. **Absolutely! It's anxiety inducing! What if they don't like you back? What if your breath smells weird or you laugh too loud?**

HOW CAN I TELL IF SOMEONE LIKES ME?

Well, in all likelihood, you can't! But here are some clues. Generally speaking, when someone is attracted to you, they will find excuses to be in your orbit, in ways that range from subtle to very obvious. You may notice that they are in the same classes or do the same activities as you. You might catch them looking at you—not just a quick glance—more like every time you look, it's like they've been waiting for you to notice them. **Honestly, they probably have.**

Let's take Jesse and Remy as an example. They were in the same class for years, but suddenly in the sixth grade every time Remy walked into the room, Jesse got butterflies in her stomach and she felt like her heart was going to beat out of their chest. Day after day, the crush increased: her hands would get sweaty and she would become tongue-tied every time Remy talked to her. The more Jesse ignored her true feelings, the more painful it became to be in the same room as Remy. Finally, Jesse asked Remy to talk after school. Filled with energy—her fingertips felt electric—Jesse told Remy about the crush. Remy smiled and said, "I like you too." And in that moment, Jesse felt like she could look into Remy's eyes for the rest of forever.

Here's the thing: It's difficult to know if the other person is feeling what you are feeling. But there's a way that you can try to figure that out. By being conscious of your TCB skills, you can get more comfortable with listening to your instincts, instead of overthinking. **Or, you could also—you know—ask. Or at least ask their friend. I was the queen of sending a messenger to find out if my crush liked me in elementary school! But also, never force things. Sometimes, you're just not that person's type.**

HOW CAN I MAKE MY CRUSH NOTICE ME?

Be yourself. That's right. It really is that simple. **Because you know what? It will attract the right person. The person who sees you for you.**

While being yourself, there are ways to catch someone's attention:

- Eye contact
- Smile at them
- Talk to them
- Really, **talk to them**

What doesn't work: stalking your crush in the hopes that will get their attention. Knowing their every move isn't going to do much except make you well-informed.

Christian had a huge crush on Evan. So they followed Evan on Instagram, Twitter, Snapchat, and TikTok. Every time Evan posted, Christian liked and commented. Christian watched and reacted to every Snapchat and Instagram story. Evan never responded or followed back. So Christian doubled down. They went to Evan's follower list and followed everyone that Evan followed. Soon, Christian was consuming everything that Evan liked, even though Christian didn't like following "hot girl" and hockey-related accounts. Even though Christian knew what Evan's bedroom and dog looked like, Evan didn't know Christian's name. Evan knew Christian's handle, but that's it. Even after all of their hard work, Christian didn't get Evan's attention. Instead of getting noticed, they felt invisible.

Following someone and watching their story isn't going to do much but drive you nuts. Sure, they can see that you saw their story or liked their post, but what does that mean? You might squeal when you see that your crush liked your post. But a like is not chemistry. You may feel like it means everything, but it means nothing.

What you can do is focus on yourself. Through focusing on yourself, instead of stalking your crush's Instagram, maybe you can learn to play the guitar like you've always dreamed of doing. It really is that simple: if you want to attract the kind of people you'll feel comfortable with and be able to turn crushes into healthy relationships (whether they end up as a friendship or a romance), you need to become comfortable with yourself first.

Here's what you have to remember, though: focusing on yourself doesn't mean forcing yourself into a particular image. It is never a good idea to put your physical and mental energy into fitting into someone else's definition of how you should look or act. **Preach!** Don't ever give that kind of control to another person. When our culture tells you that girls who look a certain way are more attractive, look for voices that disagree. **This also goes for how you define yourself. If you don't fit into a certain mold, that doesn't mean you are unattractive.**

If you start to feel like you have to act a certain way to fit in with a particular group, try hanging out with a new crowd. Remember to **trust** you will find someone who likes you for you; practice some self-**compassion** by acknowledging the things that you know are great about you—and the things that other people say are great about you—and remember that you get to determine your **boundaries** when it comes to how you act around others.

Christian learned things the hard way. As soon as they realized that Evan wasn't interested, they unfollowed all of the "hot girl" and hockey accounts. Afterward, Christian focused their energy on training for basketball tryouts. And you know what? They made the team. And soon after, River went to all of Christian's basketball games because they loved basketball. After a game, River came up to Christian and said, "Good job." Christian felt fireworks go off in their chest. They were tongue-tied, but happy. They didn't have to pretend to be someone else.

QUIZ
Should I Take My Crush to the Next Level?

It's always so easy to fantasize about your crush blossoming into something more, but sometimes a crush should remain a crush. Here are some questions to consider:

Have you had a chance to see how they treat other people?	Y/N
Can you imagine actually talking to them in person?	Y/N
Have you ever had a conversation with them that made you genuinely laugh?	Y/N
Do you know something about their real life?	Y/N
Are you currently single?	Y/N
Are they currently single?	Y/N

If you circled YES more than NO, then it's definitely go time. However, if you circled more NO than YES, it's probably better to leave the crush in the fantasy realm.

If you've decided you're ready to get up and get out there, start a conversation with your crush by choosing a low-stakes approach:

Wait till they're in a group and then say hi to everyone: "Hi, y'all."

Ask them a question: "Hey, did you finish the homework?"

Compliment them: "You're really good at math/basketball/dance/etc."

Or put it all other there. Be flirty and tell them how you feel: "I think you're real cute. Want to hang out sometime?"

OKAY. I DID IT. I TALKED TO MY CRUSH. NOW WHAT?

Once you have made contact and it is clear there is some mutual interest, it's time to move things forward. But how? And how do you know if you even should? And what if you get rejected? For lots of reasons, the answer is: put yourself out there and keep the conversation going. **There is always the option to just be transparent about your intentions. Sure, that opens you up to rejection and embarrassment, but at least you're taking your fate into your own hands.**

We're not saying to dive right into talking about your feelings for the other person. Instead, ask questions about something that interests or excites you, and then see what their answers tell you about the prospects for a deeper relationship. If you ask, "Have you seen the new Star Wars movie?" And they say, "I hate all those Star Wars movies," you've got your first clue about how compatible you're going to be. If they say, "No, but I'd love to. Are you watching *The Mandalorian*?" you can assume things are looking good.

Pay attention to opportunities to make plans. "I haven't seen it, but I know it's out now, maybe we can hang out and watch it?" Don't push too hard. Give the other person plenty of room for proper con-

sent. Don't immediately jump to suggesting a place and time. Give it some room to breathe. If they are interested, *then* start to talk about when and where. If they hesitate or look for reasons to end the conversation, *let it go*. If they end the conversation without agreeing to hang out, but don't start avoiding you, maybe bring up Star Wars again. Don't open with when and where you want to hang out, just get the conversation back on mutual interests and give *them* the chance to bring up the idea of hanging out.

HOW DO I SAY NO WITHOUT HURTING FEELINGS?

This is a hard one. Because in my experience, someone always ends up with hurt feelings. For me, it works to practice total honesty. "I'm just not interested in you that way." Also—everyone (but girls in particular)—some advice: Don't say "I'm sorry" before you let someone down. You might feel bad about breaking unwanted news, but you never have to feel "sorry" about maintaining your boundaries! Having compassion by understanding that the other person may feel hurt can help you choose your words carefully. The more transparent you can be, the less confusion there will be. Feelings may get hurt, but what's most important is that you maintain your boundary.

There are also ways to gently shut down a conversation or decline an offer. For instance, if someone says, "Do you want to go to the game with me Friday?" you might say, "You know, I'm thinking of going. But if I do go I will probably be hanging with Sarah." It may take a couple of rounds of "non-no answers" to get someone off your case if you choose this gentle approach. But they should eventually give up.

But some people just do not pick up on subtlety. The reality is sometimes you will need to be very direct, and you *will* hurt someone's feelings. And sometimes, by just not being particularly interested, you can crush someone. Remember what we've discussed about not catching feelings (see page 19 if you need a refresher). The reality is that how someone responds to disappointment is on them. You don't have an obligation to be enthusiastic or to say yes just to make someone feel good about themselves. You're a good person; you don't want to hurt anyone. But if the other person keeps pressuring you, that's aggression. And aggressiveness may need a firm response, in which case a simple "no, thanks" is all you need to say.

I feel like there is still more pressure for girls to respond positively to boys. But you *always* have the power to consent or not, even if it's consenting to continue to talk with someone. And if someone continually rejects your answer of no, then they are violating your boundaries in an inappropriate way. And you should say whatever you need to say to get them to back off. My go-to is to say "I'm already in a relationship" (which is totally against my policy of brutal honesty, but sometimes it's what it takes to let someone back off without channeling their hurt pride into aggression toward me).

Along the same lines, you need to hold good boundaries around contact that isn't in person, too. If you've been talking with someone on your phone or computer and they won't stop, you should mute or block them.

OOPS! I EMBARRASSED MYSELF IN FRONT OF MY CRUSH!

This type of embarrassment usually falls into the category of socially awkward acts, like walking into the wall because you're staring so hard at them. The reality is that minor mishaps actually make us more appealing to other people. **I couldn't agree more. The more we can learn to laugh at ourselves, the better off we are. I embarrass myself constantly, and I'm better for it.** At the same time, when it comes to a crush, at least some of your feelings can be very secretive, and feeling exposed in any way makes us feel threatened and vulnerable. **There's nothing wrong with being vulnerable, and there's nothing wrong with looking a little bit stupid. Laugh at yourself and shake it off. Life will go on.**

GETTING "FRIEND-ZONED"

The friend zone is that place you get trapped in when you have a crush on someone, but they just think of you as a friend. It doesn't matter how much desire is burning in your heart, the other person just does not have those same feelings. Feelings or no feelings, the person with the crush often has to settle for the role of friend. Now, this can be the foundation for a great friendship, *if* you've got the right balance of trust, compassion, and *especially* boundaries. **Otherwise you can find yourself in some uncomfortable and embarrassing situations. If you are the one with the romantic feelings, you have to be very clear that it will be possible for you to let them go. If you can't put those feelings away, you are not being truthful about why you are hanging around the other person—and that can damage trust.**

Don't hang out in the friend zone thinking you can make the other person change their mind and become interested in you. Romance almost never grows out of the friend zone—the only time

I have seen it happen is when people reconnect years later. But that doesn't mean you can't establish a genuine friendship with someone you are attracted to. If, amazingly, the other person admits they have reciprocal feelings for you but, say, they are in a committed relationship, then once you've told them how you feel, you need to leave that person alone. **There's nothing wrong with being vulnerable. But there is something wrong with forcing someone into doing something they are not sure about. Trying to get someone to cheat on their partner is violating the rules of TCB and consent!**

TOP THREE TAKEAWAYS ABOUT CRUSHING ON SOMEONE

1 There are two forms a crush can take: infatuation and liking. Infatuation is a powerful force that can override reason. Liking is an attraction that drives us toward intimacy with a person. Both infatuation and liking have an important role in helping you learn about romantic relationships.

2 It is just as important to take a risk and talk to a crush as it is to spend time with people you think you might like. Socializing is a skill. You need to practice. Initiate conversation with your crush in an open-ended fashion, but if the person looks for reasons to end the conversation, *let it go*.

3 Generally speaking, when someone is attracted to you, they will find excuses to be in your orbit. So pay attention.

chapter 10

DATING: DO WE CLICK?

You know you've seen this movie:

The year is 1952. There's a girl in a poodle skirt and a dude in a leather jacket. Her with her perfect grades and virginity, him with his devilish good looks and need to break any and all rules. The two are inseparable, though her parents would choose otherwise. They lean across the table to hold hands in a booth with red vinyl seats at their small-town diner. They can't look away from each other for a single second. They are so in love. A waitress wearing horn-rimmed glasses and bright coral lipstick comes up and says, "Orders up!" before she places a strawberry milkshake with two straws in front of them.

"Thanks, Kathy!" they say in unison.

*They lock eyes before leaning in and taking a sip from the milkshake. A cartoon heart floats up over their heads—*RECORD SCRATCH! Wait a minute. That doesn't happen anymore! That was, like, seventy years ago? And while that may have been your grandparents' scene, we know your *parents* are still asking: What are the kids even doing these days? We, of course, know y'all are up to *something*. And it's not as easy as sharing a strawberry milkshake at a diner. But should it be?

DATING AIN'T WHAT IT USED TO BE

Researchers from San Diego State University and Bryn Mawr College conducted a survey of a half million high school seniors between 1976 and 2016, the results of which were published in the journal *Child Development*. This survey showed that the number of seniors who said that they had been on at least one date dropped by 20 percent over that time period. And while it may not feel this way at your school or in your friend group, overall statistics show that teen sexual activity is also much lower than in previous decades. Another study showed the percentage of US high school students who had ever had sex decreased from 54 percent in 1992 to 40 percent in 2017. And get this: in the same time frame, an average of only 19 percent of teens said they were currently in a relationship! So if you're not dating, there's nothing wrong with you. **And you're not alone.**

THE CASE FOR DATING

We're actually big fans of dating. But what do we mean when we say that? For the purposes of this book, we are talking about dating *specifically* as an activity: spending one-on-one time doing a planned activity with another person that you are attracted to (who is also attracted to you). **We know that saying that you are "dating" can mean all kinds of other things people do to express their romantic and sexual interests—connecting online, texting** constantly, hanging out, or hooking up. That makes our definition seem pretty formal, right? But on a scale from crushing, to hanging out, to in a relationship, to married, dating falls somewhere in the middle. Think of it as "together without a label."

Over the course of your life, you're going to be attracted to different people, so how do you figure out if that attraction will translate to a deeper relationship? How do you decide who is worth the time and emotional investment? When I used to tour around the country and talk to college students, one of my favorite questions to ask them was, "Can you describe a social experience that would happen before sex, where you felt like it let you be who you really are?" Maybe someone would venture an answer, "Like, a party, maybe?" But more often than not, the room would be silent. Finally someone in the middle lower third of the lecture hall (you know, the type that always raises their hand) would say, "I wish someone would just sit and talk to me."

At this point, I could practically see the thought bubbles over the guys' heads. "What does talking have to do with sex?" "There's science," I would tell them. Researchers have proven a connection between intimate conversation and sex drive. Which makes sense! Because sex is a way of getting to know somebody. And if you don't want to spend time talking with them first, then maybe that's a hint.

My follow-up question was, "Would it be too awkward just to meet to talk? What if you weren't planning to have sex right away? What if there was food involved?" Heads would start to nod; yes, most agreed, food would give them something else to focus on if the talking was awkward. I pushed it further: What if you had food and talked more than once?

The aha moment was always the same, for both girls and guys: "I'd have time to decide if it was really someone I wanted to hook up with."

So that's what dating is: taking the time, in real life, to spend time with someone—in person, to talk with them, in a low-stakes situation, often more than once, to help you decide what you want. And by now, I know you know that it all is easier when you go into dating with the intent of building a relationship where attraction and chemistry are enhanced by trust, compassion, and boundaries.

"PRE-"DATING

1. **INFORMATION GATHERING.** You've got a crush, so you start your research. Maybe you follow them on Insta. Maybe you ask your friends what they know.

2. **"TALKING."** Whoa, not so fast. Not *actual* talking in person. Maybe you add them on Snapchat. Maybe you start texting. You're still information gathering, but now they're participating, too.

3. **HANGING OUT.** In groups or one-on-one, you casually start spending time together in person. This is a key because it's how your body does information gathering. In other words, here's where instincts and intuition can help you decide if you are ready for something more.

WHERE ARE ALL THESE POTENTIAL DATES?

So it's clear: dating is a necessary step in deciding whether or not you are compatible with someone else. But the big question is: How do I meet someone I actually like? You can't predict when you're going to meet that person. So, all you can do is move through your life with trust, compassion, and good boundaries. Then, if you're lucky, you might meet someone who sparks your interest.

If you are under the age of twenty, school is where most relationships will form (and break). Honestly, as hard as social stuff at school can be, this is also where it can be the easiest to get some practice in dating and relationships before it gets more complicated out in the "real world." Middle school, high school, and college are all ready-made pools of people in your age group that already share some interests and experiences. So:

1. Go to class.
2. Go to lunch.
3. Walk through the halls.
4. Join a club or a sport.

Some of you may meet friends and romantic partners online, and we'll talk about this later in the chapter. This, of course, makes adults very nervous. How do you know that someone is who they say they are? So speaking as an adult who has eyes wide open to the potential hazards of online romance, I've got one hard and fast rule that you need to follow: **If you are going to meet someone from the internet, make sure your parents**

know every detail. Once they know every detail, only then can you meet your online relationship. And only in a public place. Never, *ever* meet someone for the first time in a private place. And if you can't do this, then you need to keep the relationship online!

HOUSE RULES

By middle school, most kids are caught up in a swirl of hormones and attraction. Dating is a natural part of social development, so if you've moved through the three steps of information gathering, talking, and hanging out, you might feel like you are ready for some one-on-one time to see what happens. **That's a date, btw! But don't be shocked if your parents have opinions or even *rules* about dating, especially if you go to different schools or live in different areas. If you don't drive or have access to public transportation, you're going to have to get some other people (probably your parents—gulp!) involved.**

As a parent myself, I can predict what they're going to want to know:

- Who is this person you're interested in?
- Where are you planning to go?
- Will anyone else be there?
- How will you get there?
- How will you get home?

If your parents control the answers to all of these questions, then the real question is: When do they think is the right time to start dating? Some of you may have parents who say, "You can date when you get married," and others who are fine with whatever. It's time to have a real talk with your parents (see chapter 8 for some tips on how to ease into these potentially awkward conversations). Hanging out socially, meeting someone for coffee or a meal, or seeing a movie together are very healthy behaviors and skills that need to be cultivated.

ASKING FOR A DATE

It can be nerve-racking to ask somebody out. But with great risk comes great reward. Here are some ways to ask that special someone you've been talking to on a date:

- Start out the conversation as you would normally: "Hey, how's it goin'?"
- Establish common ground through mutual interests: "I love playing Super Smash, too!"
- Show your interest: "You're the most exciting person I have ever met."
- Ask them out on a date, while specifying the date activity: "Want to get ice cream with me after school?" Or "Do you want to go to a movie Friday night?" Or "Can I buy you a slice of pizza tomorrow night?"

CATCH A BODY, MOVE ON

In my day, "hooking up" just meant hanging out with somebody. You would "hook up" with someone after making a plan on the phone. Simpler times. Now, hooking up means engaging in sexual activity. A hookup can be as simple as kissing, or as complicated as full-on intercourse. It's a broad term for a wide range of activities.

When people talk about "hookup culture," are they talking about a cultural phenomenon of people having sex? Yes. But young people have always had sex. In the past, they may have waited a little longer and gone on a few more dates before moving on to sex, but they were doing it. But in the past, people often felt that having sex without it leading to a deeper relationship was somehow "wrong," and so people could be reluctant to admit to it. Now you shoot a text or a DM. You figure out who you like (or might like), and then you do physical things with them because you have physical desire, and maybe something more will come of it, and maybe not.

What you need to know is that the problem with a hookup *isn't* that people are having sex, it's that the assumption is that both people involved are *having sex without further expectations—or a real connection.* In a hookup, people only assess whether or not they want to get to know somebody after the sex is over. Which is crazy! As my student said the other day, "Catch a body, move on. Once you've hooked up, it is already over." The problem with hookups isn't that the sex is happening outside of a committed relationship. The problem is that the people involved aren't practicing TCB when they are having sex.

MYTH: HOOKUPS ARE WHERE FEELINGS START

Shorty sent Jason a text: meet me under the bleachers after school. Shorty knows Jason has feelings, but she does not. They meet under the bleachers and she gives him a blow job. It's his first; he's into it. And he decides to ask Shorty to go to the dance next weekend. Later that night at the football game, Jason can't catch Shorty's attention. Halfway through the game, he looks her way and sees her friends pointing and laughing. She's not just ignoring him, he realizes. She's actually making fun of him.

Hookups are casual connections (where the implied intent is consensual, noncommitted sex) or centered around partying, neither of which leaves space for spending quiet time getting to really know someone you are interested in. And having sexual contact with someone you don't really know doesn't leave a lot of room for follow-up. As Jason learned the hard way, hookups are not a signal that both people involved are developing feelings and moving into a relationship.

Hookups don't build lasting feelings between people because there isn't enough time to develop trust. It is possible to have compassion for that person and to express clear boundaries, but trust is something you can't fake. In order to build trust and profound feelings, it takes more than one physical encounter.

I once heard someone say, "Kids give each other blow jobs like they're handshakes." And this seems to be true for Shorty! But a blow job is as likely to get you a committed partner as a handshake

in an interview is likely to get you the job. What Jason couldn't have known was that Shorty had bragged to her friends that she could get any guy at school and her friends had dared her to hook up with him. That's why they were all laughing when they saw him. Being sexual to get attention is a transactional tactic: if I do this (a sexual encounter) for you, I expect something in return (love, exclusive attention, positive affirmation, even a sense of power). The problem with transactional sex is that you have to go into it pretending that neither party is supposed to have feelings about it. No one wants to admit that they feel anything; no one wants to deal with labels—and yet it's very likely that one person *does* have feelings. And that's why hookups put you on shaky ground when it comes to TCB and consent. **If you have to suppress your feelings, how can you trust your feelings? Where is the compassion for yourself? Or for the other person, if you are the one with no real feelings? A hookup is an implicit lowering of boundaries. How do you know whether or not to trust that person with your body? And don't even get me started on whether or not you're exercising healthy consent!**

I'm not immune. In college, I was supposed to be chill. I wasn't supposed to want to go on a date, because that was only something you did when you really liked somebody. I would drink to have (mediocre) sex with someone I barely knew. The more relaxed I was with their boundaries, the better. Heck, I didn't even know where my boundaries were. And because I didn't, I did things that I didn't really want to do. Hookup culture left me feeling disposable, empty, and confused.

If you haven't even kissed someone, we realize this may all

sound terrifying. However, you don't have to hook up to prove anything. Sex should only happen with someone you trust, someone who exercises compassion, and someone who knows and respects your boundaries.

QUIZ
So . . . Is This a Date?

Sometimes it's hard to tell what something is. Is this just a hangout? Or is it something more? Let's break down the key components to a date: two people, a public place, a planned activity. After the date takes place, you should feel like you know the other person better, and you should have a better sense of whether or not you want to pursue things further. Let's see whether you can tell what is and what is not a date:

1. Frankie invited Lola over to his house when his parents were out of town. Lola came over and they hooked up in his basement.

2. Lili and Yoshi met up to see a movie. After the movie ended, they had ice cream and talked about what they found funny.

3. Sitting on the bleachers after school, Houston and Blue chilled. Houston even taught Blue how to ride their skateboard.

4. At the party at Megan's house, Kevyn and Jacob sat on a couch and flirted and shared beers.

5. Freda likes to sit on Connor's lap on the senior patio. They hook up behind the gym every day after school.

The verdict: only scenario number 2 is a date. The pair met in a public place, they did an activity, and they took the time to actively get to know each other. Ultimately, a date should precede any physical encounter, so that you can get to know the person before you decide if you want to take things to the next step. Because Lili and Yoshi took the time to spend an afternoon together, they consciously decided to go on another date to get to know each other even better.

DOOMED TO BE ALONE?

Sean actively wants a girlfriend. Every Friday, he goes on a date—with a different girl. The more he dates, the more he realizes that he hates dating. He has taken girls out for pizza and a movie and ice cream and roller skating. And yet, on every single one of his dates, he can't seem to get a conversation flowing. It's not that he isn't trying, it's just that he isn't sure what to talk about. He doesn't really have any hobbies and he doesn't really feel passionate about anything. And so, nothing really happens past the first date. The more dates he goes on, the more he feels as though he will never find anyone to love.

All of this is to say: **focus on yourself and pursuing your passions; real friends and romantic partners—the kind worth having—will come.** First things first, figure out what your passions are. Whether it's running, or meditating, or playing music. Go back to chapter 3 and take stock of who you are, and the things you really like about yourself. Make your health and well-being a priority. Focus on activities that help cultivate your passions, no matter what they are. Then the right person may come along.

There's another thing to keep in mind: you are in the years when everyone is much more concerned about themselves than anyone else. Everyone around you is looking at themselves with the same critical—or approving—eye that you are using on yourself. No one is going to remember so much of what goes on now. So if someone directs negativity toward you as you pursue your interests, what they are really doing is showing something about themselves. **Hear that? How people treat you shows you how they treat themselves. If they treat you like dirt, you best believe their internal monologue is intolerable.**

If, on the other end of the spectrum, you go through relationships faster than a bag of Skittles, you need to pay attention to your process of attraction. It could be you have what I call a "broken picker," which means you are attracted to the wrong kinds of people. The reasons for this are complicated and have to do with how you see yourself (doing some of the exercises in chapter 3 can help give you a clearer picture) and of how well you are balancing trust, compassion, and boundaries. **For me, it's because I don't think I can do better. Or, I'm afraid of being alone. For a long time, I was convinced that it was being in a relationship that would make me feel better, even if that person I was in the relationship with was a jerk.**

One clear sign of a "broken picker" is if every single relationship starts with a lightning bolt of attraction. I often coach people to look for *butterflies, not lightning bolts.* In other words, see what happens if you hang out with someone you like, instead of someone who turns your life upside down. If you soon find the likable person boring, or you sabotage the relationship, you need to consider talking to a therapist. (You can read more about why this might be happening in chapter 13.) If you find that you can hang with someone who is not quite so exciting, you may be rewarded with a deeper, more meaningful connection. **Got it: butterflies, not lightning bolts. And maybe get honest with yourself about why you pick the people you do.**

DO YOU LIKE ME FOR ME?

When Jaxon asked Claire out for sushi, she said yes because she loves sushi and Jaxon makes her laugh. But in the days leading up to their date, she thought about every girl she knew he had dated before her, and she couldn't help but notice a pattern: they were all Asian, and Jaxon is white. When the date arrived, Jaxon pulled out the chair for her to sit at the table. No one had done that before. Perhaps there was no reason to worry. However, when they were about to order, Jaxon asked, "Did your grandma make you sushi growing up?" To which Claire replied, "No . . . I'm Korean." Suddenly Claire couldn't help but remember the pattern.

I think in this situation, it is easy to say that Claire is being fetishized for being Asian. Which is to say, Jaxon is sexualizing her for her ethnicity, rather than seeing her as a full living, breathing person. Jaxon's comment may seem like an innocuous way of trying to get to know Claire, but taken with the fact that he always dates Asian girls, and given that he is making an assumption about her culture, it's clear he isn't motivated to fully understand Claire's background.

I know from friends of mine that it is often hard to trust whether you are being fetishized or if you are being chased after because it's you. I think it's ultimately important to trust your instincts: are they making comments that make your skin crawl? "Where are you really from?" "Your English is actually really good!" "Can I touch your hair?" If yes, get out of there. Block their Insta and never speak to them again. However, it is possible that you were asked out on a date because you are you! Beautiful you! A person who is genuinely interested in you will not only ask you questions about yourself, but share things about themselves to build that mutual trust. A healthy relationship is where someone wants to get to know the whole you.

As you should ask yourself in every relationship, consider: Do you feel seen, heard, and respected? Is there trust, compassion, and clear boundaries? Additionally, if someone claims a "preference" for a specific ethnicity, alarm bells should go off. Though someone's ethnic and racial identity can largely inform a person, it should not **define** a person. Where can trust live if there is not enough compassion to get to know the particulars of someone else's experience?

Remember how part of being a good friend means being a good ally? Remember to MOTIVATE (see page 132): it's your job to do the work of better understanding your potential romantic partner within their lived experience. Additionally, this is yet another way to address your own unconscious biases: check yourself to avoid hurting both your intended romantic partner and the relationship you are trying to develop.

TAKE A CHANCE, TAKE A CHANCE ON ME

On the last day of school before summer, Riley asked Blake if they could talk for a sec during lunch. Riley really likes Blake. They think they're cute and funny and they would like to take them out. Before lunch ended, Riley pulled Blake aside and asked the big question: "Want to hang out this summer?" Blake looked down at their feet and said, "Maybe not." Riley crumpled like a paper sack as Blake walked away.

There's really only one thing you need to keep in mind when you get a rejection, and that's **consent**. Everyone has a right to make their own choices. To be more informed about why consent matters and why you need to respect someone's choice, even if it hurts your feelings, go back and read chapter 2!

Of course, when someone says no to you, you're probably not thinking, "Oh well, they have the power to consent or not." In fact, it more likely feels like the world is ending. Rejection stings. It feels embarrassing. And it probably doesn't make you feel better if I tell you that a no from someone you like is only one of many experiences with rejection you'll face in your lifetime. And you probably don't want to hear me tell you that rejection can be a good thing—an opportunity to grow, to become more resilient, and to explore new ideas you might not have considered before.

As a dad, I'm sort of enjoying the irony of Paulina's advice, because I *really* know from experience that my advice (which, funnily enough, now sounds exactly like my daughter's) also might not get through right away. So instead, here's the best way to practice some self-care while your ego heals. Just decide to **PLEASE (take care of yourself):**

Physical wellness matters when you're hurting emotionally.
Let your friends be a positive distraction.
Eat healthy, well-balanced meals.
Avoid alcohol or mood-altering drugs.
Sleep at least eight hours a day.
Exercise in ways that feel good for your body
(run, dance, do yoga, take a walk).

And after you've taken care of yourself, use this as a learning opportunity. Rejection is a part of life. You'll be rejected from schools, jobs, and people. That's just how it goes. How you handle yourself in the face of rejection is going to dictate how you handle yourself in the face of acceptance. If you can take rejection and move forward, then you are only opening yourself up to more opportunities. And we promise you, there are so many opportunities ahead!

UGH, WHERE'D YOU GO?

One of the most painful things you can do to a person is deny that someone exists. Most people find this feeling intolerable. **And, listen up: ghosting is denying that someone exists. Denying that they deserve an explanation. And when you walk away, with no explanation, that other person will find it difficult to find closure.**

I've been ghosted. And, I'm embarrassed to admit, I've ghosted. The stakes were low: usually on a dating app after one conversation. But more than anything, I ghosted because it had been done to me, so I did the same to others. It's a terrible excuse. It's a terrible habit.

Why do people ghost? Well, usually it's easier. **But you know what? That ain't using TCB.** If you've been ghosted, you need to know that it's not you that has a problem. It's them! Still, it's almost impossible not to take things personally. We are just set up that way—particularly when we are young, and our identity and self-esteem is very tied up with what peers think of us. If you've been ghosted, don't waste your time pursuing the person who has disappeared. It may be hard to pretend they don't exist, but it's not worth it for you to remain emotionally involved with someone who has chosen to disappear. And if they suddenly reappear, you should be very careful about letting them back into your life. **Healthy, respectful relationships are built on good communication. Even—or especially—when the things that need to be said are hard to say.**

ONE LAST REMINDER: TAKE IT OFFLINE!

It would be naive to assume that all of this is going to happen without your phone and the internet getting involved. Which is why we wanted to talk about how the internet has influenced teens today. The Pew Research Center conducted a research survey in 2015 with teenagers from all over the United States in order to see how social media affected their romantic lives.

Researchers found that one in four teenagers hooked up with or dated someone that they met online. I can't even imagine where to begin with the potential issues! How do you know that they are actually who they say they are? I've had experience meeting a lot of potential romantic partners online. But what makes me nervous is when I hear about teens doing it. (Wow, did I just channel your parents there, or what? Sorry, but I'm feeling protective.) Makes me sound like a hypocrite, I know. But it comes from experience: you can't trust everyone you meet online.

The Pew Research also found that half of all teens let someone know that they're interested in them by friending them or following them online. I, for one, have liked multiple posts in a row to show interest. Mostly in potential friends, not really romantic partners. As much as I hate to say it, I get it. A follow or a ton of likes is flattering. Especially from that special someone. Makes your stomach all fuzzy.

Even though social media can be a way to create a connection, it can also lead to unsavory situations. Twenty-seven percent of teens with dating experience have had their whereabouts tracked by their significant other checking their social media. Another 27 percent say they've become jealous or unsure of their relationships because of social media.

All of this is to say: the romantic landscape y'all are traversing is challenging. There's an opportunity to connect with a world online, in addition to the world you face day to day. The internet and social media has changed the way that teens deal with romantic relationships, but all we have to say is: How can you tell if you have chemistry through a screen?

When you're swiping in an app (which I have a lot of experience with), you can clock attraction. When you finally meet, no matter how attractive they are, you're either smiling so much that your face hurts after or you're so bored you could scream. Which is to say: you can play games and flirt by following and liking comments. But that, my friends, is not going to tell you whether or not you have chemistry. You've gotta go on a date to figure that out.

TOP THREE TAKEAWAYS FROM DATING

1 The case for dating: it allows you to get to know someone. Whether or not you find true love, dating helps you develop social-relating skills while figuring out what you do and don't like.

2 You can't clock chemistry through a screen, only attraction. It is important to go on a date with someone to see if it's something special.

3 If you're not dating yet, don't worry. It's perfectly normal, and everyone has their own timetable.

chapter 11

READY TO PUT A LABEL ON IT

So, I heard that you've found somebody you like. You've hung out. They're exactly what you're looking for. So then . . . how do you get to the next step? It's as easy as that old rhyme, right?

YOU and YOUR SWEETHEART, sitting in a tree,
K-I-S-S-I-N-G!!!
FIRST COMES LOVE,
THEN COMES MARRIAGE,
THEN COMES THE BABY IN THE BABY CARRIAGE!

Not so fast. Let's take a second to think about what's really going on. **Yes, no babies yet.** That's part of it. But more importantly, in our culture, the way we think about romantic love is a little bit twisted. Raise your hand if you think that **intensity** is the ultimate value in romantic love. **I would say intensity is the basis for all first relationships.** It's actually a little more compli-cated than that. As someone who's spent most of my career treating addicts, I know for a fact that confusing intensity for love is the foundation of big relationship problems.

I give you the original love addicts, poster children for an intense relationship: Romeo and Juliet. Sure, their love story was portrayed as full of soaring emotions and poetic circumstances, but if you jump ahead to the ending, the romantic duo ends up dead! Okay, not a dream relationship!

So if intensity isn't what we should be building a committed relationship on, what is? I mean, intensity is common in a first relationship, or at the start of many romances. How could it not be? This person is exciting enough to kick up feelings in your chest that you've never really felt before!

When I met my first real boyfriend, I had never felt that way before. We were in a summer school class together, and I tried to talk to him after every class. Soon enough, I found out his screen name. (Yes, I am dating myself here.) We started out as friends. Talking. But we were both harboring crushes, even though I had a boyfriend at the time. But once that boyfriend dumped me, I verbalized my crush. After that, my summer school romance and I dated for two and a half years. An eternity!

But I'm not just going to share my personal history here; we're gonna talk about the psychology of it all. What helps us build the foundation for a successful, healthy long-term relationship? Well, my friends, we are going to figure it out together.

THE HOLY TRINITY

Just like there are three building blocks to a healthy relationship (say them with me: *trust, compassion, boundaries*), there are also three components to a successful romantic relationship: intimacy, passion, and commitment.

INTIMACY is the feeling of attachment, closeness, and connectedness you feel with that someone special. You know how it feels like you can just be yourself? That's because of the intimacy between y'all.

PASSION, which Romeo and Juliet had a little too much of, is the engine of a sexual relationship. The heart-rate-revving, rational-thinking-disrupting, powerful feeling of *needing* that other person. Romantic and sexual feelings start with—and thrive on—passion.

COMMITMENT is what turns passion into something that doesn't burn out. Decisions about your relationship in the short term and the long term are dependent on this commitment to one another. You both make a choice to take care of the thing that is between you. And, if you've been with someone long enough, you can more easily and readily make long-term decisions (don't make long-term plans too soon!).

In a healthy, committed romantic relationship, you need all six factors: trust, compassion, and boundaries; intimacy, passion, and commitment. Remember how if one of the elements of TCB is off, you can't really consent? Well, if one of the components for a healthy romantic relationship is missing or fades, then the relationship will ultimately break down or fizzle out.

FROM WANTING TO HAVING

So what happens when you get what you want? A relationship starts as a desire. After some dating, you can determine if that person is worthy of your time. Then what happens when you have everything you want? Including that person?

Jenny and Bethany met in their first year of high school. They were both starting at a new school, and they immediately became friends. And then, one day, Jenny reached for Bethany's hand during a movie. An electric current went up Bethany's arm. Shortly after, they made it official. Now they've been dating for two years. They have lunch together every day, they hang out after school. Their friends say they are the perfect couple. Jenny and Bethany don't just talk about going to prom next year, they talk about how they'll manage things long-distance when they go to college.

There's a certain cycle to a committed relationship: first there's attraction (infatuation), where it's fun and exciting to do ordinary things just to be close to the person. Then dating (passion), when you both put time and energy into doing special things, because the attraction is mutual. The excitement usually ramps up in this phase; you might fight or argue, but you're willing to shift your opinion or change. **And you feel like you're growing as a person and emotionally, and that maybe they are too.** Finally, the next step (commitment) is deciding whether to be in an exclusive relationship, because you feel like this is your person—for you, they tick all the boxes.

Wanting and having can clash when it comes to deciding to be in an exclusive relationship for the long term, because those exciting and passionate feelings from the dating phase can wax and wane. For some, this makes the stakes for picking one person higher. Even if you think you want a relationship, you can be afraid of choosing the wrong person. Or you may think you will miss out on the right person. This is especially true if you come from a place of seeing dating as a game (which is promoted by the formatting of dating apps). With so many options, you might wonder how to settle into what you have. According to data from the General Social Survey, 51 percent of Americans between the ages of eighteen and thirty-four do not have a steady romantic partner. **It seems like no one is willing to commit. Or maybe they just haven't found the right fit.**

I'm currently in the third significant long-term relationship in my life. But before I started dating my current boyfriend, I had been single for three years. If you've been in the dating pool for a long time, it really can start to feel like a game. Swiping left and right. People treat you like you're disposable. Heck, I was treating

people like they were disposable, ghosting people constantly. I was not living with TCB. Needless to say, it did not feel good.

For me, the power of a relationship was more about wanting a relationship. The constant yearning, the daydreaming, the fantasy. However, the deep relationship I found was nothing like the romance I was chasing. I traded my fantasy of feeling intense desire day in and day out, and wanting to find someone who would fill all of the holes in my chest, for someone whose love is steady. Someone who is compassionate about my fantasy for the big romantic moments, but has good boundaries that keep those fantasies from overwhelming what is real between us. Because, in the end, it's TCB that makes relationships last. That, and holding hands.

DESTROY THE FANTASY. FIND TCB.

The first step in getting closer to a long-term relationship is getting real about what you want and what you need. Bear in mind that those two things can be very different. Wanting is the fantasy—wishing for something to make up for something that you think is missing. Needing is about fulfilling an essential aspect to enrich your life. Let's spend some time differentiating what we want and what we need.

WHAT MATTERS TO YOU IN A COMMITTED RELATIONSHIP?

1. You trust that person.
   ☐ Want   ☐ Need   ☐ Doesn't Matter

2. They write you a love letter every day.
   ☐ Want   ☐ Need   ☐ Doesn't Matter

3. They are popular.
   ☐ Want   ☐ Need   ☐ Doesn't Matter

4. They have nice hair.
   ☐ Want   ☐ Need   ☐ Doesn't Matter

5. You have chemistry with them.
   ☐ Want   ☐ Need   ☐ Doesn't Matter

6. They hold your hand.
   ☐ Want   ☐ Need   ☐ Doesn't Matter

7. They treat others with compassion.
   ☐ Want   ☐ Need   ☐ Doesn't Matter

8. You feel like you can say anything to them.
   ☐ Want   ☐ Need   ☐ Doesn't Matter

9. You feel safe with them at all times.
   ☐ Want   ☐ Need   ☐ Doesn't Matter

10. You really, really want to jump their bones.
    ☐ Want   ☐ Need   ☐ Doesn't Matter

What did you find out? What do you want and what do you
need from your relationships? And if certain things "don't matter"
to you, ask yourself why you feel that way. Is it because you feel
you don't deserve to be treated in certain ways? Or is it because
you are willing to overlook surface things like appearance in favor
of character traits, like compassion? One important thing: if you
answered "doesn't matter" to questions 1, 7, 8, or 9, you need to
take a step back from focusing on what you want in a relationship
with someone else and consider your relationship with yourself. You
are allowed to "need" trust, compassion, and good boundaries in a
partner, and if you don't think you deserve these things, you need
to work on understanding why. **Ultimately, it's up to you to decide
what you want—like chemistry, or someone with great hair—but
trust, compassion, and boundaries should be nonnegotiable.**

I THINK I'M READY TO BE EXCLUSIVE. AM I THOUGH?

If you're clear that you and your partner solidly exercise TCB (trust,
compassion, and boundaries) and have the holy trinity (intimacy,
passion, and commitment), it's time to take the next step. But before
you do, we need you to answer one more question. **And you need to
answer it honestly: Do you think this relationship is going to make
you feel more secure about who you are and what you want in your
life right now? Is this the person who is going to make everything
feel good all the time? Will this relationship "complete" you?**

If your answer to any of these questions is yes, then we're going
to have to ask you to take a moment for some self-reflection. **If you
do not feel secure in yourself, adding someone else to the equation**

might make that insecurity worse. The person you choose to be in a relationship with should be an equal partner, not a savior. Starting out with the idea that they are a magic problem-solver pretty much guarantees that you will be disappointed.

Consider the positives: Having that person who provides a safe base and who is someone you can explore intimacy and closeness with is good. There is a sense of security that being in a steady relationship can offer. It can be a relief to get away from all that comes with being single. But you need to make sure that you are not running into an exclusive situation to run away from dating. Spending quality time with someone who interests and excites you is a way to confirm what you do and don't want. And most importantly, what you need.

And weigh the negatives: In a steady relationship, you limit your opportunity to meet different people so you can figure out who you are in relationships and what you are looking for (this is why dating is good!). And exclusive relationships, especially when you are young, can limit your emotional growth. Experiencing ups and downs, in love and in life, helps build resilience.

YEP. I'M REALLY READY. NOW, HOW DO I GET INTO A COMMITTED RELATIONSHIP?

So you're ready to move from dating to an exclusive, long-term commitment? Well, it doesn't just happen. But it's not that hard, either. Sure, there are people who just sort of slide into something and it's never formally declared. But for the sake of clarity, you should assume that you're going to have to talk it out.

Remember "relationship math"? Where 1 + 1 = 3? Getting into a committed relationship means you're ready to make that "3" official. And have people pay attention to *it,* as well as to you. Here are some ways to open up the conversation with your soon-to-be-exclusive significant other:

- Hey, I like you. Wanna make it official?
- Hey, what is this we've got going on? I think it's _____.
- You are the most exciting person I have ever met. Will you be my girlfriend/boyfriend/partner?
- I hate labels. But I like you. Can we be exclusive?

Of course, how you approach the conversation depends on your relationship. Are you both mushy-gushy? Are you both cool and sarcastic? The words don't matter, but the approach needs to be the same: Even if you have been spending time together, you won't know what the other person is thinking until you talk about it. Make things extra clear and use your words.

IF I HANG AROUND LONG ENOUGH, THIS WILL TURN INTO A RELATIONSHIP, RIGHT?

Gary is a twenty-three-year-old who feels like Becky is "the one." They had dated for a minute, but when she wanted to cool things down, he decided that it was because she wasn't ready for a serious boyfriend. So Gary stayed around. He was a shoulder to cry on when things didn't work out with other guys Becky dated, and he took care of her cat when she had to travel for work. It's been two years of proving that he will always be there for her, and Gary thinks it's time to make his move. He's going to ask Becky to be exclusive.

Gary does realize that Becky isn't into him, right? That she probably sees him as a friend?

Bizarre, right? Because he had been stuck in a time warp waiting for his fantasy relationship to become a reality, this guy hadn't dated, or even considered being interested in someone else. As a result, he had no idea how to interpret cues in a romantic relationship. **It sounds like a guy who doesn't listen to women. To me, it sounds like she made it pretty clear that she didn't want him to be her boyfriend.**

I want to be clear here: this kind of stalking behavior (and it is stalking behavior if you keep hanging around with an intention that is different from how you are behaving) is not how to move into a long-term relationship. **It's not that guys and girls can't be friends. I have a ton of friends of every gender, but in this case there's a subtle boundary being crossed, in addition to an ulterior motive.** She is trusting him to have only the intention of friendship, while not being clear about her boundaries. **I mean, what kind of a mixed message is it when you keep a guy around just so he will cat-sit for you?**

To avoid this kind of situation, you need to take people at their word. When someone says they want to date you, decide if you are romantically interested, or cut them loose (kindly), and if someone says they want to be friends, trust that they want to be friends. **In either case, try dating other people. Then you can get experience in interpreting romantic cues. And that way, you won't be caught in the friend zone when you're looking for more.**

WE COME FROM DIFFERENT BACKGROUNDS, WILL THIS EVER WORK?

Tammy's parents always go silent when her boyfriend, Roger, comes to pick her up. "I'm sorry my parents are like that," she always says as soon as they get into his car.

Esther's mom always reminds her: "He's not Jewish, sweetheart."

Gwen feels eyes on her when she is pushing David's wheelchair while out in public together in a way that she doesn't when she's alone.

Just because someone does not share your race, religion, or ability does not mean that you can't be in a loving, nurturing relationship with them. Within any relationship there are bound to be ruptures and repairs; however, when it comes to interfaith, interethnic, and interabled relationships, there may be a million tiny ruptures that come from difference of experience, or worse: from other people.

For example, my first serious boyfriend was Muslim. The comments grownups made are not worth repeating, but what I learned was that a lot of the complications of being in an interfaith relationship ultimately had to do with what other people thought rather than with the bond itself.

Like any relationship, you've got to have TCB. But something important to consider is the way in which you or your partner will navigate systemic oppression. In what ways are things more difficult because of how social structures treat each of you differently? What do you need to understand about each other to be mutually sup-portive? Unfortunately, people may stare when they see you as a couple. People may say awful things. But much like how being a good friend means being a good ally, being a good partner means shutting down negative or ignorant comments. It means standing up for each other whether you're together or apart.

That being said: the two of you need to discuss boundaries so that you don't drown the other person out. When it comes to fight-ing systemic oppression, everyone has a personal approach. Discuss how each of you feels most comfortable addressing bigotry and the uncomfortable bits. You know that you are coming from different experiences, so make sure you have a boatload of TCB: trust that you're not going to purposefully hurt each other, have compassion for one another when either of you opens up—or messes up. And, like we said above: get clear on your boundaries!

Even though it may feel serious to have to consider differences of race, religion, or ability, remember why you're doing it in the first place: you like, or maybe even *gasp* love, this person! And just because there's more to learn and more to wade through doesn't mean it's not worth it.

WHY DO I FEEL SO INSECURE IN MY STEADY RELATIONSHIP?

Is your partner doing something to make you feel self-conscious or insecure? It can be very difficult to tell whether the feeling of inse-curity is the result of your partner not providing you with a strong foundation of TCB, or if this is just your own deep-seated issue.

As a teenager and into my early twenties, my self-esteem was very,

very low. It didn't matter what my partners told me; I believed that I was unlovable and unattractive. However, that changed. Through therapy, I learned how to heal my own wounds and build my self-esteem.

When in doubt, ask yourself these questions:

- Do you really feel you can trust your partner, that they will look out for your feelings and interests?
- Are you accustomed to abandonment or being let down because of what you experienced in your family or in other relationships?
- Are you afraid of being let down and so possibly you self-sabotage—getting out of something before you suffer an anticipated hurt?

If any of your answers to these questions were a yes, then it is time to work on **boundaries**. The insecurity that you think is coming from your partner is really coming from inside of you.

That being said: if your partner is doing something to make you feel insecure, like calling you mean names, talking critically about your body, putting their needs ahead of yours without real *compassion,* or behaving in a fashion that jeopardizes your relationship, the problem ain't you, my dear. So gather up your confidence and get out of the relationship. You are good enough as you are!

THREE BIG WORDS

It's the question that comes with all serious relationships: When is the right time to say "I love you"? You practice saying the words in your head day and night. Sure, it may be sliding into obsessive territory, but this is going to have a better ending than *Romeo and Juliet*.

And then you just sense that the time is right . . . and you say it: "I love you."

Now, there are two ways this can go down: they say "I love you" back, or they don't. If they do, amazing! What a beautiful moment! If they don't, don't push. It may hurt a little, but they just might not be ready to say those three words. It's a big thing to confess your love for somebody. Everyone has their reasons to say it or not say it.

And if they never say it? Then, my friend, it's time to get out of there.

HOW TO BREAK UP

Let's check back in on Jenny and Bethany . . .

It's spring of senior year, just a month before prom. Bethany and Jenny have picked their colleges, and they are going to be in different states. And even though they had a plan for the perfect senior spring (and summer), Jenny is having second thoughts— things are just seeming kind of routine. And she's been talking with a girl that she met at dance camp last summer. The conversation is getting kind of sexy. Jenny is starting to wonder how she knows if Bethany is "the one." Maybe she's just the one for right now? Before, Jenny couldn't keep herself from touching Bethany. But now it's just not as exciting. Jenny doesn't want things to end, but she's unsure of how to proceed.

Anyone who's been in a breakup sees where this is heading. Jenny starts telling her friends that things are feeling kind of . . . ordinary. Bethany starts acting overly possessive. Suddenly Jenny feels a bit bored, even trapped, by their daily routines. For sure this relationship is at a crossroads. These are two people who know, accept, and like each other better than anyone else they know—and have for years. But it's not like either are ready to raise a family together right now. And sometimes you have to acknowledge that the person you chose to be in a committed relationship with is only one very special person in your still-developing life.

No matter the reason, if the relationship is no longer serving you, no matter how long you've been together, it is not fair to the other person to stay in the relationship. So if you, like Jenny, find yourself in a steady relationship but think you need a break, there are a lot of options that may seem like they might work, but that are devastating to the trust, compassion, and boundaries that make it possible to be honest and gentle in ending it! So if you think you want to break up with someone, here's what NOT to do:

- Do NOT try to create drama in the hopes it will bring you together.
- Do NOT cheat, to test your "real" feelings.
- Do NOT stay together because you're afraid you won't meet anyone else.

- Do NOT break up to make up.
- Do NOT get back together to avoid the pain of the breakup.
- Do NOT have sex just to keep things moving forward, especially if you haven't had sex with this person yet.

Before breaking up with someone that you have been in a committed relationship with, you need to respect that relationship. Sit down with your partner and lean on TCB. Do you still trust each other? Do you both exercise compassion? Are both of you exercising your boundaries in a way that keeps you both intact and healthy? Are you both respecting each other's boundaries?

Even if the answers to the big TCB questions are yes, you may still decide you want to end the relationship. Breaking up with someone is never easy. But if you've been part of a long-term relationship, it is important to do it in person.

First things first:

1. Pick a time and a location.
2. Let your friends and family know what is going on so that they can be there for you when it is over.
3. Prepare to deal with not only your emotions, but the emotions of your partner.

The only exception to the "breaking up in person" rule is if the other person has been abusive. In that case, you owe them nothing and your only concern should be to get away. **Your safety is of the utmost importance!**

So what I hear you saying is, don't break up over text . . . Except, I don't know anybody who breaks up in person anymore. I think that breaking up over text is the most common way. It feels easier to say exactly what you feel, since you don't have to do it face-to-face. I remember the first time I heard about someone breaking up over text and I was literally in disbelief. How could someone be so disrespectful and cruel as to not even say what they needed to say in person? Ultimately, you need to deliver the message ending the relationship in a way that is respectful and safe. How about a compromise: If you've never met the person and you haven't been on a date—fine. Or if it's a second request from someone on the first date and you're just not into it, then, by all means, go ahead and text. But we are talking about committed relationships here. And if you've been dating and in a serious relationship, that person deserves the respect of a face-to-face breakup.

Here are some things you can say to make the breakup kind, but straightforward:

- I really appreciate our connection, but I think we should take time apart.
- I haven't felt the same since _____. I'm sorry, but I can't do this anymore.
- I think you're a fantastic person, but I don't want to be in a relationship with you right now.
- We need to break up.
- I've met someone else that I'm interested in and we need to break up.

Talk about what it means for the both of you after the conversation and the relationship ends:

> **Mutually decide to cut off communication for at least half the length of your relationship.** Contact can reset the clock on getting over the relationship and mourning properly. No cyberstalking, and definitely no hanging out.

> **Make a plan for social media: Change your relationship status. Agree to unfollow/unfriend each other until you can approach each other on amicable terms. Delete pictures and put them on a flash drive so that you don't have to look at them. Delete text threads. Delete their number from your contacts.**

Be clear. Don't defer or back down. **Just because your ex feels bad does not mean you should compromise on what you need. This is going to be painful, but it is necessary.** Don't stay in a relationship that you don't want to be in anymore.

HOW TO SURVIVE A BREAKUP

I'm so sorry your heart is broken. Know that I've been there too. I was broken up with for the first time when I was fourteen. My boyfriend was at summer camp and he dumped me over the phone. I had never cried so hard in my life. Well, maybe when my cat died.

Top tips for getting over a break up:

- Tell your friends and family.
- Get some exercise: take a hike, go for a run, hit the gym.
- Cry your eyes out.
- Eat a pint of ice cream (preferably with a friend).
- Listen to sappy love songs.
- Take a bath, or engage in other forms of self-care.
- Feel regret—sit with it. Don't do anything about it.
- Block their phone number. (Seriously, no texting.)

Mostly, give yourself the space to feel sad. The first time you go through a breakup, the process is going to be unique to you. The second and third times might feel completely different. At any time, you need to be kind to yourself. **Trust** that you will be okay and that you'll find someone to love again. Have **compassion** for yourself. Dive into what you find pleasurable. And if you need to cry? Don't be afraid. Make sure you give yourself space to feel all the feelings. Remember the importance of setting a mutual **boundary**: no social media contact, no one-on-one contact at all (we know how hard it can be to totally avoid an ex when they are in the same history class as you!).

I love that TCB works just as well to get through a breakup as it does to start a relationship. And when you're ready, go back and remember those good times. Acknowledge what you shared together, be grateful for it, and respect it for what it was. And after you've healed your heart and gotten yourself back together, don't feel bad about making a new action plan. Congratulations, you've had your heart broken. And you survived.

TOP THREE TAKEAWAYS FOR COMMITTED LONG-TERM RELATIONSHIPS

1. The three components of a thriving long-term relationship are intimacy, passion, and commitment. If one of those elements is off, the relationship will not thrive.

2. What you want is different from what you need. A want is a desire and a need is a necessity. Only through knowing what you want will you be able to explore TCB with someone else.

3. Please, PLEASE, don't break up with someone over text. Pick a time and place and be straightforward.

chapter 12

BOW-CHICKA-WOWOW: HAVING SEX

"Sex is an emotion in motion."

It feels entirely appropriate to start this chapter with a quote from the queen of sex appeal, Mae West. If you don't know her, you should definitely look her up. She was amazing. She was the ultimate sex symbol. She started in vaudeville but would go on to write and star in movies. (She even got arrested for one of the plays she wrote! An icon!) With quick quips and a breezy attitude, she was a woman who was in command of her sexuality. And she wasn't afraid to talk about it. Which was unprecedented in the early twentieth century.

Remember how in the last chapter we talked about the holy trinity: intimacy, passion, and commitment? Well, my friends, if passion has got you going, there are more things we want you to know to make sure that it's taking you down a path you want to be on. So, let's talk about the birds and the bees! We are beginning with a quick biology refresher that might be a little different from what you hear in health class.

THE SCIENCE OF SEX

Most of you are aware of the basics of sex. And if you're a little hazy, there are tons of resources online (Google "biology of intercourse") or check our Resources and Recommended Reading section. What you may not know, however, is how the different hormones that flood your system during puberty influence not just your physical body, but your emotions and behaviors. If you accept that your hormones push you in one direction, you can check in with TCB—for yourself and for others—to make sure you are exploring sexual desire, attraction, and encounters in healthy ways. I've observed that some important biological differences are rarely talked about, resulting in the potential for confusion and conflict when it comes to interpreting how someone else is feeling about sex. Here's one example: there is research that suggests that women can experience high levels of sexual *arousal* without a corresponding *drive* to have sex. **Which is to say that women are able to see someone they're attracted to, and not necessarily want to have sex with them.** For example, a girl may think the barista at the local cafe is hot, but that does not mean she wants to have sex with them.

Research also tells us that most men are pretty much the opposite; arousal and drive are strongly linked. **In other words, if men see someone sexy, they want to (and sometimes feel like they absolutely must) try to have sex with them.** So a guy might think the barista is hot, and he *of course* would very, very much like to have sex with them. But just because this is how someone is wired, it doesn't mean they should be having sex indiscriminately.

WHEN HORMONES AND GENDER EXPRESSION DON'T MATCH

Here's another reason why paying attention to your hormonal impulses is important: instead of "guys" and "girls," think about sex drive in terms of estrogen and testosterone. Because you all know that sex and desire is not as simple as all guys and all girls wanting the same thing. What is specific are the hormones flooding your body, *not* the gender orientation you're expressing. So, absent any hormone therapy, if you are a trans woman (who still has plenty of testosterone), you may find your sex drive expressing itself in a way that is different than a cis female, even though your gender identity is that of a woman. And if you're a trans man, you may have a lower sex drive than a typical cis male, even though your gender identity is that of a man. (And if your brain is reeling from these terms, head back to chapter 4 for a refresher on gender identity!)

The other way in which your hormones can mess up your game is in how receptive you are to someone making a move. "Receptivity" is an experience that is enhanced by the predominantly female hormone of estrogen. **Which means that when estrogen is flowing, there's a sense of relaxation and openness. This attitude lends itself to the willingness and ability to accept new ideas or feelings.** When testosterone is the dominant hormone, the dynamic switches to one of increasing drive. So instead of feeling open and relaxed, someone who is testosterone-dominant will encounter a snowball effect where they feel an urge to move to the next level, especially in a sexual encounter. In other words, a rush of testosterone can cause some individuals to push past boundaries. And if their partner is feeling open to things—until they aren't—there can be some real confusion when it comes to having sex.

Brodie and Eden have been hanging out together for a couple of months. They text every night and there's an undeniable attraction. At a keg party in the woods, they hook up in Brodie's car. Things are getting hot and heavy and Brodie makes a move. Eden's not sure, but Brodie pushes it. "You know we're good together. You've been wanting this for a while, I know it. Besides, everybody already thinks we're doing it. Why wouldn't we?" Eden's still not completely sure, but it's not like what Brodie is doing feels bad. But when it's over, Brodie seems distant and Eden just wants to cry.

So, folks with testosterone, what this means is you need to be super aware of taking a moment to check in. And for all you estrogen-heavy people out there, you need to make sure that you are checking in with yourself and your boundaries and not letting your partner sweep you along if you're not ready.

DOING THE DEED

We've done the science, and now we're moving on to the math: the 1 + 1 = 3 relationship calculation is perhaps most relevant when it comes to having sex. A sexual relationship *is* a "third thing" between two people, and it should be something that both are willing to pay attention to. If you're not willing to give the sex the attention it deserves, you're probably hooking up, and you might want to go back and reread chapter 10 so you know what you are signed up for.

> *Grey and Ellis have been dating for all of sophomore year. They agree that even though they are only sixteen, they are both committed to one another. Their physical chemistry is powerful, and they're each other's best friend. They both feel ready to take the next step. On a Friday night in the school parking lot, they had a long conversation about contraception, timing, and the deep, deep desire they feel for each other. They set a date: the next Friday after the football game.*

Having healthy, meaningful sex with someone means being able to have healthy meaningful communication. You need to be willing to expose the most intimate and vulnerable parts of yourself. **Which means that you shouldn't venture into sexual territory if you're not bringing along TCB. If you cannot *trust* your partner (to really listen to what you are saying and/or not saying); if you don't have *compassion* (to understand how ready—or not—someone is to take this big step); and if you can't respect *boundaries* ("no" means "no," and "I don't like that" means "stop right away"), then you are NOT ready to take it to a sexual level.**

But if you think you are ready, we want to make sure that you are 100 percent in touch with your personal boundaries. Because knowing where your own boundaries exist is particularly important when you are about to flirt with literal boundarylessness. **Having sex means fusing your body with another body. And you get to choose who you fuse your body to!**

In the boundarylessness experience that is a sexual encounter, it's important to remember:

SEX SHOULD BE A CONSENSUAL DECISION (notice how much this sounds like "consent"). **Both partners should really, really, reallllllly want to do it. No lukewarm. Blazing hot!**

SEX IS NOT TRANSACTIONAL. You're not doing something to get something. **If someone says that you have to have sex with them to get what you want, you need to dip out ASAP.** Sex should be a decision made between two people who know themselves, trust themselves, and know their own boundaries. **And more than that: trust each other, have compassion for each other, and respect each other's boundaries.**

QUIZ
Are You Ready to Have Sex? 10 Questions to Ask Yourself Before Getting Down to It

1. Do you wanna have sex?
   a. Yes
   b. I'm not sure
   c. No

2. Do you know why you want to have sex? Are your reasons healthy ones?
   a. My partner and I have talked about it. We both want to. We both feel ready.
   b. Because everyone else is doing it.
   c. My partner wants to and I want to make them happy/don't want to make them mad.

3. Are you aware of all safe sex tactics?
   a. Yes. And I'm ready to make sure we use them all.
   b. Sort of. I mean, I'm on the pill/I'm sure she's on the pill.
   c. Of course I'm aware. But sex is supposed to be spontaneous. You can't always be 100 percent prepared.

4. Do you have your preferred sexual contraceptive (and a condom)?
   a. Yep. Birth control and a condom. Check.
   b. Birth control is covered. I'm sure he has a condom/Got the condom, I'm sure she's on birth control.
   c. Why would I need more than one form of birth control?

5. **Do you trust your sexual partner?**
   a. One hundred percent. We've been together for a while and we can talk about anything. I am sure this is what I want.
   b. Why not? They seem nice enough.
   c. What does it matter? We're just hooking up.

6. **Do you trust yourself?**
   a. Yes. I'm sober and fully consenting.
   b. I mean, I guess so. They'll know what to do.
   c. What does it mean to trust myself?

7. **Are you open and receptive to hearing what your partner likes?**
   a. Sure. I want this to feel great for the both of us.
   b. What if it's something weird?
   c. I'm experienced. I know they'll like what I do.

8. **Are you prepared to talk about what's going on while it's going on?**
   a. Definitely. I want to know what they're feeling and if everything is good.
   b. I'm really not into talking during sex. They'll be able to tell if I like it.
   c. Sex is physical. Why talk about it?

9. **Are you and your partner in agreement that anyone can say stop at any time during a sexual encounter?**
   a. Yes. We've talked about it and both agree that "stop" means a full time-out and a check-in.
   b. I'm sure if I say stop, they'll stop. And if they want me to stop, I figure they'll say so.
   c. Why would you want to stop once you get started?

10. Are you really ready to have sex?

a. Yes. I'm old enough to make this decision. I'm making it of my own free will. I trust my partner and we agree on what consent means.

b. Yes. We haven't worked out all the details, but I'm really attracted to my partner and this next step feels right for the relationship.

c. Who isn't?

Mostly As: If you answered mostly As, your head is in the right place. You're prepared physically, emotionally, and sexually. You know your partner and what they need. And if you have any doubt, you know that you will work it out together.

Mostly Bs: You could be in better shape. You definitely have the desire, but you haven't communicated enough with your partner. In order to get more TCB, you need to do a little contraceptive research and talk to your partner about your boundaries.

Mostly Cs: Just because you have experience doesn't mean you are ready. Each sexual encounter is different, which is why it's important to have an open line of communication between you and your partner. Additionally, please refer to our Resources and Recommended Reading section to find out more about sexual contraceptives.

THREE THINGS YOU MUST KNOW BEFORE HAVING SEX

Knowledge is power, and while there's a lot of information about sex out there (see our resource section for some good options), there are three key things we want you to know:

ADOLESCENT HEALTH EXPERTS AGREE THAT SIX-TEEN IS GENERALLY THE AGE THAT THE HUMAN BRAIN MATURES TO THE POINT THAT IT CAN REA-SONABLY HANDLE THE FEELINGS AND RESPONSI-BILITIES THAT COME WITH SEXUAL ACTIVITY. Any younger and your brain literally hits its limits in process-ing, and a sexual interaction—even if you think you're ready—can leave residual trauma. So respect the power of brain biology and wait until you're at least sixteen!

PROTECT AGAINST STIS. NO EXCEPTIONS, NO EXCUSES! Anyone having sex with anyone with a penis should have condoms on hand. Even if you or your part-ner is on birth control, there is still a risk of contract-ing a sexually transmitted infection (STI). For the sake of safety and your future partners, *you must always use a condom.* Even if you have been having sex with your partner regularly, you *still need to use a condom!* And don't make the mistake of thinking if there's no penis, there's no need for protection. STIs like herpes, HPV, and HIV can be transmitted during oral sex. Dental dams are thin, latex (sometimes flavored!) barriers that are placed over the vagina or anus and can help protect you and your partner. The Planned Parenthood website offers all the info you should know about safely using condoms and dental dams. (Find the link in our Resources and Recommended Reading section in the back of the book.)

CONSENT TO HAVE SEX CAN ALWAYS BE TAKEN BACK—no matter how far along you are. And if you worry that you won't be able to say no once things have gotten under way, head back to chapter 2 for a refresher on the power of consent, and how it's yours to use.

PRACTICE SAFER
SEX WITH TCB

Some of you may have had abstinence-only education. And while it may seem simple—*one rule: no sex*—such an approach can keep you from being fully informed about what healthy sex adds to a relationship. The truth is that no sexual encounter is guaranteed to be completely safe; if you're not abstaining, you're taking risks. Physically, you could get pregnant; you could get an STI. Emotionally, having sex is a deeply vulnerable experience. You can be hurt in ways that don't show and can't be treated with a visit to a clinic. **But here's the other side: Sex feels good. And having sex can deepen and grow a relationship in ways that are powerful and important. We've all got hormones, and drive. Sometimes passion takes over and you-**

don't-even-know-what-you're-doing-but-it-feels-so-good-and-you-don't-want-it-to-stop-and-suddenly-you're-having-sex! But getting carried away won't be as dangerous if you are already using TCB to keep your relationship healthy (and knowledge about contraception to keep your body safe). SO, LET ME SAY IT AGAIN: when it happens, sex should feel good—with no regrets!

Let's go over the ground rules for *safer* sex with TCB:

Mutual **trust** is essential. And trust is built on an expectation of honest words and consistent actions. Whether you're having sex early in the relationship or after you've been together a while, disclosure of any potential risk to your partner is a nonnegotiable conversation. In other words, you must, muuuuuuuust tell them your STI status. And if you don't know? Get tested immediately. Whether you've been with one or more partners, it's important to get tested. Until you have been exclusive for a while and have 100 percent trust your partner has too, it is smart to get tested once every six months. If you test positive, make sure you are taking medication to prevent spread to a partner. Everyone: talk to your doctor about getting the HPV vaccine if you have not yet had it. You can get it at any age and it can help to prevent future cervical and other cancers.

Compassion is key in a sexual relationship. It helps you feel emotionally connected and safe, and shores up trust. The best sex isn't just something you do with your body. Sex stirs up all kinds of feelings, which can sometimes feel overwhelming. Remember that your brain is still wiring all kinds of connections, some of which help you manage your emotions. And strong feelings can leave you confused, or even upset, without really understanding why. Have you ever had sex and felt like you had an emotional hangover for days? Maybe you wanted to cry for no reason. Or you felt an adrenaline rush that wouldn't quit. Be compassionate with yourself. Share your feelings with your partner—in a healthy relationship, they'll respond with compassion. If you are in a sexual relationship and are struggling with feelings that your partner can't—or won't—acknowledge, talk to someone you trust. A trusted adult might help, either by listening or providing you with the resources that can help you figure things out.

Boundaries. Where to begin with boundaries and sex—considering that sex is a time when boundaries can melt (in a good way)? Whether it's the expectation that you'll keep your feelings in check during a hookup, or the wild rush of trusting someone enough to let physical and emotional boundaries down to let them in, or the fact that contraceptives *literally* create boundaries that keep you from getting STIs or becoming pregnant—whew!

Even though boundaries may be the most important part of TCB to have in place when it comes to sex, there's so much working against them: they can be weakened by passion, intensity, and drive. They can be too rigid, getting in the way of trust and vulnerability. They can be made fuzzy by alcohol, drugs, or peer pressure. Knowing yourself so you feel confident in your boundaries is maybe the most important thing you can do to make sure any sex you are having is healthy and enjoyable.

Finally, and critically, good sex requires that both people are fully and enthusiastically consenting to the experience. If you're at all confused about how it works to consent to a shared experience, go back and reread chapter 2 and don't have sex until you really, really understand what it means for you—and your partner—to consent to sex!

PUBLIC SERVICE ANNOUNCEMENT

If you are hetero, two forms of contraception are best. So if you are on the pill, he needs a condom. If you have a diaphragm or IUD, he needs a condom. If you've got a penis—it's condoms for everyone, every time. If oral sex is on the menu: reach for a dental dam. No, it does not kill the mood. You know what kills the mood? An STI. If you are queer, you still need protection. If you are having sex with a new partner, always, always, always use protection. You and your partner get to decide which type is the best for you. You can find all kinds of condoms and dental dams at drugstores, Planned Parenthood, doctor's offices, and online. Sometimes, they're even in vending machines. They're probably at your school's health services office. So no excuses!

GETTIN' IT ON!

We want to be realistic about how these things go down: love isn't the only reason to have sex. And you do not have to be in a committed relationship to have sex. (And by sex, we mean not just intercourse, but anything you define as sex. It could be a super-hot make-out session with all your clothes on. The same rules still apply.) **It feels a bit scandalous telling you that. However, we don't want you to confuse casual sex with being treated poorly. Even sex with someone who is not your steady partner needs to have mutual *consent, trust, compassion,* and healthy *boundaries* as well as the spark of mutual passion. And respect. Mutual respect.**

There are lots of good reasons sex happens: you're both so aroused that you simply might explode if you don't do the deed;

you do it because you want to; neither of you wants to fight the attraction; you both consented. We're not here to make you feel bad for your choice. It's normal to want to express your sexuality. And if anyone shames you for it, it's more about them than it is about you. Sex should feel good. So feel good about it! As long as you feel good about yourself and you feel good about having sex outside of a committed relationship, then go for it. For some, this may feel unimaginable. And that's okay too! When, how, and with whom you have sex is for you and you alone to define.

SO HOW DO I KNOW WHAT I LIKE?

So now that we've started getting into some real talk, guess what's next? Masturbation. This, my friend, is my call to action to get down with your sexy self. Go masturbate! I know, I'm going to upset some adults with that statement. But really, masturbation is a key part of knowing your body. You should never feel shame for it. Just because other people feel ashamed of their body doesn't mean you have to.

But more importantly, how are you supposed to communicate to your partner what feels good to you if you don't know yourself? Masturbation is normal, healthy, and as Paulina points out, a great way to get to know what feels good sexually.

As a doctor, I'll say that inserting objects (including penises) into a vagina can alter its pH balance, and may cause itching or irritation. Anal sex may also cause irritation and/or light bleeding, especially if you have not used enough lubrication. None of these scenarios are reason to panic or to avoid masturbating or sex—but it does require a call to your doctor. **Please note here that lots of other things marketed to vagina owners (like feminine washes/douches and tampons) can throw off the balance of your vaginal environment! So, to go back to masturbation . . . Don't be afraid. Start with your (clean) hands. Feel things out and be patient. You'll figure it out.**

DO I HAVE TO BE EXPERIENCED TO HAVE GOOD SEX?

After the second date, Davenport knew they wanted to take things to the next level. Davenport had never been intimate with anyone before, whereas Lila had some experience. But that didn't lead to jealousy and distrust. If anything, it deepened their trust for each other that they could talk candidly about their sexual experiences (or lack thereof). Six months in, Lila approached the topic: "I think I'm ready to have sex." After a discussion about their boundaries, they took things to the next level in the back of Lila's car. Though the setting wasn't all that romantic, they caressed and fondled each other lovingly. Through open and honest communication, they have learned how to trust each other more deeply, in addition to exploring each other physically.

You do not both have to be equally experienced to have good sex. What matters is being clear about your boundaries, your intentions, and your vulnerabilities. **Good communication and TCB will make for a deeper, more meaningful experience than whatever you've learned from past partners.**

WHAT ABOUT "FRIENDS WITH BENEFITS"?

The summer before college, Tristan and Robbie started hanging out. They played video games, they fooled around. They discussed their expectations and boundaries, so as not to cause confusion. Neither of them had expectations of anything becoming more—they were both leaving for college in the fall, so they didn't want to get into anything serious. They both had been tested within the last month, so they could trust each other. They didn't talk much about their feelings, or about anything all that deep, but they had a lot of fun together.

A casual encounter, or friends-with-benefits situation, is only harmless if you truly trust each other, have compassion for each other, and are extremely clear about where boundaries lie. It is easy to get into sticky territory if you assume that being "casual" means you can let compassion slide. Just because you aren't in a committed relationship doesn't mean you can be a jerk. Sex without a committed relationship can be complicated if there isn't a clear line of communication. In my experience, almost always someone develops feelings in this setup. And if communication and expectations aren't clear, someone will get hurt. So make your choices carefully when you're choosing a friend with benefits.

WHEN THINGS AREN'T RIGHT

Mistakes are common, disappointments are common, things don't always go right. Maybe what your partner is doing doesn't feel good to you. You don't want to stop having sex, but how do you let them know what will make it better for you without making things awkward? Choosing to have sex is a high-stakes emotional game. And you should approach it that way. Here are some things you can say to help make your sexual encounter feel better.

1. You can tell them what you like: "I like when you _____."
2. Ask for what you want: "Can you _____?"
3. Give them a firm command: "Faster/Slower."
4. Take a break: "Can we pause and talk?"

WHEN IT COMES TO SEX, I KNOW WHAT PEOPLE LIKE BECAUSE I WATCH PORN.

Whoa there. If you think that you are ready for sex because you've watched porn, then you need to slow down and pay attention! First: Porn is a performance. It is a fantasy. What those actors are selling to you doesn't necessarily feel good—to them, or to your partners. We do understand that, in terms of figuring out stuff about sex, porn is an accessible resource. And you can get answers to questions you might be embarrassed to ask. So, yes, you might learn things from porn. But the physical features and mechanics of sex scenes are not representative of real life, with all its imperfections and emotions. Your sexual relationships are not scenes in a movie and you are not actors! **That's right. Porn is not real sex. Porn is not real life.**

I HAD UNPROTECTED SEX, WHAT DO I DO?

Get tested. Some STIs take time to manifest, which is why you should talk to a doctor, nurse, or someone at a Planned Parenthood center. If you had unprotected vaginal intercourse with someone with a penis, there is a risk of pregnancy. There are emergency contraceptives that can be bought over the counter (AKA the morning after pill), and they can be purchased and effective up to five days after the sexual encounter. However, the sooner you take it, the more effective it is.

If your partner is showing symptoms of an STI, get tested. If not, still get tested. Some STIs are undetectable. Some, like HPV, only manifest in people with vaginas. A penis can have HPV and not know it, spreading it around. **Do your part and be responsible: get tested at least once a year if you've had unprotected sex. And heck, even if it is protected. It's important to know your status.**

I'M HAVING SEX WITH SOMEONE MUCH OLDER THAN ME, IS THAT WRONG?

First of all, go back to chapter 2 and brush up on **consent**. It may be illegal for you to be having a sexual relationship with someone older than you. Different states have different laws, and even if you are consenting to the relationship, someone else can report it and the older person will suffer the consequences.

It can be difficult for adolescents to pick up on power imbalances and manipulations, but when you've got an unequal power dynamic, you've got unequal balances of **trust, compassion,** and **boundaries.** Having sex with an adult, or someone significantly older than you, may make you feel special or chosen. You may feel like that person sees your maturity. But, you can easily trust the wrong person just because it is someone who "seems" mature. Question the fact that the older person is looking for someone younger—are they incapable of having a relationship with an adult? Are they looking to exploit? Do they think children are attractive? These are difficult questions. But when someone is older, they inherently have more power. You are not in an equal relationship, even if they tell you that you are.

This is especially true if you are involved with someone who has authority over you (a boss, a teacher, a coach, or a group leader). People with authority are the ones responsible for teaching you about **boundaries.** It is their job to hold good boundaries and protect the people in their care from harm (emotional *and* physical). Our advice when it comes to dating, or having relationships with, or having sex with, someone more than a few years older than you is: *just don't.* It's not healthy for you emotionally and it's certainly not practicing TCB in the way you should.

TOP THREE TAKEAWAYS ABOUT HAVING SEX

1 Having sex can be awesome when you're ready for it and can deal with what it means for your relationships and emotions.

2 There's no having sex without some risk. (Maybe that's why it's so exciting sometimes.) Be honest and prepare yourself for the responsibility of having sex.

3 Healthy sex means both people want it at the same time, can express the way they want it, and fully consent to the shared experience.

PART 5

THE HARD STUFF

While TCB makes good relationships even better, we want to acknowledge that things aren't always so easy. You may find yourself in situations that are harmful, or more serious than a simple miscommunication or misunderstanding. To navigate the hard stuff that life can throw at you, it helps to remember the lesson from chapter 3: part of who you are, and how you relate to other people, is shaped by events and relationships that have taken place throughout the course of your life up until this moment. This is true for everyone around you. Anyone can carry invisible baggage that has nothing to do with you. Keeping this in mind can help you be compassionate to yourself and to others when evaluating complicated relationships or painful situations.

Hard truth: sometimes bad things happen to people who don't deserve it, and sometimes good people do bad things. It's important to feel like you have some solid tools to help you decide what to do and where to turn when things get tough. In this section, you'll see how you can face even the worst situations by using TCB to trust your instincts, be more compassionate with yourself and with others, and be aware of boundaries, especially when your relationship to a person feels particularly challenging or unexpectedly confusing.

chapter 13

BIG "T" AND LITTLE "†": NAVIGATING TRAUMA WITH TCB

WHY YOU NEED TO UNDERSTAND TRAUMA

Before we get into talking about some of the really hard stuff that comes along with human interactions, it helps to have a basic understanding of what can make some of it so hard. There's a difference between feeling awkward about a situation and having an acute psychological reaction. For some people, there are things that have happened in their lives and relationships that make it challenging to create healthy connections. And knowing a little bit about how that works can help you be more compassionate (to yourself and others!).

If you've suffered trauma, this chapter might help you understand some things about how you act, or react, in relationships. And if you have not suffered trauma, you probably know someone who has (whether you know what that trauma is or not).

As you read through this chapter, you'll notice there are no quizzes, no funny asides, no jokes. That's because this chapter covers some heavy stuff. An important part of my job is helping people to see the bigger picture of their lives, and I have learned that it is important for everyone to have some understanding of how trauma can work against healthy relationships and how TCB can help. Experiencing trauma or addiction can leave people feeling like they are missing a part of themselves—and they are. Acknowledging these missing pieces, and learning (with the help of therapists or counselors) how to own them, lets people make sense of how their current behavior is rooted in past experiences.

WHAT IS TRAUMA?

Trauma is the name for a psychological and physical reaction that happens when a single or repeated experience causes an overwhelming threat to one's very being; one traumatic event, or repeated traumatic events, can literally cause the brain to rewire—changing how people receive and process emotions, and shaping how they approach situations and relationships. **In other words, there are specific things that happen to you where you feel so endangered that your brain literally changes tracks.** And that rewiring fundamentally affects the way that you behave in certain situations, including in relationships. These types of experiences are often referred to as big "T" traumas, and they are more common than you might think. Examples of big "T" trauma include:

- Violent physical attacks: According to the CDC, homicide is the third leading cause of death for young people ages ten to twenty-four. Each day, about fourteen young people are victims of homicide, and about 1,300 are treated in emergency departments for non-fatal assault-related injuries. Black adolescents and young adults are at higher risk for the most physically harmful forms of violence (e.g., homicides, fights with injuries, aggravated assaults) compared with white youth.

- Fear for safety at school: Eighty percent of transgender students report feeling unsafe at their schools because of their gender identity.

- Intimate partner violence: A CDC report on teen dating violence documents that nearly one in eleven high school females, and approximately one in fifteen high school males, report having experienced **physical** dating violence in the last year. About one in nine female and one in thirty-six male high school students report having experienced **sexual** dating violence in the last year.

- Sexual abuse: The CDC reports that one in three females between ages eleven and seventeen is a rape victim, and nearly one in four males between eleven and seventeen years old is a rape victim. A briefing paper from the YWCA states that approximately 40 percent of Black women report experiencing coercive sexual contact by age eighteen.

- Physical abuse and neglect (absent parents, most often because of drug addiction or mental illness): Conservative estimates from the CDC indicate that each year at least one in seven children have experienced child abuse and/or neglect. Rates of child abuse and neglect are five times higher for children in families with low socioeconomic status compared to children in families with higher socioeconomic status. BIPOC teens are at an increased risk of experiencing traumatic events—such as displacement, sexual abuse, poverty, witnessing violence, or experiencing racial discrimination, and are much less likely to receive treatment to address trauma.

- Mental health concerns: According to the YWCA paper, girls of color, particularly Latina girls, experience a much higher prevalence of mental health concerns like feeling sad or hopeless, seriously considering suicide, and attempting suicide, compared to other groups.

- Discrimination: It's important to note that LGBTQIA+ kids report significantly more big "T" trauma than their peers. The 2019 inaugural national survey on LGBTQ mental health from the Trevor Project (thetrevorproject.org) reports that 78 percent of transgender and nonbinary youth reported being the subject of discrimination due to their gender identity and 70 percent of LGBTQ youth reported discrimination due to their sexual orientation.

- Suicidal thoughts: More than half of transgender and nonbinary youth in the Trevor Project survey had seriously considered suicide.

When someone has experienced a big "T" trauma, especially in childhood, it's like a part of them disconnects without them being aware of why that happens. **Imagine your phone battery keeps running down really fast and you can't figure out why. You know it's supposed to hold a charge longer, but it just doesn't. So you just decide to suffer along with a phone that only works for a few hours of the day. Or you may go to an expert and ask what's wrong, and what that expert discovers is that you have a battery-draining app running and that something has happened to your phone that has kept you from seeing that. That app had a big impact on your whole phone system; it wore down your phone's energy and made it less efficient.** Big "T" trauma is like that. Those who have experienced a big "T" trauma often ignore—or learn to live with—the disconnect. **Without knowing why they are struggling, they go along without having their full emotional system operating.**

ACE SCORE AND TRAUMA

Trauma survivors will typically say things like, "I'm over it" or "I don't think about it anymore." The fact is that the effects of that trauma are not gone, and what they don't think about is the low level of distress that is always running in the background of their emotional system. The Adverse Childhood Experience (ACE) screening test (which you can find online at acestoohigh.com/got-your-ace-score) asks ten questions. **A positive score of four or more means you will benefit from talking with a counselor or a trusted adult.** Talking to someone about your trauma will help you develop *resilience,* which is the characteristic of being able to recover and adapt in the face of adversity. Ignoring a score of four or higher all but guarantees that you will struggle with trust, compassion, and boundaries in your future relationships.

Having had Adverse Childhood Experiences is linked to chronic health problems, mental illness, and substance misuse in adulthood. ACEs can also negatively impact education and job opportunities. The toxic stress from unaddressed ACEs can change brain development and affect such things as attention, decision-making, learning, and response to stress.

TRAUMA, DRAMA, AND TCB

In addition to the big "T" traumas we talk about above, there are what we think of as little "t" traumas. These are situations where you feel helpless or afraid—but not to the degree where your brain is literally convinced you are in mortal danger. Verbal bullying, a bad breakup, a stressful family situation, or being ostracized from a friend group can all create little "t" trauma. **When little "t" trauma** happens, TCB collapses. You may struggle to trust the person caus-ing the trauma, you'll feel like you are not being treated with com-passion, and it's likely you'll feel like your boundaries have been steamrolled. That's because you, yourself (the part of you that you worked so hard on in chapter 3 of this book), is being distilled down to an object not worthy of TCB. You don't have to have been physi-cally abused or hurt. Whenever you trust someone who betrays you, you are at risk for suffering trauma to some degree.

Think of it this way: In big "T" trauma, trust, compassion, and boundaries have vaporized and are replaced with *terror, chaos, being in fear of danger*. In little "t" trauma, you'll find TCB dissolves into *tears, confusion, and betrayal*.

WHEN DRAMA HIDES TRAUMA

Sixteen-year-old Isolde had always acted in ways that were screaming out for attention. She was popular at school because she always had some big drama and wasn't shy about pulling everyone in to help her "solve" it. No one but her therapist knew that Isolde had been sexually abused by her uncle, who was a drug addict. He would stay with the family for a few days, get kicked out, then reappear with money or gifts, and the cycle would start over again. Isolde told her therapist what her uncle had done, but that it didn't really bother her anymore. What she really wanted to know was why guys she was attracted to would disappear after she had sex with them. She knew her friends thought she was just into the drama, but what she really wanted was a committed relationship. For Isolde, the trauma in her childhood was repeating in her romantic relationships. The expectation that guys would drop into her life, offer sex instead of affection, and then disappear, felt familiar—almost comfortable.

Are you someone who can't help causing drama in your relationships? If you keep getting drawn into the same kind of situation over and over again, you may be unconsciously reacting to a trauma in your own life. **You might not notice it at first—in fact, you might enjoy the attention you get—and you will get attention. Many people are entertained by being spectators to drama in other people's lives. Someone with trauma in their background can't read these signals and shift gears. And if their friends get tired of being constantly pulled into another messy scene, they'll just look for another audience.**

For example, if like Isolde, you come from a family that was abusive, chaotic, and unable to access TCB, you may do more than attract drama, you may keep it going because it feels comfortable engaging with dramatic people once they find you or you find them. In other words, trauma sets up wiring of attraction in our brain to similar people and circumstances to those who initially perpetrated the trauma. And of course these similar people and circumstances result in the same outcome. The psychological term for this is *traumatic reenactment.*

It's important to know the difference between behavior that comes from having trauma in your history and behavior that comes from having a dramatic personality. If you're a drama queen by nature, pay attention to whether or not being center stage is so important to you that when the audience leaves, you immediately go in search of another, just to keep the drama alive.

Drama follows Jordan. Or, rather, Jordan creates drama. If their friend has a crush on someone, they kiss that person first. If someone is getting more attention than them, they do or say something outrageous to refocus the conversation. However, they know when to pull back. Jordan's outsized personality works; they're one of the most popular people at school.

If you can shift gears and leave the spotlight, that's a healthy sign. But if you suffer emotionally when you are not the center of attention—whether it's positive or negative—talking to someone can help you understand why you're driven to play out the same scene over and over again.

TRAUMA, CONSENT, AND BEING TRIGGERED

Trauma has a very specific impact on your ability to consent. One of the most common things that happens is that you freeze instead of being able to say no. It's important to remember that **silence is not consent**.

I froze one time when a guy started to undress me. We were making out, but I wasn't expecting it to go further. The next thing I knew he had pulled my shirt off, unhooked my bra, and was just staring at my body. I felt violated. Even though I see myself as confident, loud, and in control, I froze. I didn't say no. I didn't say a word. I just thought: this can't be happening to me. But it was. I finally managed to get myself out of the situation before it got worse, but I kept asking myself later: How could I have frozen like that? Why didn't, why couldn't, I say no?

Often, right before your brain checks out from a traumatic situation, it sends you an SOS message that "this can't be happening." When you are feeling threatened, your brain tries to protect you. The feeling that "this can't be happening" is your brain's effort to protect you from the reality that something awful actually *is* happening.

If you have been in a situation that has triggered a freeze response, the first thing you need to know is that whatever has happened *is not your fault*. The next thing you need to know is that you *must tell someone what happened*. If you do not have a trusted adult in your life, call one of the hotline numbers in our resource section or text the crisis line. It is possible to retrain your brain to address traumatic situations, but this is not work you can—or should have to—do on your own.

The other way in which past traumatic experiences can cause a spiral of depression, anxiety, or grief is when trauma hijacks your reactions to "normal" events. When it comes to understanding trauma, being "triggered" means more than having an unpleasant feeling. Trauma can trigger very real and painful reactions. Events or people that, intentionally or unintentionally, cross a **boundary** in a way that is not **compassionate**—even if it is subtle—can damage the **trust** between the people involved. And it helps to have a strategy in place when you know you are going to encounter these scenarios. If you believe you might have triggers, you should not feel ashamed or embarrassed to bring them up.

Something I know is that I cannot get weighed without feeling triggered. I had an eating disorder for all of my teenage years—and I still struggle with my body every now and again. However, after eight years of therapy and a lot of work on myself, I no longer struggle in the way I once did: unless I get weighed. When I go to the doctor, I tell them that I don't want to know how much I weigh. I don't explain that it will be triggering for me because I don't have to. If a doctor presses, then I'll explain. But ultimately, *I am not consenting to hearing a number.* I allow my doctor to weigh me, for medical purposes. However, I know myself, and knowing how much I weigh is actively detrimental to my mental health.

HOW TO GET HELP

If, after reading this, you suspect that you might feel better if you talked with someone **(or even more telling, if the thought of talking to someone makes you feel scared and ashamed),** here's what you can do:

- Allow any and all emotions to wash over you; don't try to push feelings away.
- Choosing who to tell is a big step. Think of someone who you know you can trust. Whether that's a friend, teacher, or a parent depends on who you think can offer compassion and hold firm boundaries. Find someone who you think can listen without judgment,

and not rush in to try to fix things (unless you ask them to help).

- If you can't think of anyone in your personal life you can talk to, there are professionals who can help. Try talking to a guidance counselor at school, or tell your doctor or therapist.
- Call or text one of the hotlines listed in our resource section.
- Write about what you consider to be your trauma in your journal.

ACKNOWLEDGING TRAUMA WITH TCB

Whether you are aware of past trauma or dealing with a traumatic situation in your life right now, the best thing you can do is learn to talk about it. Being the victim of a traumatic experience is not a reason to be ashamed. And realizing that you may struggle with trust, compassion, and boundaries is the first step in being able to identify the areas where you need to focus in order to make your relationships healthier.

When handling how to approach the topic with someone you love, allow TCB to guide you:

- **Trust** that what you are feeling is real. Listen to what your body needs: screaming, crying, hugging, sighing. Make space for it all.

- Have **compassion** for yourself: you are not responsible for what happened to you, no matter what people say.
- Establish a **boundary**. You can say, "I just need for you to listen to what I am going to say."

If you want to let your friends know about triggers or trauma, try to explain what you experience *before* you are in a triggering situation. Be clear about how you react and where it comes from. For example, if you have a parent who is abusive when they drink, you may find parties where everyone is drunk to be triggering. Tell your friends if you think you need to leave. Ask if someone will be your sober buddy if you need one to make you feel safe. Close friends will help you navigate triggering situations.

It's equally important to support your friends, and help create a safe space where they can share their experiences. All you need to be a source of support is to be clear with TCB. Let your friend know they can trust you to understand their triggers. Have compassion—even if their behavior seems silly or like an overreaction to you. Keep your boundaries strong; don't "catch" their powerful emotions. Romantic relationships, especially, can often open up the dynamics of trauma. Being a good partner to someone with trauma in their past means listening carefully to their fears, understanding their destructive or self-sabotaging patterns, holding good boundaries to make them feel secure—and loving them despite their struggles.

WHAT IF IT'S ALL TOO MUCH TO HANDLE?

Sometimes your own or someone's else's emotional baggage can be too much to bear. You have to honestly assess: What can you realistically handle at this moment? Acknowledging when you, or someone you love, needs help is an important step in a healthy direction.

If you need to disengage because a situation feels triggering, trust your instincts, but act with compassion. Here are some things you can say to press Pause on an intense conversation:

- "You know what? I'm really not ready to talk about this yet."
- "I think this is a conversation meant for me and a therapist. I appreciate your concern, but I need space."
- "I don't want to talk about this anymore."

TOP THREE TAKEAWAYS ABOUT TRAUMA

1 Just because you don't think about it anymore doesn't mean it is not affecting you.

2 Whether big "T" or little "t," trauma affects TCB and relationships. If you know you have trauma in your life, check your relationships; if your relationships have a consistently toxic pattern, check your trauma.

3 Freezing is a natural adaptive response to an overwhelming threat, but it has consequences on our brain, particularly in childhood, that can last throughout our life if not properly addressed.

chapter 14

ALTERED: NAVIGATING SUBSTANCES

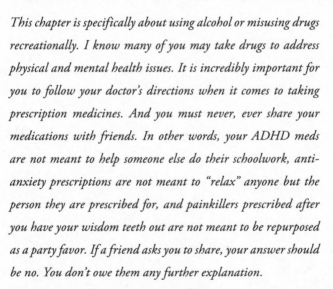

This chapter is specifically about using alcohol or misusing drugs recreationally. I know many of you may take drugs to address physical and mental health issues. It is incredibly important for you to follow your doctor's directions when it comes to taking prescription medicines. And you must never, ever share your medications with friends. In other words, your ADHD meds are not meant to help someone else do their schoolwork, anti-anxiety prescriptions are not meant to "relax" anyone but the person they are prescribed for, and painkillers prescribed after you have your wisdom teeth out are not meant to be repurposed as a party favor. If a friend asks you to share, your answer should be no. You don't owe them any further explanation.

Let me repeat: prescription medications are meant to treat specific issues, and can be critically important to helping a person function in a mentally or physically healthy way. If you are

> *someone who takes a daily medication, you* **should not, ever,** *use other drugs (not even marijuana) or alcohol. The results could be deadly.* **If you choose to ignore this advice, please make sure that you are truthful with your prescribing doctor about your recreational use of alcohol or other substances.**

My dad came to talk to my class about substance abuse junior year of high school. That day, we all filed into a room full of empty fold-out chairs. Once we took our seats, he started to talk about drugs and alcohol. I remember that day clearly. I could have done the talk in two minutes, because what I want to say to anyone who is thinking about using, or actively using, alcohol or drugs is: JUST DON'T! Need more reason than my decades of experience as a doctor who treats people with drug and alcohol addictions? Here are my top three:

1. Using drugs and alcohol has a very concerning effect on your developing teenage brain.
2. You are prone to taking physical and emotional risks when you are drunk or high, increasing your chance of hurting yourself or others, and disrupting your ability to practice the building blocks of good friendships or other relationships (and we're talking about TCB: trust, compassion, and boundaries).
3. No one who is under the influence of any substance is able to give **consent** for any activity—whether it seems to be their idea or not! Remember how, in chapter 2, we talked about "legal, ethical, and moral" issues around

consent? News flash: if you are intoxicated—which means your ability to think clearly, speak, move, or manage your emotions is compromised—and you are under the age of twenty-one, you are in dangerous territory when it comes to all three. You are engaging in illegal behavior, you have muted the moral voice in your brain, and you may behave in ways that are unethical. None of this is good news for relationships, for sex, or for consent.

So here's my take as a parent, and as a doctor who has spent decades treating addicts and people who are sick or made sicker from substance abuse: DON'T DO IT. And when your parents set **boundaries** meant to keep you safe by limiting how much you experiment, understand that having to evaluate whether or not a risk is worth taking helps your brain lay down strong connections between risk and reward. In a perfect world, I'd end this chapter right here, having given you the best prescription for dealing with drugs and alcohol. But we're going to go a little further here, because we respect your intelligence and want you to know the science and psychology behind waiting to drink or use drugs until you are at least twenty-one, if not older.

When my dad came to talk to our class, I hadn't consumed any illicit substances. Not one. I was too scared to, if I'm being frank. I mean, MY DAD was the one who came to talk to us about substance abuse. That being said, I'm an anomaly. Most of the teens I knew during high school at least drank. Which is why we have this chapter. *We are never, ever going to tell you that drinking or doing drugs is good for you. It's not.* But I personally want to offer guidance for how to move through the world. If you're going to do it, at least think about it, and know what you are risking when you try it.

THIS IS YOUR DEVELOPING BRAIN . . .

If you're rolling your eyes because you think that you are totally in control of your alcohol or drug use, listen up. There's a reason you don't want to believe us, and it's grounded in proven *science*. No matter how mature you are, or feel, the basic neurological fact is that your brain has not finished the work of fully wiring the frontal lobe—which is the command center for evaluating risk and reward. **So when your brain is already working overtime to clarify what is risky behavior and whether or not it's worth a risk to gain a thrill, then adding intoxicants to the mix completely confuses the situation.**

And while we are talking about what happens to your brain, let's just take a minute to understand what happens when you "black out" while partying. **Having a blackout while drinking is not the same as passing out. A blackout means there's a big black hole in your memory beginning after you started drinking (and sometimes memories even prior to drinking can be affected).** When you are passed out, you are effectively unconscious, and in a dangerous health situation. When you're in a blackout, everyone else may just think you are drunk, but when you wake up the next morning you won't remember things about the night. You might not know how you got where you ended up. You might not know who helped you get there. **Passing out is like having anesthesia and then waking up, whereas blacking out is like getting a concussion and not remembering what happened after you were hit.**

Blacking out happens because there is a part of your brain—the hippocampus—whose job it is to make and store memories. Binge drinking (consuming an excessive amount of alcohol in a short period of time) interferes with the process of storing information in your memory—and the more you drink, the bigger the gap. **So once the alcohol hijacks your memory center, you can lose the memory of whatever you did while drinking, from conversations to having sex.**

One more thing about binge drinking: I suspect that for some of you the idea of drinking to get drunk—and get drunk fast—seems perfectly normal. But binge drinking, no matter what anyone tries to tell you, is not a "normal behavior." The *DSM-5* (*Diagnostic and Statistical Manual of Mental Disorders,* a tool used by psychiatrists and psychologists to give standard definitions to mental disorders) defines "binge alcohol drinking" as a genuine disorder characterized by dangerous or unwanted consequences. And those consequences can affect more than just your developing brain.

Gigi woke up the next morning not remembering much from the night before. She remembered getting ready with her friends before the party, and doing shots to pregame. She remembered having another drink—or two—at the party. She felt sore but wasn't certain about why she was sore. It wasn't that she was concerned about having had sex. That had happened before. But she couldn't remember if she had used a condom. She had a thought: Am I pregnant?

Gigi's got several serious things to deal with here, including a possibility of pregnancy. And they are all a result of her relationship to alcohol. Here's what *could* go wrong in this scenario: Since Gigi was in a blackout, she wasn't able to consent to having sex. So whoever her partner was, they could be guilty of assault. She's worried she didn't use protection. So she could have an STI and/or be pregnant. Maybe even more concerning to me, Gigi is not upset about the fact that she might have had sex while she was in a blackout state.

Gigi needs to take action! She needs to take care of her physical self and see her doctor (or visit a Planned Parenthood clinic) to get evaluated and treated. She needs to seek help for her drinking. (See our Resources and Recommended Reading section for ideas on where to start.) And she needs to understand what is driving her risky behavior. If you have a friend like Gigi—or suspect you're kind of like her yourself—find someone to talk to. If you trust an adult close to you, tell them what you're worried about. If you are afraid to tell the adults in your life, see our Resources and Recommended Reading section for some places to turn for advice.

ALCOHOL ABUSE

Do you have a problem with alcohol? Answering yes to just *one* of these questions means you need to examine your relationship to drinking:

- Has your use of alcohol resulted in poor performance at school or work?
- Do you forget about responsibilities when you are drinking?
- Have you been in trouble with the law because of drinking?
- Do you drink and then drive?

If you continue to drink despite alcohol causing trouble in your social, school, or work life, or if you continue to drink despite physical consequences (blackouts, hangovers, drinking until sick or unconscious), you are *abusing* alcohol and should seek help. Don't assume you'll "outgrow" your need to party. The consequences of ignoring that you have a problem can be life-altering.

DRUGS, ALCOHOL, AND YOUR EMOTIONS

When you are using substances recreationally **(meaning in any way other than prescribed by your doctor, and for the sole purpose of getting high)**, whether it's alcohol, weed, or Xanax, you're altering the function of your brain, minus the knowledge that comes with having a medical degree. And research shows that even with very low levels of exposure, your judgment can be affected. You have a harder time controlling your own emotions and reading the emotions of other people. In other words, when you're altered, things can seem exciting and hilarious, or terrible and depressing—or a mix of them all at the same time.

Raise your hand if any of these things happened when you were partying:

- You suddenly started to cry.
- You ended up in a screaming fight with your date.
- You got physically violent—punched a wall (or a person), threw something.

- You couldn't figure out if your friend was mad at you or just worried.
- You couldn't tell if someone was quiet because they were angry or because they were sad.

Drugs and alcohol can mask your feelings and suppress your emotions. Being physical with someone is an experience that you should feel completely comfortable with. It's not right if you feel like you need to numb yourself before getting physical with someone. **Meaning: if you don't want to have sex when you are sober, you shouldn't be doing it at all. Getting intoxicated and proceeding is only going to make you feel terrible afterward.** And denying your feelings is the exact opposite of having **compassion** for yourself. Bottom line: you should not have to reach for an answer outside of your body in order to manage your feelings—in any situation, but especially when it comes to your physical relationships with others.

Melissa got super drunk at the party last Friday and kissed Archie—who wasn't drunk at all. Archie is in her English class and has a rep as a player. But Melissa identifies as queer, even though she's not open about it. In fact, she and a girl she was starting to see had a big fight over the fact that Melissa didn't want to go public, and now they're not even talking. It's just that she was telling Archie how sad she was, and he was being so understanding, and then he told her that she was beautiful and perfect—and then they were kissing. Melissa doesn't think she likes guys that way, and when she sees Archie the next day, it's definitely awkward. Archie's making it worse by telling everyone at school what happened. Meanwhile Melissa is having a hard time wrapping her head around the whole situation.

So maybe Melissa is sexually curious and maybe she isn't. But that's not the issue: Melissa was drunk. Archie was not. And whether he meant to or not, Archie manipulated Melissa into having strong emotions that he then took advantage of. Whether Archie just saw an opportunity because Melissa was drunk or whether he was into her, he was wrong to take advantage this way.

We don't know if Melissa and Archie are platonic friends. But even if they are, Archie has some apologizing to do. Unless there was a clear signal from Melissa that she was interested in experimenting (before she started drinking), Archie crossed a boundary. It might be hard for Melissa to trust Archie after this, especially since he seems to be bragging about what happened between them. I've seen a ton of friendships end over these kinds of drunken scenarios. If someone's drunk and you think it's the perfect time to make a romantic move, think again. It's not worth risking a friendship or your reputation. And it definitely puts you in precarious territory when it comes to TCB and consent.

TCB UNDER THE INFLUENCE

The biggest problem with TCB when you're under the influence is that your own ability to use trust, compassion, and boundaries in your interactions with other people is compromised. **You might violate a friend's trust by sharing a secret that you'd promised to keep. You might be so caught up in the party mindset that you can't have compassion for a friend who is not having a good time and wants to leave, or needs your help. For sure, your boundaries, both physical and emotional, can get sloppy. And you could find yourself in real trouble.**

Making things even more complicated, while your fuzzier boundaries might make it hard to contain your emotions, your ability to read other people's emotions is simultaneously impaired. **You might put your trust in someone who does not have your best interests at heart. Like Melissa with Archie, you might mistake manipulation for compassion. And you might misinterpret when someone is trying to hold a boundary and, even without meaning to, push them to do something they don't want to do.**

And if TCB isn't working, **consent** isn't happening. You already know that if you are intoxicated or high you cannot truly give consent. But what about this? What if you are not under the influence, but you're making out with someone who is? Have both of you really consented to what you're doing? Should you **trust** someone who is not in their normal state of mind? Is the person who is under the influence able to exercise **compassion**? What happens if you tell them you want to stop until they sober up? Will they understand your point of view? Will they respect the **boundary** you are trying to establish? **Already, the lines are blurry. As we can see, it's almost impossible to ensure that both people are practicing TCB no matter who is under the influence.**

CONSENT

If you've gotten this far and still don't know whether or not using drugs or alcohol will have an effect on your ability, or your partner's ability, to ask for or give consent, go back and reread chapter 2 (really, it's important!) to understand why anyone who is under the influence is **unable** to give or ask for consent that meets our (and we hope your) criteria of balancing **trust, compassion,** and **boundaries**!

Gus and Devon were only in their first year of high school, but they decided to go to one of Saskia's "legendary" pool parties while her parents were out of town. They made a pact that they would stick together no matter what. But once they got to the party, Devon started drinking—a lot. Gus stuck with him. It was pretty funny at first. Devon wasn't usually so outrageous. But then one of Saskia's brother's college football teammates started egging Devon on, getting him to do shots and a keg stand. Gus tried to get Devon to leave, but Devon was loving the attention. It just made Gus more and more nervous. This guy was so much older. And bigger. And definitely drunk. And there was definitely sexual innuendo in his comments to Devon. And then the guy asked Devon to go upstairs with him. "I'm good," Devon told Gus. "Go have fun at the party." But Gus remembered their promise and wouldn't leave. Finally, the guy gave up. "You're such a baby that you can't even party without your babysitter," he said as he walked away. Devon wouldn't talk to Gus the whole way home. He didn't return texts the next day. It was radio silence all weekend, and Gus couldn't decide whether he was more worried he'd lost his best friend or angry with Devon for wanting to ditch him. They'd made a promise. Either way, Gus was dreading school on Monday.

Gus was being a good friend. He can't control Devon's reaction, but he should at least feel confident that he did what was right. He rightly understood that a drunk Devon couldn't consent to going upstairs with the guy. And even if he wasn't calculating the age difference, at best he stopped what would legally be considered criminal assault. At the very least, Gus helped Devon avoid a choice he likely would have regretted.

Remember how we talked about questioning the motives of someone much older who wanted to hook up with someone much younger? And remember the part about how your teenage brain can't accurately process risk—even when sober? Gus needs to be *compassionate*. Clearly Devon was flattered by the attention, but he was too drunk to read all the signals that were being put out. Hopefully Devon will come around in time and apologize and *trust* that Gus was looking out for him. After all, Devon was the one trying to back out on a promise to stick together. Being a good friend is more important than not having your friend get mad at you for stopping them from making a potentially dangerous choice.

JUST SAY NO . . . TO PEER PRESSURE*

Plan your answer ahead of time and practice, so you're ready to confidently look the person offering in the eye and say no in a friendly way. If they continue to pressure you, don't worry about explaining, just remove yourself from the situation.

Remember that peer pressure is a two-way street. If you find you are trying your hardest to sway a friend who keeps saying no, take a step back and check in with TCB. Compassion can help you remember how it feels to be pressured by a friend you trust. Acknowledge that respecting boundaries is important. Someone who is repeatedly making excuses no matter how much you try to convince them may be (politely) trying to hold their own boundary—for their own reasons. Stop pushing and think about why it's so important to you that your friend does what you are urging.

- "No thanks." You don't ever owe anyone an explanation for what you choose to do or not do with your own body.
- "I tried it before and got really sick." This is a useful social white lie.
- "I'm taking another med right now and the interaction is really bad." Depending on whether you do or do not take other prescription medications, this is either another social white lie or an important fact. Alcohol (a depressant) can counteract the effects of antidepressants like Prozac and others. Alcohol can also interfere with antibiotics, making them less effective or even damaging to the liver. Marijuana can interfere with seizure and asthma medications, in addition to virtually all psychotropic medication.

- "It's just not for me." Notice how this way of saying no does not blame, shame, or judge the person offering. If they continue to pressure you, they're not being a good friend and taking some space is probably the right thing to do.
- "It's against my (personal/religious/cultural) beliefs." This is (yet another) way of asking someone to respect your boundaries without blaming, shaming, or judging theirs.

*As we write this book, the "sober curious" movement has been gaining steam. Unlike choosing a "sober" lifestyle, which can imply having dealt with an alcohol disorder, sober curious means claiming the power to choose, question, or change your drinking habits in order to focus on your mental or physical health. So be confident in naming your desire to refuse peer pressure. Your lifestyle: your choice!

IF YOU'RE GOING TO PARTY ANYWAY . . .

Okay. We've given you all the warnings. You know that our best advice is to avoid using alcohol or other substances until you are at least twenty-one. Do we think you will follow this advice? My experience tells me that's unlikely. **We know drinking and drugs happen. I mean, if you go to college (and maybe even high school), you've probably encountered this scene at a party: spilled liquor coating the floors and everyone smooching in the dark. By the** way, this is not a reason to be scared of the social scene on a college campus. College rules. It's also when people get to try new things all the time. And sometimes trying things means learning where your personal boundaries are—or should be. So yes, alcohol and drugs and a raging party scene are problematic. So how can you do your best to navigate it?

HERE ARE OUR RECOMMENDATIONS FOR TAKING PERSONAL RESPONSIBILITY WHEN ALCOHOL OR OTHER SUBSTANCES ARE INVOLVED:

SET YOUR INTENTION BEFORE YOU GO OUT. Is tonight about dancing? Do you want to get kissed? Do you just want to be with your friends? Do you feel like you can have fun without any substances? Make sure you say out loud what you want to happen for the night to yourself and to your friends. Write it down if you have to!

STAY IN TOUCH WITH YOUR OWN BODY; CHECK IN WITH YOURSELF AT LEAST EVERY THIRTY MINUTES. How is the substance hitting your system? Do you feel in control or are you about to get sick? If you feel like you are about to get sick, then you are not exercising a healthy relationship with a substance. Assess and reassess. Much like how consent is a continual conversation with someone else, engaging with substances is a continual conversation with yourself.

KNOW WHO'S ON YOUR TEAM. Be with people who you love and who make you feel safe. This isn't about perpetuating the misogynistic idea that women are responsible for what happens to them when they drink. More than anything, you should be engaging with people who make you feel good and safe. Check in with them throughout the night. Are they pursuing the intention that they set at the beginning of the night? Are they having fun? Or are they intoxicated as well? In which case you cannot rely on them to be there for you. How can you be there for them?

TUNE INTO REALITY. Is your body safe? Are your boundaries being respected? Is someone being too aggressive? Does someone feel sick? Do you feel sick? Don't shy away from seeing the situation for what it is. Remember, your ability to perceive boundary violations is compromised if you are intoxicated.

DON'T BE AFRAID TO GET HELP. If you saw a crime, you'd call 911—use that same judgment at a party. *No matter what, remember: if someone is unconscious, unresponsive, having a seizure, breathing irregularly, freezing cold, or their skin has turned blue or pale, call 911.*

TOP THREE TAKEAWAYS FOR USING SUBSTANCES WITH TCB (AND A BONUS REMINDER)

1 Set your intention. Take your own temperature. Know who's on your team. Tune into reality.

2 If you are intoxicated (meaning your ability to think clearly, speak, move, or manage your emotions is compromised), you cannot consent.

3 Regardless of whether you think you can "handle it," being under the influence of alcohol or other substances carries the risk of every adverse health outcome to yourself or to others that you can measure: illness, injury, death. MEANING: be careful with this stuff.

BONUS REMINDER: In our opinion, it's better to not experiment with substances until you are of legal age (i.e., twenty-one), with your all-important brain development nearing completion.

chapter 15

SOMETHING HAPPENED TO ME . . . NOW WHAT?

When you encounter tough situations—you will be better equipped to get through them if you can be aware of whether those relationships have the right balance of trust, compassion, and boundaries. But sometimes things that happen to you are bigger than you can deal with alone. You may think the advice in this chapter sounds kind of the same, no matter what's happening between the people—and you're sort of right. That's because you shouldn't have to manage problems that feel overwhelming to you on your own. As a doctor, I know that when a prescription is working, there's no need to change it. So when we tell you to take your problem to a trusted adult, it's because it is the right thing to do in a serious situation.

I'm echoing my dad here because repeating things emphasizes their importance. And the important advice in this chapter is:

When something in a relationship seems wrong, always check the balance of trust, compassion, and boundaries. And, there are situations that are too big, and too emotionally or physically dangerous, for you to try to handle on your own.

Checking in with trust, compassion, and boundaries doesn't take long. If you can answer yes to even one of these questions, then your instinct is right: something happened to you and you don't have to just "get over it."

1. Was your trust violated?

   "I thought that my coach was trying to help me when they took video of me at practice, but then I learned that they were showing it to other teachers in the lunchroom and laughing. I don't trust them now."

2. Did someone do something that was devoid of compassion?

   "When I told my friend that someone in our class got grabby with me and said that if I didn't like it, that meant I was gay, my friend told me I should be flattered that such a popular person liked me."

3. Were your boundaries violated?

   "I told the people at the party that I didn't drink. So someone spiked my soda. I spent the whole night crying and throwing up while all my friends laughed at me."

DOS AND DON'TS
FOR GETTING HELP

DO tell someone what is going on. Holding things in doesn't help you in these cases. When someone does something wrong to you, it's okay to ask for help to solve the problem.

DO pick an adult you are comfortable with—a parent, a teacher, a counselor at school, your doctor—any trusted adult.

DO pay attention to whether or not your situation is having an impact on your ability to function. Have your grades dropped? Does it seem unimportant if you shower or get dressed? Have you stopped hanging out with your friends? Are you having trouble sleeping? Or is it hard to get out of bed? Have you lost your appetite? Or are you suddenly eating constantly? Aggression, skipping school, sexual acting out, or substance use can all be ways of masking depression or anxiety.

DO NOT be afraid to ask for help if any of the behaviors above continue for more than a day or two. One bad grade on one test will not hurt you. Skipping class for a week might have a bigger impact. One day of feeling too sad to eat dinner is fine. A week of trying to control your life by controlling your food (either not eating or eating your feelings) is not. Your parents, teachers, or school counselors can work with you to find ways to take the pressure off as you take care of yourself.

DO NOT think that your best friend's advice is the best—or only—advice. Of course you should tell your most trusted friends how you are feeling, even if you don't want to share details. Their *support* is critical during tough times, and it's true that their advice can be useful in dealing with a peer situation. But if you are feeling that any situation is *very* wrong—and you should always trust your gut on this—then bring in an adult perspective as well.

DO NOT get discouraged if the first adult you tell doesn't listen to your concerns or immediately react in the way you want them to. Sometimes adults can misunderstand what you are trying to say. If you're not feeling better after taking your problem to one adult, take it to someone else. Or call a volunteer-run helpline (see some listed in our Resources and Recommended Reading section in the back of this book).

THE DANGER ZONE

I THINK I'M BEING STALKED.

Tamber and Danni met online and had been texting for about a month. But Tamber was getting really insistent about Danni telling them all kinds of personal information. Danni was holding back. When Tamber asked for nudes, Danni told them she wanted to stop talking. Then things started getting weird. Tamber started texting Danni things like: "You looked great in that sweater today" and "Do you always walk home after school?" and finally "I don't need nudes when I can watch through your bathroom window." Danni was starting to get scared. She didn't know if Tamber was really watching or if they were just trying to freak her out.

This is just another harsh reminder that the internet is a dangerous place. There is no way to know who someone really might be out there in cyberspace. **You can't *trust* someone you've never** met in person. You've got to see them in flesh and blood to really, truly know they are who they say they are.

Here's the real truth: there are criminals out there trolling for images of young people that they can then sell to a dark underworld. And there are people out there who are even more dangerous. Whatever is going on here, Danni is *not consenting* to it. And she has every right to try to make it stop. **And despite our cautions about online relationships, *Danni has done nothing wrong.*** And so she needs to tell her parents what is going on. Tamber may actually have personal information about Danni, or they could be a high school kid who gets their thrills through online bullying. There are ways for the local police to report this kind of harassment to cybercriminal units to ensure there is no dark intent. And this is what should happen here. **Danni needs to *trust* that her parents will protect her, have *compassion* for herself for misjudging Tamber as a person, and establish a *boundary* by documenting this harassment.**

I GOT ACCUSED OF DOING SOMETHING I DIDN'T DO.

Zack was hanging out on the fields after school with a group of his friends. They were drinking, but he wasn't. When the football coach caught them, he hauled the whole group into the principal's office (even though Zack was protesting that he was not drinking). The principal called everyone's parents. It was all Zack could do not to cry. He was sure he was going to get in so much trouble.

Zack's got some TCB work to do, even though his only mistake was sticking around when other people were doing things that they should not have been. Hopefully he's got TCB with his parents and their **trust** in him will remain intact (although he can't be offended if they question his good judgment in sticking around when the drinking started). When kids get caught in a bad situation, parents may decide to tighten up on the family rules for a while. For some parents, this might mean more frequent check-ins, or agreeing to take a break from a friend group. Others may want to take it further: making you sign into a geolocator like Find My Friends, or tracking the GPS on your phone or car. Some parents may ask their kid to take a drug screening to prove they haven't been using substances. In this case, Zack knows he's done nothing wrong, but he needs to find a way to have some **compassion** for his parents, who are trying to protect and guide him.

Hopefully his parents also have compassion for Zack and demonstrate it by respecting his *boundaries*. After all, part of being a teenager is making mistakes and (hopefully) learning from them. Trust me on this one! If you feel like your parents are becoming excessively up in your business, you can help establish a boundary by proving your trustworthiness. And that means, first of all: telling the truth (remember, trust takes time to build, but only a second to destroy). And, second, work to keep the lines of communication as open as you can. See chapter 8 for advice on how to have those awkward conversations with your folks.

I DIDN'T SAY YES, BUT THEY MIGHT HAVE THOUGHT I MEANT YES.

Last summer, Nina was swimming in a lake with a boy she liked. Flirting, she wrapped her legs around his waist. Without asking, the boy slid his penis inside of her. She yelled, "Stop!" and he stopped. Nina isn't sure what happened, but she doesn't think it's the guy's fault because she was flirting—and he did stop.

The first thing Nina needs to know is that what happened was a nonconsensual, unprotected sexual act. The guy didn't ask if she wanted to have sex. She didn't say she wanted to have sex. But sex happened anyway, and there could be consequences: Nina could get a sexually transmitted disease. She could be pregnant. Depending on her age and the age of the boy involved, a sexual crime may have been committed. This is serious, and Nina has some complicated feelings about it. She shouldn't be expected to navigate this on her own.

Nina needs to trust that she is the one who gets to make choices about her body and that flirting does not mean she wants to have sex. She already seems to have compassion for the boy (who she feels just "took it too far"), but she needs to have compassion for herself as well, as she is clearly struggling to make sense of what happened. Her body is not just an object for some guy's enjoyment. In this case her boundaries were not respected.

As hard as it is, Nina needs to take some steps to protect her sexual health. If Nina feels like she can't tell her parents or another trusted adult, she should look for an online or community resource.

Trained staff at an organization like Planned Parenthood or RAINN (see our Resources and Recommended Reading section in the back of the book) can provide information on local resources. And even though she says that it's not a big deal now, Nina's feelings about what happened can change over time. If the incident starts to cause her stress or depression, she needs to talk it out with a trusted adult.

I SAID YES, BUT ONLY BECAUSE I FELT LIKE I HAD TO.

Andrea was lying next to Hollis in their dorm room bed when they slid their hand up her shirt. Andrea liked Hollis. She wanted to get to know them better. When they texted to ask her to come over to "study," she showed up at their room (even though she knew what they were really looking for). Andrea felt like jumping out of the bed, but instead she stayed put. Hollis proceeded to unhook her bra. Andrea closed her eyes. She had said yes when Hollis asked her to come over, so she kind of felt like she had agreed to this. That made her feel like she couldn't say no, now. So she didn't say anything at all.

It is a big deal to do something that you do not want to do. When it comes to physical contact, you have the power of consent (and if you need a refresher on how to feel confident about saying what you do and don't want, go back to chapter 2). Andrea knew where things were likely to go if she went to Hollis's room, and if she was being honest with herself, she was hoping that a casual hookup might bring them closer. This is catastrophically problematic thinking. Hooking up is not a strategy for relationship building. Physical intimacy should grow out of a relationship, not be the starting point.

Still, it can feel difficult to tell people no when it is easier to say yes. Especially if you are at all confused about the circumstances. But the more you disregard your own boundaries, the more you lose the ability to trust and have compassion for yourself. Andrea could have been truthful with Hollis and said, "I did want to come over, but I don't want to do this." A little TCB can go a long way in helping you feel confident in finding your voice.

I SAID NO TO SEX, BUT THEY DIDN'T STOP.

The party was getting crazy and Cassie was feeling pretty wasted. Her friends had all left and she wanted to get out of there, too. When Parker offered to walk her home, she agreed. Parker said he wanted to get his coat, and Cassie went upstairs, too. Parker locked the door to the bedroom and pushed Cassie onto the bed. She was dizzy and disoriented; the room was spinning. "I don't want to do this," she said when Parker unzipped her jeans. "Stop. No." It was like Parker didn't hear a word she said. Or didn't care. Everything faded out for Cassie until it was over. "Hey, thanks for coming up to my room," Parker said as he unlocked the door to go back to the party. "Feel free to take a shower if you want."

This is a hard and ugly word, but what happened to Cassie was rape. Nonconsensual sexual assault is a crime. It doesn't matter if either of them were drunk; it doesn't matter if they were flirting, or how they were dressed; it doesn't matter where they were at the time it happened. It doesn't matter if she froze while it was happening or if she said no in a whisper or a scream.

If you have been sexually assaulted, nothing that happened is your

fault! If you said no and sex still happened, *you are not to blame.* It is a crime, and the worst violation of **TCB**. And you are not alone. According to the National Sexual Violence Resource Center (nsvrc .org), the self-reported incidence of rape or sexual assault more than doubled from 2017 to 2018, from 1.4 victimizations per one thousand persons age twelve or older in 2017 to 2.7 in 2018. Based on data from the survey, it is estimated that 734,630 people were raped (threatened, attempted, or completed) in the United States in 2018.

If you have been sexually assaulted, here's what you need to do:

First of all, make sure you are safe. If you can get to a safe space, get there. If you are injured or in immediate danger, call 911.

Call someone you trust; seeking help will be easier if you have support. No matter where you are, you can call the National Sexual Assault Hotline at 800-656-4673. They will be able to refer you to a health facility near you that can take care of survivors of sexual assault.

A specially trained medical professional will examine you, treat any injuries, and collect DNA evidence. (If you go straight to the health facility without showering or changing your clothes, it will be easier for them to collect this evidence.) This examination should be free. It is likely a staff social worker will visit you to offer mental health support services.

You may choose to report your assault to law enforcement. This does not have to happen immediately. RAINN (rainn.org) has extensive details on what you can expect.

Remember: none of these professionals will judge you in any way. Something happened to you that you did not ask to happen. Expect to be treated with compassion.

WHAT IF I THINK I'M THE VICTIM, BUT EVERYONE IS TREATING ME LIKE I DID SOMETHING WRONG?

Tiff woke up to a bunch of angry texts from her friends: "How could you do that to Niki?" "Are you stupid?" "You totally went overboard last night . . . What else did you expect?" "Everyone saw what was going on there." The scary thing was that Tiff had no idea what they were talking about. All she knows is that she started the night at her birthday party, and Brandon, Niki's boyfriend, was flirting with her. He brought her a drink and challenged her to chug it. And then . . . she isn't sure of what happened after that. All she knows is that her muscles feel sore. She has bruises all over her body. And no one will tell her what happened.

What happened to Tiff was simply terrible, completely violating her trust (in Brandon and her friends), compassion (as everyone piles on in defense of Niki), and boundaries (as she has physical evidence of injury . . . for starters). As hard as it may be, she needs to act.

In a scenario where everyone is blaming you—even if it's not as worrisome as this one—and you have no idea what you did wrong, your impulse can be to try to smooth things over with the accusers by apologizing, or just hiding in the hopes that it all somehow goes away. But if I heard this story from a patient, I would have to examine whether or not they had been sexually assaulted. Tiff needs to go for a medical evaluation. She also needs a support team. Whether this is her parents or her friends, someone needs to go with Tiff to the emergency room and report what happened. She may have been drugged (in which case a crime was committed). She may also have had some sort of a reaction to alcohol leading her to black out, meaning she wouldn't know what happened after she began to drink. Tiff's physical soreness may also be evidence of a crime.

This is the kind of event that can absolutely cause trauma (see what kind of fallout results from traumatic events in chapter 13), and Tiff will benefit from some counseling. I would expect her to struggle emotionally and psychologically even if she can't remember what happened.

On top of all of that, the way everyone is piling on with accusations may make Tiff feel guilty, even though she has nothing to feel guilty about. But Tiff—or anyone who finds themselves in this kind of a situation—did nothing wrong! They were not able to *consent,* so anything that happened was a violation of TCB in the most serious of ways. And one final note: NEVER take a drink from someone at a party or at a bar. Always serve yourself.

MY BOYFRIEND/GIRLFRIEND HURTS ME PHYSICALLY.

It's happened more than once. When they get into a fight, Jack tends to get physical. It's not that Jade doesn't trust him. It's just that every time things get heated, Jack grabs her wrist or her hair and screams in her face. After every fight, he promises it won't happen again. Inevitably, it does. Jade feels too embarrassed to tell her friends what is going on. She has told no one, but her friends notice the bruises.

An organization called Violence Prevention Works (violencepreventionworks.org) is dedicated to helping teens deal with dating violence (also called intimate partner violence). Stats from their website support the fact that the situation Jade finds herself in with Jack is not uncommon among young people.

- One in three high school students will be involved in an abusive relationship. And only one third who are in a violent relationship ever tell anyone about the abuse.
- Forty-five percent of teenage girls ages fourteen to seventeen say they know someone their age who has been hit or beaten by a boyfriend.
- Nearly 80 percent of girls who have been physically abused in their intimate relationships continue to date their abuser.
- Intimate partner abuse is a particular risk for Black women and girls. According to a 2019 report from the American Civil Liberties Union (ACLU), approx-

imately 22 percent of Black women across the United
States have experienced rape. Forty percent will experience intimate partner violence, and Black women and
Black transgender or gender nonconforming women are
killed at a higher rate than any other group of women.

- People across the gender spectrum can both be abused
by a dating partner and be abusers.

Like many people who are caught in a cycle of abuse, Jade is too
close to it to see clearly what is happening. She's embarrassed about
what people will think if they find out—about her and about Jack.
She's afraid that if she tells anyone, they'll encourage her to break
up with Jack—but she loves him. Her parents would kill Jack if they
knew. Or maybe they'd be mad at her. Every time Jade tries to think
of a way out of the situation, her head starts to spin. And then it just
seems easier to stay, and to try to keep Jack from getting mad.

People who are violent with their partners follow a specific
and highly predictable pattern, and there can be hints from their
backgrounds that certain people may be prone to violent outbursts.
Jade needs to get some space from Jack, and with that distance will
come some perspective. If Jade has been with Jack for a long time,
she might need some professional counseling to help her get into
a place where she values her safety over the relationship. Because
she has been keeping this a secret (even though her friends can
probably guess what is happening if they really pay attention), it
tells me that she is still invested in the relationship, making it easy
for Jack to manipulate her into staying with him. Jade needs to get
real about whether her relationship with Jack follows the classic
pattern of abuse:

Tension-building, in which the victim starts to feel the aggression or anger building and begins to walk on eggshells around the abuser in the hopes of avoiding becoming the target.

Acute violence, when the emotional and or physical outburst actually occurs.

Reconciliation/honeymoon, when the abuser apologizes and usually says that their actions are driven by the intense love they have for the person they are hurting; they promise it will never happen again.

Calm, established as the victim forgives the abuser . . . and then *the cycle ALWAYS repeats.*

Let me repeat that again: the cycle of abuse always repeats. If you are in a circumstance where you have been mistreated or abused, do not kid yourself that it will get better. It gets worse. In order to ensure your safety, the first task is to go to a safe place, and then the second is to ask someone for help. And because we want to make sure we recognize the importance of compassion, once Jade is safe, it is fine for her to hope that Jack gets the help he needs as well. But once out of the relationship, she needs to keep strong boundaries: it's not her job to help him.

TOP THREE TAKEAWAYS FOR GETTING HELP WHEN SOMETHING HAPPENS

1 If something has happened to you, start with applying TCB to your own situation. Trust that you know what has happened doesn't feel right. Have compassion for yourself: you've done nothing wrong. Believe that you are entitled to define your own boundaries and allowed to ask for help in protecting them.

2 If the situation can't be fixed with some TCB, it's time to call in a trusted adult.

3 The cycle that is abuse is bound to repeat. However, you can break it. But it will be difficult work.

chapter 16

I THINK I DID SOMETHING . . . NOW WHAT?

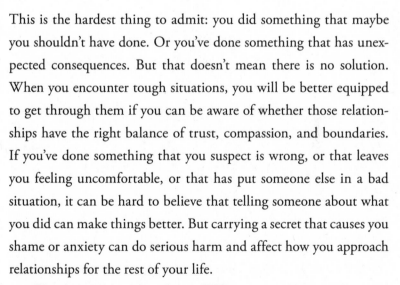

This is the hardest thing to admit: you did something that maybe you shouldn't have done. Or you've done something that has unexpected consequences. But that doesn't mean there is no solution. When you encounter tough situations, you will be better equipped to get through them if you can be aware of whether those relationships have the right balance of trust, compassion, and boundaries. If you've done something that you suspect is wrong, or that leaves you feeling uncomfortable, or that has put someone else in a bad situation, it can be hard to believe that telling someone about what you did can make things better. But carrying a secret that causes you shame or anxiety can do serious harm and affect how you approach relationships for the rest of your life.

Checking in with where TCB—trust, compassion, and boundaries—might have gone off track can give you a framework for sharing with someone else. This doesn't mean there won't be consequences when you let someone know what's happened. But you have to trust that getting things out in the open and accepting responsibility for your actions, and the consequences that come with them, is an important part of growing up.

Checking in with trust, compassion, and boundaries doesn't take long. If you can answer yes to even one of these questions, then you might want to start to think about how you can make things right, and who you can call on to help you.

1. Did you violate someone's trust? *I stole money out of my mom's wallet because I already spent my allowance.*
2. Did you act in a way that was without compassion? *I laughed when I saw my friend throw a nerd up against a locker.*
3. Did you violate someone's mental, emotional, or physical boundaries? *My girlfriend said she was too drunk to want sex. But we did it anyway.*

DOS AND DON'TS FOR STEPPING UP AND COMING CLEAN

DO tell someone what is going on. Holding things in doesn't help you in these cases. Whether it's apologizing to someone you hurt or confessing a bigger worry to an adult, you'll feel better if you're not holding on to it.

DO think about who should know—a parent, a teacher, a counselor at school, your doctor? And understand that all actions have consequences. You know how your parents are likely to react to wrongdoing. If you are in an abusive household, keep yourself safe by finding another adult who will keep your confidence. If your school has a student handbook, you may want to read through to anticipate if there are consequences that apply to your actions. Doctors will keep patient confidentiality, but they will also share all the facts with you about what your health risks might be.

DO pay attention to whether or not worrying about your situation is having an impact on your ability to function. Have your grades dropped? Does it seem unimportant if you shower or get dressed? Have you stopped hanging out with your friends? Are you having trouble sleeping? Or is it hard to get out of bed? Have you lost your appetite? Or are you suddenly eating constantly? Aggression, skipping school, acting out sexually, or substance use can all be ways of masking depression or anxiety.

DO NOT be afraid that your "life is ruined." I've spent a lot of time with people who by a reasonable person's standards had "ruined" their lives, and I can tell you that it is amazing how people can get their lives back on track when they take responsibility for their actions. Everyone makes mistakes, and most adults understand that making the wrong choice is a part of growing up. Even if you feel bad about what you did, you should feel good about being brave enough to admit you will take responsibility.

DO NOT think that someone else is going to solve this for you. Rely on friends for support, of course! But don't use them as messengers or ask them to take the fall for you.

DO NOT get discouraged if people don't forgive you just for coming forward. Understand that there will be work to do to repair trust and invite compassion.

Before you take your problem to another person, don't think about how to excuse your behavior. Instead, try to examine what was behind your action. Was it accidental? Or purposeful? Was it out of habit or was it done for the sake of fitting in? Then evaluate how your problematic behavior violated **trust**, **compassion**, and **boundaries**.

ENABLE, RESCUE, OR CONTROL?

Sometimes a person will ask you to get involved with something that feels sketchy or wrong. Whether it's helping them think through a particular situation, figure out how to avoid trouble, or actively help them to do something you know isn't right, you need to be aware of whether they're asking you to help, rescue, or enable. If your underage friend asks you to steal your sister's ID and lend it to them so they can buy beer for a party, because they totally promised they'd bring something—and you do it—then you are **enabling** that person. Your friend is in the process of creating a situation based on bad choices that might have serious consequences. **Know that if things go bad here, you are just as likely to be blamed as anyone else. After all, you're now an accomplice to bad behavior.**

Rescuing is a broader category of behavior that can include enabling. **Like if you always lend someone your class notes because they were skipping class to hang out with a girl they have a crush on.** Sometimes rescuing is appropriate, but more often, a rescue interferes with the person learning from their actions. Experience is a powerful teacher, and for it to have its full effect, consequences must be felt. But if it is your opinion that the consequences are too great, it may be appropriate to rescue. **If you take a minute to think about it, you'll quickly see the difference between enabling (allowing someone to avoid consequences that will teach them an important life lesson, but not endanger them) and rescuing (saving someone from real danger, whether physical or emotional, like answering that text to pick your friend up from a party if they are too altered to drive).**

Be careful of getting in a situation where your offer to help someone becomes a way to **control** the relationship. Don't link your value to someone to your ability to "save" them. Jumping in to rescue someone who hasn't asked for your help makes the situation about you, rather than them. Stepping in to solve someone else's problem can be another form of enabling where your role as protector can morph into a dynamic that lets the other person avoid consequences and avoid growing up.

DID SOMETHING?
SAY SOMETHING.

SEXTING: I SENT ONE.
I SAVED ONE. I ASKED FOR ONE.

Bobby had sexted with his now ex-girlfriend, Z, during his first year of college, but never with pics. During winter break of junior year Bobby was bored, so he sent Z a text: "nudes?" Even though the breakup was Bobby's idea, they're still friends. Bobby is chill, Z is chill, they had been texting for weeks. But Z's never sent nudes. Still, she likes that Bobby is thinking of her, and maybe if he remembers how much chemistry they had they could get back together . . .

Facts first: If you send a nude and are under the age of eighteen, and you get caught, you will be charged with creating child pornography. If you receive a nude, and the subject of that nude is under the age of eighteen, you are breaking the law. And if you ask for one from a minor? That is also breaking the law. Received an image and shared it with someone? That's trafficking child pornography and also . . . breaking the law. Get the idea? If you think you are going to get in trouble for your activities on your phone, in order to protect yourself and those involved, you may want to ask a lawyer for advice before you say anything to anyone else (we realize this may mean involving your parents). But if there are legal proceedings about to go down, and you are not protected, the consequences could be life-altering.

Another thing: Deleted photos aren't ever really deleted. Not even Snapchats. Your nudes will live on a server where they can be subpoenaed and used as evidence. **So don't send nudes**. Here's what digital safety expert Dr. Lisa Strohman says can happen once a nude is online: hackers in European and Asian countries have systems that monitor every image sent by text in this country. Their software screens for youthful characteristics, captures these images, and sells them to pedophiles on the dark web (a part of the internet that is invisible to search engines and requires special software to access). This sounds dramatic, but it's true. **Look, sexting at your age is just a terrible idea. I think we should all be proud of how we look. And it's not wrong to celebrate that your partner finds you sexy. Just save the sexy poses for when you're together. And then rely on your memory or just use words.**

You can call on TCB to help you know how to act if you find yourself on the receiving end of unrequested images from a third party. You know something from a third party has to be a violation of **trust**, not to mention **boundaries. Be a friend to the person whose images come into your hands and stop it now. Delete it. Tell the sender that you're letting the person in the picture know that their image is circulating and you are doing** your part to stop it. Don't judge someone for sending nudes in the first place. Be **compassionate**. If their pictures are being sent around, they are being exploited. Tell them you are sorry that this is happening, and that they have a friend in you.

I THINK THERE WAS A MISCOMMUNICATION AROUND CONSENT. AND I THINK IT WAS MY FAULT.

At the end of their date, Rebecca grabbed Tony's hand. She smiled. He smiled. Rebecca figured it was a matter of time before Tony made a move. But when he didn't, she leaned in and kissed him. He kissed her back. Things got a bit more heated, and Tony slid his hand up her shirt. Rebecca tensed up. "Please stop!" she said. Tony stopped, but ever since, Rebecca has felt like things are awkward between the two of them.

This sounds as if Tony was trying to read Rebecca's signals and he misinterpreted them. It happens. They started on the same page as Rebecca took things from hand-holding to kissing. And when Rebecca was clear about wanting to stop, Tony listened. But it seems as if he was confused when his attempt to move things forward wasn't what Rebecca wanted. Think of all your encounters as a chance to learn more about how to use TCB to make relationships stronger, even if something awkward has happened. In order to get back on the track, they both have to be honest about what went down. **It might be hard to start this conversation, but it's clear some practice in saying what they want** would help to make sure their desire is in sync with consent. And if they still like one another, either person can be the one who says, "Hey, can we talk about what went on the other night?"

It's not easy to open up a conversation about consent after you've gone past a boundary. Don't protest that it's not your fault. Don't point out that the other person seemed to like it. That they were as into it as you were. This is a passive way of denying the other person's experience in order to protect yourself from admitting you made a mistake.

You need to be sincere, so the other person can **trust** that you are trying to make things right and communicate real feelings. At the same time, you need to be **compassionate** and receptive to hearing how the other person experienced your actions. If they say you went past a boundary and made them uncomfortable, you need to take them at their word, apologize, and ask, "What can I do differently to make you feel comfortable?"

I KNEW THEY PROBABLY WANTED TO SAY NO, BUT I PRESSURED THEM INTO A YES.

Phoenix and Rowan were hooking up in Rowan's room. A few minutes in, Phoenix realized that they were tired and wanted to go home. "Stay a little longer," Rowan whispered. Phoenix replied, "Really, I'm tired. I have a test tomorrow morning," but Rowan insisted, "Baby, I'm so close. Please just stay and finish me off." Phoenix rolled their eyes. But they stayed. When Phoenix finally left to go home, much later than they planned, Rowan felt kind of guilty. But they rationalized that Phoenix wouldn't have stayed if they didn't want to.

What's really missing here is compassion. (Well, that and a respect for boundaries!) Phoenix is tired, has a test, and wants to leave. Rowan's clearly focused on their own needs. On the one hand, maybe Phoenix stayed because it's nice to be wanted, and being persuasive is different from being coercive (in that one is more like asking pretty please and one is using force). **On the other hand, you shouldn't have to persuade someone. They should be an active and willing participant in what is a mutual experience. I feel like Phoenix stayed just to get Rowan to stop asking. And while that's Phoenix's boundary issue, I don't think it's fair of Rowan to take advantage of it.**

The bottom line is that if you badger someone into submission, that is not the TCB way. You're missing **compassion** for whatever is making the other person hesitate and you're pushing at a **boundary** you sense is weak. Of course you are free to express your desire. But the other person also has the freedom to take care of their own needs.

In the end, it's the fact that Rowan felt guilty that signals they need to take some action. Guilt can be a useful emotion if it motivates us to stop or redirect a problematic behavior. If you are feeling guilty about something, then you are probably doing something you shouldn't. Stop, check in with TCB, change your actions, and learn from your behavior. It happens. No one is perfect, and we all do things we regret. **Bottom line: If you find yourself persuading or egging on a specific action, especially for selfish reasons, that is not consensual. So, more than just listening to your guilt: listen to your partner.**

I CROSSED A LINE WITH MY FRIEND'S BOYFRIEND/GIRLFRIEND.

Best friends Andie and Theo went to a party at Andie's boyfriend's house. Andie had been dating her boyfriend, Nick, for a few months. When Andie went to the bathroom, Nick pulled Theo onto the dance floor. He grabbed him around the waist and whispered into his ear, "You're hot." Theo leaned into Nick. "You are too," he said. When the dance ended, Theo escaped to the bathroom. Andie was just coming out when he was going in. Theo felt awkward and couldn't meet Andie's eyes when she asked him if he was having fun. Did she suspect that Nick would flirt with him? And why the heck did he flirt back?

This is another time to listen to your guilt. Theo knows he did something wrong; he betrayed his friend's trust. (So did Nick, and if Andie finds out, it's fair if she never trusts her boyfriend again.) But Theo needs to do the most difficult thing: tell his friend what happened. And it'll be up to Andie to decide what to do.

Hoo boy. This could mutate in the worst way possible: Andie blames Theo and continues seeing Nick. Theo probably suspects that this could happen, too. She could get really mad at him; she could break up with Nick (who would then blame Theo). When you're in a triangle like this, it's virtually impossible to imagine a good outcome. But ultimately, you must come clean about your part in it!

Whether Theo wants to admit it or not, he betrayed his friend's **trust** and crossed a **boundary**. He could have just said "no thanks" when Nick asked him to dance. In order for Theo's relationship with Andie to stay in balance with trust, compassion, and boundaries, he needs to be transparent and accept the consequences, whatever they may be.

THEY SAID NO. I KEPT GOING.

Tyson whispered into Skylar's ear, "Want to go upstairs?" Skylar smiled and nodded. They'd been flirting for the past year in chemistry class and had been dancing and laughing and talking all night. They entered a dark room and tumbled onto the bed, making out. "Wait, wait, wait," Skylar said. "I need to stop." They both sat up on the bed. But then Skylar kissed Tyson again. After a few minutes, Skylar said, "No, wait." But Tyson kept going. Skylar didn't mean it the first time, so why would they mean it the second time?

This scenario should remind us to educate young males. They are often stunned to discover the impact of these inappropriate behaviors that seriously violate boundaries. We have to raise their understanding—so let's start here: according to RAINN, 94 percent of women who are raped experience PTSD symptoms. Nearly a third of victims still have those symptoms nine months after the rape, and 13 percent of women who are raped attempt suicide. **Additionally, as we discussed in chapter 2, consent can be taken back at any point during a sexual encounter. It is not a matter of "believing" someone's intent. No means no, even if there has been a yes. If there is any confusion surrounding this concept at all, please turn back and reread chapter 2.**

Since Skylar said no, it's a painful reality to acknowledge that

Tyson committed sexual assault. If you come to terms with the fact that you have committed sexual assault, you must tell your parents, because you may face legal repercussions. If you have any more questions, you can go to the RAINN website (in our Resources and Recommended Reading section), where they offer information about laws by state.

I CHEATED ON MY BOYFRIEND/ GIRLFRIEND/SIGNIFICANT OTHER.

It happened at summer camp. It had been a couple of months since Rae saw her steady boyfriend, Johnny. And everyone at camp was just so close. She couldn't help herself: she kissed her cocounselor. It was just once, but then the flirtation was heavy and daily. She still wrote letters to Johnny, and she still loves him very deeply. She just had a crush and it played out. Nothing like it has happened since she's been home and back with Johnny. She doesn't need to tell him . . . does she?

Cheating on a partner says more about that relationship and/ or your feelings about your partner than anything about you, the person you cheated with, or even your ability to be faithful. So Rae needs to be honest with herself: When she cheated, did she feel guilty? Or concerned about breaking the trust that she had with Johnny? Because she hasn't told Johnny, and has basically rationalized her summer fling, she's probably not feeling either of those things. **The fact is, cheating puts all of TCB in jeopardy. You've broken the trust between you and your partner. You weren't able to put yourself in your boyfriend/girlfriend's** shoes and imagine how you would feel if they cheated on you. And finally, you've done some real damage to the boundary that keeps your relationship secure.

If you're cheating as a way of sabotaging the relationship, you're trying to control the course of your relationship by provoking a reaction in the other person. If Rae is spending the summer worrying that Johnny is not thinking of her just because he's not returning her texts right away or saying "I love you" all the time, she might be so scared that he's going to leave her that she acts in a way that makes sure he does. **That way, Rae proves to herself that she was right. That being apart over the summer was more than Johnny could handle. If she hadn't cheated on him, he would have cheated on her and she would have been hurt.**

The thing that's the same about either of these scenarios is that cheating has more to do with you then it does with the person you're cheating on. Since you've pretty much abandoned TCB in the relationship, even if the other person doesn't know it yet, you need to do the right thing and break up. Rae doesn't need to tell Johnny she cheated—that might cause unnecessary pain. But she does have to tell him that her feelings have changed and she needs to take a break from their relationship.

I'M STALKING MY EX ON SOCIAL.

Jack and Hillary broke up a year ago. They decided to stop following each other on social media, but Hillary couldn't stand it. So, she made a fake account and followed Jack. And that's how she found out about his new girlfriend, Melissa. On the fake account, she followed Melissa. She watches her story every day.

Hillary needs to go back to chapter 11 and read up on how to be compassionate with herself after a breakup. Then, it's gonna be hard to do, but she's gotta delete the account. Unfollow. And start thinking about what she needs. In this hyperconnected world, it is easy to keep tabs on people. But does keeping tabs on your ex and their new partner serve you?

Let's think about how TCB can be a road map away from heartbreak for Hillary: She needs to **trust** that she will get over Jack, no matter how sad she feels now. If she has **compassion** for herself, she'll stop comparing their old relationship to the one she sees unfolding on Instagram. What will really help Hillary is establishing a **boundary**. Plus, Hillary, honey? Your behavior's bordering on creepy. Scratch that. It's creepy. Be the bigger person and move on. You will love again. And the more you stalk and make fake accounts, the longer you will sit in this hurt. Do what you need to do to get over it. But, my God, please delete the account!

I LOST MY TEMPER AND PHYSICALLY HURT SOMEONE. BUT I'M REALLY SORRY. HOW CAN I MAKE THEM FORGIVE ME?

Syd didn't mean to punch Dale. It just sort of happened. They had been playing basketball after school, but Dale fouled on Syd. Rather than shaking it off, Syd pushed Dale. Dale pushed back. And so, Syd punched him in the face. Syd and Dale are friends, but Dale hasn't spoken to Syd since it happened. Syd just wants things between them to be cool again.

Syd can't make Dale forgive him. You can't make anyone forgive you. When you physically hurt someone, you do more than violate a physical boundary: you violate their trust. **You can be sorry for what you did—in fact, you should be. But all you can do is apologize, offer to talk about it, and wait to see what they do. They may never forgive you, and that is something you have to live with. Learn from your mistakes.**

There's another kind of violence that is more than just losing your temper in a heated circumstance. If you *repeatedly* lash out verbally, or physically, especially against someone you are in an intimate relationship with, you **must get help**. Intimate partner violence, also called teen dating violence, is a real and dangerous phenomenon, and if you're the perpetrator, we want you to know that there is room for compassion for you, too. People who have been abused often become abusers.

It's okay to let someone see your pain rather than trying to literally transfer that pain to someone else. Find out more about how to break the cycle by calling the National Teen Dating Abuse Helpline: 866-331-9474. Tell them you are afraid you are an abuser and you want help.

I LOST CONTROL WHEN I WAS DRUNK.

Tristy took a shot, then another. She took her shoes off and decided to dance on the table, so she used her arm like a windshield wiper and knocked everything off the table. Beckett dared her to take her T-shirt off. Tristy pulled off her shirt, jumped off the table, and started to dance just wearing her bra. The whole party was cheering as they took out their phones and videoed Tristy dancing amid bottles, Solo cups, and sticky liquid. When she woke up the next morning, she didn't remember a thing. But the proof was on everyone's stories.

Okay, I'll go first here. For sure this was a bad decision, but as long as it stopped here, it's not the worst thing that could have come out of Tristy's night. It's true that Tristy wasn't physically violated or traumatized. And she wasn't the object of a crime. But even if something worse had happened, it wouldn't have been Tristy's fault. Anyone who is under the influence of drugs or alcohol is unable to give consent for *anything*—whether it's being videoed, or having sex.

Let's talk about who is "at fault" in this scenario—starting with Tristy's supposed "friends" who egged her on. Anyone with your best interest should help you stay out of situations where the consequences could be harmful—or even embarrassing. How can you *trust* friends if they let you get into this situation? And videotaping someone without consent is a clear *boundary* violation. We need to look out for one another!

In chapter 14, we talked about how alcohol or other substances can take away your ability to consent and wreck TCB in relationships. An incident like this should be an opportunity to examine your relationship with alcohol. As a doctor who treats patients with addictions, I know it's never too early to start asking certain questions:

- Are you under twenty-one? If so, why are you taking the risk of breaking the law?
- If you think it's okay to drink, do you think it's okay to use other substances? Is this way of living consistent with your values?
- Does anyone in your family have a problem with alcohol? If you have a parent or sibling with alcoholism or addiction, you also could be at risk. And by the way, blacking out from drinking is a big red flag for a dangerous relationship with alcohol.

If you answered yes to any of these questions and for some reason skipped reading chapter 14 about TCB and substances, go back and read it now. If you've already read it, we hope you're rethinking your relationship to alcohol and/or other substances.

TOP THREE TAKEAWAYS FOR MAKING IT RIGHT WHEN YOU'VE DONE SOMETHING WRONG

1 If you think you've done something wrong, you probably have. Start with looking at trust, compassion, and boundaries to try to figure out what you can do to make it right.

2 Making mistakes and accepting consequences is how we learn. It's not easy, but it is part of becoming a mature person.

3 If the situation can't be fixed with some TCB, it's time to call in a trusted adult.

WE KNOW YOU'VE GOT THIS!

☆

Whether it's making friends or finding patience when butting heads with your parents, navigating what to do about your crush or dating that special someone long term, thanks to TCB you are more equipped than ever before. Now that you've reached the end of this journey, you understand what you need to look for when you start, and put into practice to maintain, strong, healthy relationships (say it with us!): **trust**, **compassion**, **and boundaries**. It may seem too simple. But what do you have to lose by trying? If you consistently look to these three guiding principles, you will be able to navigate any and all situations—from tough, to easy, to medium hard.

We see you. We know that sometimes, things can majorly suck. From your parents, to your friends, to your partners, relationships can be confusing and scary, devastating, or even violating. But also, the people in your life can make you feel really, really great. From warm fuzzies to I-believe-in-you confidence to Pop Rocks in your stomach, fingers tingling, smiling-so-hard-you-can't-feel-your-face great. Trust, compassion, and boundaries give you a simple structure to make sense of the buzzing confusion that life can throw at you.

It can be hard to find your people. It can be hard to feel worthy. It can be hard to feel empathy for people who seem so different from you. We know you're going to do awesome things: fall in love, express yourself, make great friends. But it might be awkward—or even really hard—getting there. Just remember that trust, compassion, boundaries, and consent are more than words, that they are actions that must be experienced and repeated, the more you practice, the more natural it will feel to balance them in all of your relationships.

You've granted yourself the gift of knowledge. How do we know that this is such a gift? I know because this helped me talk about things with my dad that I've never discussed with him before. I have to say, I've learned a lot in the process, too. I have been so inspired to really hear Paulina's concerns, and to share mine. (That's not to say that she didn't share things that made me want to cover MY ears and go LA! LA! LA!) But by keeping TCB front and center, our relationship has grown.

We hope we've broadened your thinking about what it means to consent—not just sexually, but in all areas of your life. When people talk about consent, we want you to remember that the whole concept comes down to **treating one another in a specific way—with integrity.** We want you to remember that knowing yourself, and being sensitive and compassionate to others, is how you create a better world; a world where you trust your instincts, create compassion and feel empathy, and respect yourself and others. A world where your voice is heard, your feelings are honored and where you hear others and honor their feelings. A world where Emma Sulkowicz would never have had to carry her mattress onto the graduation stage. A world where consent is considered a benefit in a relationship—not a transaction.

When it comes to putting TCB into action in your life, don't be afraid to act in ways that, at first, feel unnatural or uncomfortable because they are new. Trust that you can be compassionate, trust that you can learn your boundaries, and trust that some attention in these key areas will result in growth. You must be open to whatever that means.

Appreciate that imagination is a distinctly human phenomenon. No other species (that we know of) has the capacity to turn imagination into reality in the same way that we do. And if we can imagine a world where we can trust each other, have compassion for each other, and respect each other's boundaries, then it is most likely to become our lived reality. Don't be afraid to dream big. Start here, start now. Start with the people around you.

Scientists who study what makes people happy tell us that leading a life consistent with your values and reaching out to others with compassion (but also with good boundaries) leads to feelings of well-being and being of service. Although we are technically more connected than we've ever been in human history, it can be too easy to feel alienated, isolated, and alone. Real connection, the kind where you can say what you feel and feel what others intend, should be your goal.

And remember that you have the power of TCB. Trust, compassion, and boundaries allow you to consent to relationships that are healthy and help you grow. Practice these concepts in all your relationships, online and off. **And isn't that what this is all about? How you treat yourself and others has the power to create the world you want to live in. You have the capacity to become the person you dream of becoming.** And you have the ability to change the way we think and talk about consent. With TCB, you will change the way we all move through the world.

Take care, TCB.

LET'S TALK ABOUT IT

You've read the book and you've reflected on the relationships in your life. But this is just the beginning. In order to put the lessons into practice, you have to start with an open dialogue. Here are a few questions that can help start that conversation with the people in your life who matter most. Framing your questions using phrases like "I've noticed" or "I've been wondering" can keep things feeling conversational. This is not meant to be an interrogation!

TEN QUESTIONS FOR TEENS TO ASK THE ADULTS IN THEIR LIFE

1. Did you think about consent when you were my age?
   a. If yes, what did you think about it back then? Do you think differently about it now?
   b. If no, why didn't you think about it? Do you think about it now?
2. What do you think is most important in a relationship?
3. The way I communicate with my friends is so different from how you and your friends keep in touch. Do you think it's better? Worse? Just different? Why?
4. What do you think is the most important quality in a friend?
5. It seems like gender was a very different topic when you were my age. Why do you think that is? What do you think about the conversation now?

6. Did you date when you were my age? Did you enjoy it? What did you learn? Did you have a(ny) long-term relationship(s)? Have you ever gone through a breakup?

7. I've noticed that the rules for our household are different from some of my friends'. Can we talk about why you feel strongly about _____?

8. Have you ever done something you wish you had not done to another person, like a friend, partner, date, etc.? If so, what did you do about it?

9. This might be awkward to talk about, but when do you think I should be ready to be physically intimate with someone else?

10. What does it mean to you to use drugs or alcohol responsibly?

TEN QUESTIONS FOR ADULTS TO ASK THE TEEN IN THEIR LIFE

1. Consent has become an important topic, perhaps more than I had previously understood. I'm wondering, what does consent mean to you?

2. I am happy to see that people are free to express how they feel about their gender. Do you have any questions about different ways to express your identity?

3. So much about sexual attraction can be confusing. Is there something more I can do to support you as you figure out who you like?

4. Do you have a crush on anybody? I don't necessarily

need to know details if you do; I just want to know if you have any questions about romantic relationships.

5. Friendships change a lot over the course of life. I bet you have noticed some changes in your peers and in yourself. Have your friendships changed recently? How are you feeling about this?

6. It's an uncomfortable topic, but it doesn't have to be! I wonder, do you have any questions about having a sexual relationship and how you can be safe and healthy?

7. Sometimes things happen to us during our childhood that really affect us. We try to put them out of our mind, but they have a way of creeping in. Have you ever experienced anything that you feel was traumatic for you?

8. I hope that if you hurt someone, intentionally or not, you would feel comfortable sharing that with me so that we could discuss what comes next. Have you ever done something you wish you hadn't to someone you care about, like a friend or a partner? Would you like to talk about what happened?

9. We are not going to discuss whether or not I did drugs or drank when I was your age. My job is to keep you safe and well, so I have certain rules about substances. These are my rules: _____

10. I hope I can be an adult you can trust and talk openly with. But it's good to know other adults whose advice you value and who you feel comfortable going to if you want to talk about something that has happened in your life. Is there anyone you think of in that way?

RESOURCES AND RECOMMENDED READING

Good Books to Read If You Want to Know More about Physical Stuff and Sex

The Care and Keeping of You: The Body Book for Younger Girls, Valorie Lee Schaefer and Josée Masse (Middleton, WI: American Girl Publishing, 1998). Ever have questions about how to take care of yourself? This classic from American Girl fills in the blanks.

The Care and Keeping of You: The Body Book for Older Girls, Cara Natterson and Josée Masse (Middleton, WI: American Girl Publishing, 2012). Just like the first version, except for older girls!

Our Bodies, Ourselves, Judy Norsigian and the Boston Women's Health Book Collective (New York: Touchstone, 1984). The classic text to teach us about our bodies and how they work.

S.E.X.: The All-You-Need-to-Know Sexuality Guide to Get You Through Your Teens and Twenties, Heather Corinna (Cambridge, MA: Da Capo, 2016). From the founder of Scarleteen, a guide to sex and consent.

Trans Bodies, Trans Selves: A Resource for the Transgender Community, Laura Erickson-Schroth and Jennifer Finney Boylan (Oxford: Oxford University Press, 2014). Much like the classic book with a similar title, this is a comprehensive guide on how to navigate the intricacies of the trans experience.

The Vagina Bible, Jen Gunter (New York: Penguin Random House, 2019). Everything you'll ever need to know about vaginas and vulvas!

Good Books to Read If You Want to Know More about Friendships, Emotional Stuff, and Sex

Boys & Sex: Young Men on Hookups, Love, Porn, Consent, and Navigating the New Masculinity, Peggy Orenstein (New York: Harper, 2020). Comprehensive interviews serve as the backbone of this groundbreaking book, drawing on topics like locker-room culture and sex education.

Dating and Sex: A Guide for the 21st Century Teen Boy, Andrew P. Smiler (Washington, DC: Magination, 2016). With teen boys in mind, this graphic novel provides information on dating, relationships, and sex.

Girls & Sex: Navigating the Complicated New Landscape, Peggy Orenstein. (New York: HarperCollins, 2016). The underbelly of the beast cracks open: comprehensive interviews with high school girls explore the ways in which porn and sexual myths have permeated the culture.

Inventing Ourselves: The Secret Life of the Teenage Brain, Sarah-Jayne Blakemore (New York: PublicAffairs, 2018). Just like the title suggests, Professor Sarah-Jayne Blakemore offers insight into the developing teenage brain.

Queen Bees & Wannabes: Helping Your Daughter Survive Cliques, Gossip, Boyfriends, and the New Realities of Girl World, **Rosalind Wiseman (New York: Three Rivers, 2002).** This book changed the way that people look at teen girls and their friendships.

Sex, Teens, & Everything in Between: The New and Necessary Conversations Today's Teenagers Need to Have about Consent, Sexual Harassment, Healthy Relationships, Love, and More, **Shafia Zaloom (Naperville, IL: Sourcebooks, 2019).** This book answers all of the questions you were afraid to ask. A great companion read with our book!

Wait, What? A Comic Book Guide to Relationships, Bodies, and Growing Up, **Heather Corinna (Portland, OR: Limerence, 2019).** If you like graphic novels, you'll love this.

Read More about Consent

What Does Consent Really Mean? **Pete Wallis and Thalia Wallis, (London: Singing Dragon, 2018).** This graphic novel explores a group of kids processing the sexual assault of a classmate.

Querying Consent: Beyond Permission and Refusal, **edited by Jordana Greenblatt and Keja Valens (New Brunswick, NJ: Rutgers University Press, 2018).** Geared toward the more advanced reader (read: adult), this book explores what consent means in the world today.

We Know You're Going to Google . . . Websites You Can Trust (That Are Great Resources for Parents and Educators As Well!)*

Adolescent Development:
hhs.gov/ash/oah/adolescent-development/index.html

A comprehensive resource covering everything from physical development to mental, physical, and reproductive health and healthy relationships. This site also provides data on adolescent lives at the national and state levels.

AA (Alcoholics Anonymous) or NA (Narcotics Anonymous):
AA.org, NA.org

Worldwide groups for people of any age, founded on the twelve-step principle (twelve actions that guide a person to recovery, with an emphasis on personal responsibility and a spiritual component).

Born This Way Foundation: bornthisway.foundation

Born This Way Foundation was not only started by Lady Gaga, but it is doing important work in creating innovative programming and partnerships in order to help promote healthy conversations about mental wellness, both online and off.

Break the Cycle: www.breakthecycle.org

Inspiring and supporting young people twelve to twenty-four to build healthy relationships and create a culture without abuse. Their Let's Be Real movement creates online and in-person opportunities for you to have real conversations about your experiences.

Cyberbullying Research Center: cyberbullying.org

Resources for educators, parents, teens, and adult victims. Read about laws and research and current news on the evolution of cyberbullying.

Dating Matters:

www.cdc.gov/violenceprevention/intimatepartnerviolence

Teen dating violence affects millions of teens each year. This website focuses on healthy relationship skills aimed at reducing behaviors that increase the risk for dating violence.

Gender Spectrum: genderspectrum.org

Info on how to create gender-sensitive and inclusive environments for children and teens.

GLSEN: glsen.org

A national network of educators, students, and local GLSEN chapters working to ensure that LGBTQ students are able to learn and grow in a school environment free from bullying and harassment.

Go Ask Alice: goaskalice.columbia.edu

I had friends who worked for Go Ask Alice in college, and they were the most knowledgeable people when it came to sex, relationships, drugs, and alcohol. This resource is great for having any and all questions answered in a way that is accurate, reliable, and culturally relevant.

Guide to Allyship: guidetoallyship.com

An open-source starter guide to begin your journey to being a better ally.

It Gets Better Project: itgetsbetter.org

The It Gets Better Project inspires people across the globe to share their stories and remind the next generation of LGBTQ+ youth that hope is out there, and it will get better.

LGBT Youth Resources from Centers for Disease Control and Prevention (CDC): www.cdc.gov/lgbthealth/youth-resources.htm

Resources from the CDC, other government agencies, and community organizations for LGBT youth, their friends, educators, parents, and family members to support positive environments.

Love Is Respect: loveisrespect.org

The ultimate resource to empower youth to prevent and end dating abuse. A project of the National Domestic Violence Hotline. We particularly like their quiz to find out where your relationship falls on the spectrum from healthy to abusive.

NEDA (National Eating Disorders Association): nationaleatingdisorders.org

The National Eating Disorders Association provides support and guidance through eating disorders. Whether you or someone you know is struggling with an eating disorder, NEDA's website is the best place to start.

NIDA (National Institute on Drug Abuse) for Teens: teens.drugabuse.gov

NIDA shares the scientific facts about drugs and addiction, drug use among teens, and how drugs affect the teen brain and body.

PFLAG: pflag.org

The first and largest organization for lesbian, gay, bisexual, transgender, and queer (LGBTQ+) people, their parents and families, and allies.

RAINN (Rape, Abuse, & Incest National Network): rainn.org

The nation's largest anti–sexual violence organization. A great resource for finding help or resources for survivors, loved ones looking for support, or anyone looking to learn more and support survivors.

SAMHSA (Substance Abuse and Mental Health Services Administration): samhsa.gov/find-treatment

If the spiritually centered approach of AA or NA is not for you, these government agencies offer tons of information about addiction and treatment.

Stonewall: stonewall.org.uk

From across the pond, Europe's largest LGBTQ+ organization has a comprehensive glossary and a great "Young Stonewall" section. The LGBTQ+ community is worldwide. Expand your horizons!

Teens Health: teenshealth.org

This site helps teens take charge of their physical, emotional, mental, and sexual health.

That's Not Cool: thatsnotcool.com

A super-interactive site that helps teens assess relationships and learn what's healthy and what's abusive; it also provides resources and support to victims. Their "Cool or Not Cool" quiz lets you see how other teens have judged relationship scenarios.

Trans Student Educational Resources: transstudent.org

Trans Student Educational Resources was cofounded in 2011 by Eli Erlick and Alex Sennello, two sixteen-year-old transgender women, as Trans Student Equality Resources. It was and remains the only national organization run by young transgender people.

The Trevor Project: www.thetrevorproject.org

The Trevor Project is doing the good and important work of providing crisis counseling and services to LGBTQ+ youth. Honorable mention goes to their page dedicated to becoming an ally—check it out!

TrevorSpace: trevorspace.org

Meet other LGBTQIA+ teens.

University of Oxford LGBTQ+: oulgbtq.org

More from the Brits, including one of the better sections on queer relationships (search under "identity resources").

UpRoot: Resources for Consent: havenuproot.wordpress.com /resources-for-consent

Encyclopedic in their heroic efforts to cover every possible variation on the topic of consent. Bravo!

*These websites were active at the time this book was published. We hope they are around for a long time!

Important Phone Numbers

Crisis Text Line

Text HOME to 741741 to be connected to a trained volunteer counselor via text.

National Domestic Violence Hotline

800-799-SAFE (7233)

National Sexual Assault Telephone Hotline

800-656-HOPE (4673)

National Suicide Prevention Hotline

800-273-8255

National Teen Dating Abuse Helpline

866-331-9474

Trans Lifeline

877-565-8860

TrevorLifeline

866-488-7386; or TrevorText: text START to 678-678

ACKNOWLEDGMENTS

We are deeply indebted to Jill Stern, without whom this book would not have been possible. Thank you to our team at UTA, with a special shout-out to Albert Lee, who brought this project to life. Thank you to our editor, Emilia Rhodes, who was a pleasure to work with. Thank you to Samantha Shea for her guidance and support. Thank you to Jackie Stern for her steady presence and to Howard Lapides for his ever-present guidance.

We would be lost without the insight and expertise of Haylin Belay. Additionally, thank you to Kira and Amanda for sharing your stories with us.

Special thanks to the other members of our family: mom/wife Susan and brothers/sons Douglas and Jordan, who had to deal with our being ever distracted by this project. Thank you for putting up with us. Paulina and I have become quite at ease with this conversation, but we apologize for any cringeworthy scenarios as you read along.

And last but not least, thank you—our readers—for practicing a little TCB with us.